Haakon Lie, Denis Healey and the making of an Anglo-Norwegian special relationship 1945-1951

Tony Insall

Unipub 2010

© Unipub 2010

ISBN 978-82-7477-488-9

Contact info Unipub:
T: + 47 22 85 33 00
F: + 47 22 85 30 39
E-mail: post@unipub.no
www.unipub.no

Cover photos: Haakon Lie: © Arbeiderbevegelsens arkiv og bibliotek,
Denis Healey at a Labour party conference in Blackpool in 1945. Every
effort has been made to trace copyright material and the publishers
wish to apologise for any omissions.

Publisher: Oslo Academic Press, Unipub Norway
Printed in Norway: AIT e-dit AS, Oslo 2010

All rights reserved. No part of this publication may be reproduced or
transmitted, in any form or by any means, without permission.

For Nonie, Rob, Nick and Ali

Series preface

ISSUES IN CONTEMPORARY HISTORY is a series of publications from the Forum for Contemporary History (FCH) at the University of Oslo. The main focus of the FCH is on the study of changes in political culture as a means towards understanding broader social transformations in the post-World War II period. Our aim is to identify and analyse specific features and patterns of change in the fields of consumer culture, the public sphere, feminism, collective social movements, the welfare state and foreign and security policies in the Scandinavian and other Western societies in this period.

Publications in this series fall into two main categories: edited collections relating to the core interests of the FCH, and monographs primarily based on doctoral dissertations.

The present volume is a revised version of a doctoral dissertation written at King's College, London. The author analyses the close relationship between the Norwegian and British Labour parties during the immediate post-World War II period when Norwegian foreign and security policies were fundamentally transformed through its special relationship with Great Britain and its membership in NATO. Denis Healey and Haakon Lie played key roles in this process.

Contents

Series preface 5

Acknowledgements 9

Abbreviations 11

1 Introduction.. 13

2 The historical background 21

3 The development of a uniquely close relationship:
1945-1948 47

4 Information Research Department 99

5 The impact of Information Research Department in
Norway in 1948: an intimate relationship............... 135

6 Spain 163

7 The Socialist International 203

8 The relationship at work and its sudden end:
1949 to October 1951 227

9 Conclusion 273

Bibliography 283

Index 297

Acknowledgements

This book originated as a doctoral thesis written between 2004 and 2007 at King's College, London. It owes a great deal to the many people who helped and advised me during the course of my research. I am glad to have a chance to express my appreciation to them here.

First, to Jon Bingen, who unwittingly sowed the seed which eventually germinated into this project, during a long discussion when we were deep in the Nordmarka sometime towards the end of the last century.

I am also grateful to so many Norwegians who have shown an interest in this project and generously given me their time, advice and support at various stages. They include Hans Otto Frøland, Kristian Steinnes, John Lunde, Rolf Tamnes, Olav Riste, Geir Lundestad, Paul Engstad, Bernt Bull, David Aly Redvaldsen and Sven Holtsmark, who gave me access to documents from the Russian Foreign Ministry. I would like to acknowledge the considerable help and advice given to me by Knut Einar Eriksen and his staff at the Arbeiderbevegelsens arkiv, who could not have been more helpful. Anders Buraas wrote to me several times answering a long series of questions and provided me with some very useful assistance during a telephone interview.

I am particularly grateful to the late Haakon Lie, whose interviews with me provided not only answers to a wide range of questions, but also many valuable insights into the background of this subject which I could never have found elsewhere.

I have been equally fortunate with the help and support which I have had from many British friends and colleagues. They include Stephen Bird and Darren Treadwell at the Labour Party archive in Manchester, John Madeley, Clive Archer, Alyson Bailes, Peter Morley, Mike Goodman, Tony

Cowan, Adam Watson, Lady Cicely Mayhew, William Collier, Zara Steiner and Patrick Salmon, who pointed me in the direction of some promising lines of enquiry.

It is also a pleasure to have an opportunity to thank Mariot Leslie again here, not only for her generous hospitality when I was visiting Oslo, but also for her friendship and support at times when she had much more important things to think about.

I should also like to highlight the help which I have had from my supervisors, first Mats Berdal and then Joe Maiolo who, with good humour and diligence, kept me pointed in the right direction. Their critical comments and suggestions have greatly improved the final outcome.

I am grateful to the Trustees of the Liddell Hart Centre for Military Archives, King's College London, for permission to quote from the papers of Sir Christopher Mayhew. I am also grateful to the Countess of Avon for her permission to quote from the diaries of the Earl of Avon.

Finally, a project of this nature produces all sorts of domestic pressures and consequences. I am grateful to my family for putting up with them, but of course most particularly to Nonie for her forbearance, patience and loving support throughout this time – as always.

Abbreviations

AP	Associated Press
CGIL	Confederazione Generale Italiana del Lavoro
CIA	Central Intelligence Agency
COMISCO	Committee of the International Socialist Conference
DNA	Det Norske Arbeiderpartiet
EEC	European Economic Community
ICFTU	International Confederation of Free Trade Unions
IFTU	International Federation of Trade Unions
ILP	Independent Labour Party
IPU	Inter Parlimentary Union
IRD	Information Research Department
JIC	Joint Intelligence Committee
LO	Landsorganisasjonen i Norge
LRC	Labour Representation Committee
LSI	Labour and Socialist International
MI5	The British Security Service
MI6	SIS, the British Secret Intelligence Service
NATO	North Atlantic Treaty Organisation
NEC	National Executive Committee
NIS	Norwegian Intelligence Service
NKP	Norges Kommunistisk Parti
OSS	Office of Strategic Services
PCI	Partito Comunista Italiano
POT	Politiets Overvåkingstjeneste
PSI	Partito Socialista Italiano
PSIUP	Partito Socialista Italiano di Unita Proletaria
PSLI	Partito Socialista dei Lavoratori Italiani
PWE	Political Warfare Executive
SDLP	Social Democratic Labour Party

ABBREVIATIONS

SFIO	Section Française de l'Internationale Ouvrière
SILO	Socialist Information and Labour Office
SIS	Secret Intelligence Service
TGWU	Transport and General Workers' Union
TUC	Trades Union Congress
TUC (B)	Trades Union Congress (Burma)
UGT	Union General de Trabajadores
WFDY	World Federation of Democratic Youth
WFTU	World Federation of Trade Unions
WIDF	World International Democratic Federation

1 Introduction

This book sets out to analyse the remarkably close relationship which existed between the British and Norwegian Labour parties, when both parties were in government during the immediate post-war period - and the roles played by Haakon Lie and Denis Healey in developing those links. It will demonstrate the extent to which their work helped deepen bilateral relations at a time of considerable tension and uncertainty in post-war Europe. The two parties became so close that in August 1951, four senior British ministers including the prime minister, Attlee (who scarcely ever holidayed abroad) and the foreign secretary, Morrison, visited Norway on holidays which both Attlee and Morrison combined with party and official talks in Oslo. This unprecedented series of visits, shortly before Labour lost the October 1951 election in the UK, reflects the high-water mark in their relations, which before the war had been infrequent and generally distant.

The significant events of this period, in particular those which led to the creation of the two blocs represented by NATO and the Warsaw Pact, exercised considerable influence over the western world for much of the rest of the twentieth century. This was also a time of tension and uncertainty, particularly in 1948 after the communist coup in Czechoslovakia and during the blockade of Berlin.[1] Most aspects of this period have already been recorded and assessed in detail. The parts played by Britain and Norway have generally been

---

[1] Years later, the Russian Foreign Minister Andrei Gromyko agreed with Christopher Mayhew that the crash of a British plane which had been 'buzzed' by a Soviet fighter during the Berlin airlift had marked the most dangerous moment of the entire cold war. (However, this was before the Cuban missile crisis.) Mayhew, *A War of Words* (I. B. Tauris, 1998), p40.

1 Introduction

similarly well covered by both Norwegian and British scholars. Due attention has been paid to the strategic analyses which underpinned the policies of both countries, the depth and frequency of their diplomatic exchanges, the closeness of their bilateral relations and the personalities of the key figures who were involved. Their research has been based on a thorough review of the range of documentary material now available in the archives, as well as the personal accounts provided in diaries, interviews and personal reminiscences by many of the participants. What scope can there be for any further examination?

There is a further important aspect of the bilateral relationship which has hitherto gone almost unrecorded. The close relations which existed between the two Labour parties, encouraged and facilitated by the British ambassador to Oslo, Sir Laurence Collier and some of his staff, played an important part in developing the bilateral relationship and in helping to achieve objectives of importance to both sides during the early and critical years of the Cold War.

In the past, I have sometimes noticed the extent to which politicians in different countries have used their personal and political contacts to facilitate processes which they may otherwise have felt were not being dealt with adequately by their administrative processes. This characteristic occasionally featured in British-Norwegian relations. For example, as will be illustrated in Chapter Three, in January 1948 Haakon Lie wrote to Denis Healey (who at that time held no formal position in government, but who enjoyed good and wide-ranging connections in the Foreign Office from Bevin downwards), asking him to explain the background to Bevin's Western Union speech. Healey replied that he could not provide a written answer, but that he would arrange for Lie to be given a briefing in Oslo. This was actually provided by the labour attaché in the British embassy, John Inman.[2] No archival record has been found to show that the ambassador (or, for that matter, anyone else in the Foreign Office) had been consulted or was even aware that this was taking place.

The book will therefore present a study of the nature of the personal and political contacts between the parties. It

---

[2] Conversation with Haakon Lie, 14 December 2004.

will examine how close and effective they were, and in what areas. It will highlight the significance of the roles played by Healey and Lie throughout this period. It will also demonstrate the extent to which these links played a part – either outside the structure of regular diplomatic and governmental exchanges or in parallel with them – in facilitating the development of the bilateral relationship and will show in what ways both countries benefited as a result. It will consider areas where the relationship worked particularly effectively, for example in their collaboration in disseminating the large quantities of anti-communist propaganda material produced by the Information Research Department (IRD) of the Foreign Office. Finally, it will also look at two other case studies, involving Spain and the Socialist International, where co-operation was close but did not produce comparably significant results. (However, the chapter on Spain will produce documentary evidence from three separate archives which demonstrates that in 1946, contrary to its public and private statements to the contrary, the British government was indeed working to remove Franco from power in Spain. This material has hitherto not been published.)

Use of the prism of Labour party links to study aspects of the relationship between Britain and Norway helps to add to an understanding of the nature of the relationship during an especially significant period in post-war history. It provides an opportunity to demonstrate the manner in which political contacts could sometimes be maintained through links which went outside diplomatic channels. It also demonstrates how much the two parties were able to cooperate on a variety of sensitive issues, thereby helping to achieve – or attempting to achieve – some of the objectives of their respective governments. While the dissemination of IRD material will be shown to be the best example of this extensive cooperation, it is by no means the only one. Thus, Norwegian party and labour movement representatives were sent to Britain in 1946 to use their party links not only to obtain information about British policy towards Spain, but also to explore the scope for influencing that policy: they concluded that there was no opportunity to do so.

As far as I am aware, this approach – historically piecing together contacts of very different kinds, using for the

1 Introduction

most part official documentary sources which often describe aspects of these unofficial links – has not been used before to study a bilateral relationship, The conceptual issues which it addresses may therefore be of interest to a wider audience. There is more than sufficient evidence to demonstrate that the links between the two Labour parties, and the way in which they were exploited, fulfilled an important function at a time of particular significance during the Cold War. The book will therefore provide a historical insight into an important aspect of diplomacy which is normally overlooked in theoretical analysis. Most of the material on which it is based is dispersed and not readily retrievable. It has therefore avoided scrutiny or been overlooked by academics whose attention has been diverted elsewhere. It highlights some important issues, as well as the crucial role played by a broad range of both party members and officials who cooperated remarkably closely in a way which does not appear to have been replicated since.

Research for this subject has presented a number of interesting challenges. It is perhaps not surprising that there is an absence of secondary material, because the subject has not hitherto attracted much academic interest. Little has been written about it directly. Nor is it really addressed in autobiographies written by politicians from the period, although Healey does occasionally provide some valuable insights.[3] The diaries of politicians such as Eden,[4] or advisers such as Arne Ording,[5] have occasionally provided useful information, but the authors have been discreet about sensitive subjects. The value of the diaries has therefore been either as a means of cross-checking references to information obtained elsewhere, or occasionally pointing to an area of possible interest which might repay further inquiry in an archive. (Although Konrad Nordahl's diaries have only been published from 1950 onwards, some earlier entries are available in the Arbeiderbevegelsens arkiv in Oslo. They occasionally provide

---

[3] Denis Healey, *The Time of My Life* (Michael Joseph, 1989).
[4] Eden's unpublished diaries have been deposited with the Avon papers at Birmingham University.
[5] Two volumes of Arne Ording's diaries have been published covering the period from June 1942 to April 1949.

useful information, for example, about the exchanges where Nordahl sought and obtained financial assistance from the TUC following the German invasion in April 1940.)

By their very nature, party contacts tended to be less formal and were not recorded in the same way as governmental or official meetings. Apart from visits arranged for specific purposes, most business was transacted either by correspondence or when the key participants met at international socialist conferences. Furthermore, the correspondence between the parties during this period was frequently used to arrange meetings, rather than to describe their outcomes or to debate policy issues. No doubt this would often have reflected concerns about the sensitivity of the messages which might have been passed: thus - not surprisingly - there is no correspondence between Healey and Lie on IRD issues. Quite frequently, therefore, party correspondence or records provide a clue to the existence of an event which – if it is recorded at all[6] – may be described elsewhere, perhaps in a different archive. For example, an account by Aksel Zachariassen of his arrest and deportation from London in 1919 is contained in the Arbeiderbevegelsens arkiv.[7] This document encouraged research which led to the discovery of the much fuller account in the Riksarkiv, contained in reporting from the Norwegian legation in London as well as detailed reports passed to them by Basil Thomson, the head of Special Branch.[8] Similarly, Arne Ording's account of the socialist conference on Spain in Paris in August 1946, which provided the first indications of a hitherto undisclosed British policy on Spain, was also found in the Arbeiderbevegelsens arkiv.[9] It was this document which

---

[6] By way of illustration, Haakon Lie wrote to Healey and Phillips on 28 January 1950, saying that when they met he wanted to discuss with them a project on which he had been working for some time. He gave no indication of the subject, and there is no record of any discussion of it which may then have taken place. Internasjonalt utvalg, D Da 36, Arbeiderbevegelsens arkiv, Oslo.
[7] Zachariassen to Kendall, 9 July 1966, Zachariassen papers, C25, Arbeiderbevegelsens arkiv.
[8] These papers, with some Norwegian police reports, are in Boks 481, Rets A1.6, Riksarkiv, Oslo.
[9] Report by Ording on the International Socialist Conference in Paris, August 1946, Internasjonalt utvalg, D Da 10, Arbeiderbevegelsens arkiv.

provided the clue leading to the discovery of material in the Riksarkiv, recording a briefing given by Trifon Gomez to Lange and Ording in which Gomez discussed some of the methods which the British government was using in its attempts to remove Franco from power. This document explained the British policy in greater detail.[10] This in turn led to some documents in the National Archive which explained Foreign Office reactions to the inadvertent disclosure by Morgan Phillips of some aspects of this policy.[11]

Visitors were also used to carry sensitive messages, a role which the labour attachés often performed, as for example Inman did with the background briefing provided to Lie on Bevin's Western Union speech. Sometimes, the parties used official channels to send their sensitive messages, as Healey did via Robin Hankey to Lie before meetings of the Norwegian Labour Party and of the Scandinavian socialist parties to discuss Western Union in early February 1948.[12] Sometimes, too, officials were so intimately involved in party exchanges that it was they who made the arrangements or facilitated them. This happened, for example, when Kit Kenney (the information officer in the British embassy) identified the need for Healey to visit Oslo in 1947, and then made most of the arrangements as well.[13] It was therefore necessary to research a wide variety of different archives and sources in order to be able to present a composite picture of the relationships which existed at that time, and to discover what they achieved.

The most fruitful outcome of my research was the discovery of a significant volume of material on Norway in the FO 1110 series at Kew, which has to my knowledge not previously been examined for this purpose. This series describes the work of IRD following its establishment in January 1948. IRD was set up with the aim of combating communist propaganda,

---

[10] Letter from Berg, minister in Paris, 17 September 1946, enclosing Ording's report of the meeting between Gomez and Lange on 14 September, Boks 10505, 25.4/102, Riksarkiv.
[11] Western Department minuting, 18-24 December 1946, Z10586/36/41, FO 371/60371.
[12] Hankey to Oslo, 29 January 1948, N1336/34/30, FO 371/71485.
[13] Wardrop (chargé d'affaires) to Bevin, 22 November 1947, covering Kenney's report of Healey's visit, N13645/4718/30, FO 371/66061.

which was considered to be an increasing cause of damage to Western interests and influence. There is a rich vein of material on Norway which is effectively disguised from researchers because the cataloguing of the material, especially for 1948, but also to some extent during the next few years, conceals the nature of much of the contents.

These files are clearly significant. They cast new light on the development of Foreign Office strategy towards Norway in the early post-war period, on the importance which it attached to the development of closer links between the two Labour parties, and their respective labour movements, and on how it planned to achieve these objectives. They show how Sir Laurence Collier, the British ambassador in Oslo from 1945 to 1950, fleshed out policy proposals along these lines, which he had already been promoting since early 1946, to facilitate the work of IRD in Norway – and how he saw the opportunity to do so right from the outset at the beginning of 1948. In the early years, IRD work often sought to take advantage of labour movement links. However, apart from this and the British-Norwegian links which I examine, I am not aware of other significant cases where the Foreign Office sought to use the development of party relations as a tool of national policy in this way, to anything like the same extent. To substantiate this view, in addition to describing the origins of IRD, Chapter Four will examine the work done by IRD with socialist parties in three countries with very different circumstances - France, Italy and Burma. This will help to show quite clearly how the links with Norway were considerably closer and more effective.

In addition to the new information which has been obtained from these IRD files, it has also been possible to make use of the Freedom of Information Act to obtain the release of a range of documents which have also been relevant to my research. They have provided some valuable additional details, mainly but not exclusively about the work of IRD. Where they have been used, an acknowledgement has been made in the accompanying footnote.

It will be demonstrated that Collier played a crucial role in encouraging and facilitating the development of closer party links, and that he had identified the need to do this in a series of despatches which he wrote to the Foreign Office from early in 1946. He was assisted by staff who also had close links to the labour movement as well as to Norway. For example, Rowland Kenney who was married to a Norwegian, had run the *Socialist Review* and had then been the first editor of the *Daily Herald* in 1912, did information work in Norway from 1916 to 1918, served as the press attaché in Oslo in 1939, acted as an adviser to the Norwegian government in exile and was well-known to many senior members of the Norwegian Labour Party (Det norske Arbeiderparti – DNA). He served as the counsellor in the embassy in Oslo from 1945 to 1946. His son Kit also served in the embassy from 1946 to 1948, and so for a period worked as a colleague of his father . He, with others such as the labour attaché John Inman, was able to build on these links. They were especially close to Haakon Lie. There were frequent occasions, well exemplified by the visit of Healey to Oslo in October 1947, when the boundaries between diplomatic and party political work were so blurred as to be indistinguishable from each other.

2 The historical background

This chapter traces the development of links between the two British and Norwegian Labour Parties and their respective labour movements from their establishment until the end of the Second World War. There is relatively little documentary evidence describing their relationship during this period. The subject is not much covered in secondary material, except occasionally in anecdotal references. Nor is there much primary material. One of the main reasons is that almost all of the archives of DNA were confiscated by the Germans after the invasion of Norway in April 1940, and taken to Berlin. They were not recovered after the war, and had presumably been destroyed. Furthermore, the number and range of contacts between the labour movements were not great. For much of the interwar period, after it had disaffiliated from the Comintern, DNA was not a member of the Labour and Socialist International. Similarly, the Norwegian trade union organisation, Landsorganisasjonen i Norge (LO), had disaffiliated from the International Federation of Trade Unions (IFTU) for most of this same period. Both organisations were therefore outside much of the ideological and practical mainstream of the main European labour movements and thus lacked many of the opportunities for formal and informal contacts which would have permitted the development of closer relations with their counterparts. Moreover, many of the relatively few contacts which did exist, appear from the available material to have been developed for simple exchanges of information, rather than for the collaborative exchange of ideas and discussion of respective ideologies.

With the exception of the Trades Union Congress (TUC), founded in 1868, the other organisations were all established towards the end of the nineteenth century. DNA was founded in 1887 and won its first parliamentary seats in 1903. LO was established in 1899. (However, workers' organisations in Scandinavian countries had been holding joint meetings attended by labour and trade union delegates from Norway, Sweden and Denmark since 1886.[14]) The Labour Representation Committee (LRC), the forerunner of the Labour Party and also largely based on union support, was founded in 1900. It did not transform itself into the Labour Party until after the election in 1906, when it won twenty-nine seats. In the early days, both political parties depended on organised labour for a great deal of their support (many British MPs were directly sponsored by trade unions), but the Independent Labour Party (ILP), the Social Democratic Federation and the Fabian Society were also closely involved in the founding of the LRC.[15]

Early approaches

A small amount of material has survived in the Norwegian archive. The first record of contacts between the movements is a letter dated 28 January 1897 from the International Federation of Ship, Dock and River Workers, explaining its purpose, and inviting a delegate to attend a meeting.[16] There is no surviving record to show whether anyone accepted this invitation. The first letter in the British Labour Party archive is from Alfred Carter, secretary of the National Union of Quarrymen, to Ramsay MacDonald in June 1902. The union had decided to send Carter to Norway and he sought information about any labour organisation there with which he could get in contact.[17] Again, there is no record of any reply. The first significant visitor of whom there is a record was Martin Tranmæl, one of the most influential members of the Norwegian labour movement for more than

---

[14] John Price, *The International Labour Movement* (Oxford University Press, 1945), p16.
[15] Alastair J Reid and Henry Pelling, *A Short History of the Labour Party* (Palgrave Macmillan, 2005), pp1-4.
[16] Correspondence file, Internasjonale forbindelser 1896-1927, D Daa 6, Arbeiderbevegelsens arkiv, Oslo.
[17] Letter from A. Carter, General Secretary of the National Union of Quarrymen, to Ramsey MacDonald, 5 June 1902. International Department papers, Labour Party Archive, Manchester.

half a century and editor of DNA's paper *Social Demokraten* (later *Arbeiderbladet*) from 1921 until 1949. He visited the UK briefly in 1903 on his way to the United States for a study tour of the American labour movement, the first of two long visits which brought him into close contact with the new radicalism in American trade unions.[18] He went to London, where he was struck by the extent of the poverty in the East End, but was favourably impressed by what he saw of the socialist press there.[19] He had further contact with the British labour movement when he returned eight years later in 1911. On this occasion, writing for the Labour Party paper *Ny Tid,* he wanted to study the methods and tactics of the unions – particularly the seamen, dockers and railway workers, who had considerable success in strike actions which took place during that period. Tranmæl met prominent labour movement activists such as Ben Tillett and J. H. Thomas, but not Tom Mann, who was away from London where Tranmæl spent most of his visit. When Tranmæl returned to Trondheim, he held meetings with the unions there and worked out a programme for organised opposition in the Norwegian labour movement, based largely on the knowledge which he had gained in Britain.[20]

Radical groups within the labour movements

The Russian Revolution and the aftermath of the First World War produced considerable political uncertainty and social upheaval throughout Europe. Revolutionary factions within most socialist movements tried to assert themselves. However, DNA was the only major social-democratic party in Western Europe to go as far as to affiliate to the Third International, or Comintern.[21] It did so in 1919. DNA left the Comintern after considerable debate in 1923, mainly at the initiative of Tranmæl, when the party refused to

---

[18] Jens A Christopherson, "Mot Dag' and the Norwegian Left', *Journal of Contemporary History,* (1966), p136.
[19] Haakon Lie, *Martin Tranmæl. Et bål av vilje* (Tiden Norsk Forlag, 1988), p66.
[20] Ibid., pp138-142.
[21] Nils Morten Udgaard, *Great Power Politics and Norwegian Foreign Policy* (Universitetsforlaget, 1973), p20.

submit to Moscow's demand for it to exercise control. The Norwegian Communist Party, or NKP, was founded at this point from the small part of DNA which did not wish to abandon Moscow, although quite a number of DNA members remained sympathetic to aspects of communist ideology for some time afterwards. DNA was unified in 1927, when the group which had left in 1921 to found the Social Democratic Party (SPD) decided to rejoin the party. (It was only possible to achieve this by severing Norwegian links – through the SPD – to the Labour and Socialist International, or LSI.[22]) However, quite a number of radically inclined Norwegians did not rejoin DNA until rather later. For example, many of those (including Arne Ording) who coalesced around Erling Falk and formed the radical intellectual group Mot Dag, split from DNA in 1925. They did not rejoin until 1936.[23] In 1923, LO withdrew from the IFTU, which had been revived in 1919.[24] It did not rejoin until 1936: thus for a large part of the interwar period, both LO and DNA (which did not rejoin the LSI until 1938[25]) had no formal links to international labour movements.

There were similar differences within the British Labour Party, particularly among members of the ILP. By the mid-1920s a large section had begun to emerge as the most significant dissentient group within the Labour Party, after the election of Maxton as chairman in 1926, the year of the General Strike.[26] The ILP disaffiliated from the Labour Party in 1932 and after a conference vote in 1933, flirted with the idea of affiliating to the Comintern, though the negotiations came to nothing. At a Communist Party conference in 1935, Maxton also suggested a conference to establish a joint communist party which would represent every revolutionary

---

[22] Price, *The International Labour Movement*, p31.
[23] Jakob Sverdrup, introduction to *Arne Ordings Dagbøker 1942-1945* (Tano Aschehoug, 2000), pp18-19.
[24] T. K. Derry, *A History of Modern Norway 1814-1972* (Clarendon, 1973), p311.
[25] Price, *The International Labour Movement*, p45.
[26] Andrew Thorpe, *A History of the British Labour Party* (Palgrave, 2001), p58.

throughout Britain, though he subsequently claimed that he had only been talking about a federation.[27]

The activities of suspected Norwegian Bolsheviks

Although there were very few contacts between the parties until the mid-1930s, the activities of a small number of Norwegian Bolsheviks, or suspected Bolsheviks, caused significant concern to the British security authorities at this time. They were aware that contacts between Scandinavian socialists and the leaders of the Russian revolutionary movement were close,[28] and in the immediate post-war period, they were already taking steps to monitor revolutionaries who travelled from Russia to Britain via Scandinavia and Finland.[29] There is recently discovered archival evidence describing the arrest and deportation of Aksel Zachariassen, who provided money to Sylvia Pankhurst in 1919, an investigation into Leonard Aspaas in Shanghai and a long-running investigation into Arne Ording (foreign affairs adviser both to the wartime Norwegian government and later to Halvard Lange) between 1935 and 1978.[30] It is likely that knowledge of these activities would have encouraged the Foreign Office to hold the Norwegian government at arms length for much of this period.

In 1919 a young Norwegian journalist, Aksel Zachariassen, was arrested by the police in London after a meeting at which he had given £300 to Sylvia Pankhurst, the Bolshevik editor of the *Worker's Dreadnought*. He was deported back to Norway. His case attracted considerable publicity. Zachariassen subsequently maintained that he was

---

[27] Gordon Brown, *Maxton* (Edinburgh: Mainstream, 1986), p272.
[28] Patrick Salmon, *Scandinavia and the Great Powers 1890 – 1940* (Cambridge University Press, 1997), p173.
[29] Michael Futrell, *Northern Underground: Episodes of Russian Revolutionary Transport and Communications Through Scandinavia and Finland 1863-1917* (London, 1963), quoted by Salmon ibid. p173.
[30] These investigations are described more fully in an article by the author 'Britisk sikkerhetstjeneste og mistenkte norske bolsjeviker i mellomkrigstiden', *Arbeiderhistorie* (Årbok for Arbeiderbevegelsens arkiv og bibliotek, 2009).

not a Comintern courier.[31] However, there are documents in the Riksarkiv provided to the Norwegian legation in London by Sir Basil Thomson, the head of Special Branch, which show otherwise.[32] Thomson told the Norwegian Minister, Benjamin Vogt, that Zachariassen had been arrested in possession of Bolshevik literature and details of revolutionaries and anarchists living in London. Furthermore, during his interrogation, Zachariassen admitted that he had been carrying the money on behalf of Fred Ström, the secretary of what Thomson described as the Swedish Labour Party (although it was in fact the Swedish Communist Party). Thomson commented that the Swedish Labour Party had obtained the money from the Hungarian Soviet government. There was no doubt that Zachariassen had come as a Bolshevik emissary, because he was carrying messages from Bela Kun, the well-known Bolshevik who had led a coup in Hungary which led to the short-lived takeover of government there in March 1919. Zachariassen subsequently became the full time secretary of the Committee for Workers' Education in 1921 and had a long career in the Norwegian labour movement. He later returned to London to work as labour attaché at the Norwegian embassy from 1953 to 1955, where he succeeded Halvard Bojer.[33]

---

[31] Letter from Zachariassen to Kendall, 9 July 1966, Zachariassen papers, C25, Arbeiderbevegelsens arkiv.

[32] The papers on Zachariassen's arrest, interrogation and deportation are in Boks 481 Rets A1.6 in the Riksarkiv.

[33] Zachariassen must have been frustrated and disappointed at the outcome of his mission and his arrest by Special Branch. With perhaps understandable *schadenfreude,* in the file about this incident in Arbeiderbevegelsens arkiv, he placed two newspaper clippings from 1926 describing the trial and sentencing of a former senior policeman on a charge of violating public decency with a prostitute in Hyde Park. The policeman was Sir Basil Thomson, and he was fined £5. It seems that Zachariassen's attitude to Britain remained at least ambivalent for rather longer. During his posting in London as labour attaché in the early 1950s, several Conservative papers in Norway commented critically on some 'letters from London' which had appeared in the Norwegian labour press bearing the signature 'Old Boy' and which they alleged bore the imprint of Zachariassen's authorship. The letters carried distinctly partisan comment on the British general election, and the charge was made that Zachariassen was abusing his diplomatic position in London by writing such articles. Reporting this, the embassy in Oslo added that there was little doubt that Zachariassen was the author. Northern Department

The Zachariassen case was not the only attempt by Norwegians to provide support to Bolsheviks in Britain. In December 1920, Lloyd George announced in the House of Commons that two Englishmen and a Norwegian, Anker Pettersen, had been arrested in Newcastle and charged with attempting to smuggle several thousand Bolshevik leaflets into the country.[34] Pettersen was subsequently sentenced to three months' hard labour for his involvement. The consignment was linked to Folkets Hus, the headquarters of DNA. It later transpired that members of the Norwegian Seamens' and Firemens' Union had arranged the smuggling attempt without the knowledge of DNA headquarters. Commenting on this incident, the British legation in Kristiania (renamed Oslo in 1925) reported that on 30 December 1920, *Social Demokraten* had written that members of DNA were determined to continue to smuggle literature into Britain despite police efforts.[35] Shortly afterwards, the legation reported a confidential approach from the Norwegian Shipowners' Association, who were anxious that the British government realise that they were doing all they could to stop further smuggling. They asked the legation whether there was any public information available in England concerning the story that Birkeland, then Chairman of the Norwegian Seamens' Union, had taken gold to Britain in May 1919 which he had given to Sylvia Pankhurst for propaganda purposes. The Shipowners' Association thought that he had done so secretly.[36] There is no record in this file of any answer to their request.[37]

---

commented that it may have been improper for Zachariassen to mix diplomacy and journalism, but there did not seem to be quite enough evidence to warrant a complaint, particularly since he was due to leave London two or three months later. The matter was left there. Letter from Crawford to Hohler, 26 May 1955, and subsequent FO minuting, NN1905/1, FO 371/116495.

[34] This was reported in *Aftenposten* on 17 December 1920, quoting a speech by Lloyd George in the House of Commons the previous day and subsequently reported by the legation, FO 337/90.

[35] Despatch from Findley to Curzon, 31 December 1920, FO 337/90.

[36] Letter from Findley to Curzon, 31 December 1920, FO 337/90.

[37] However, the Shipowners' Association quite frequently passed on reporting about communist activities, mainly among seamen, to the legation during this period. See, for example, a report on the Pettersen case given to G. Warner on 23 December 1920, FO 337/90.

2 THE HISTORICAL BACKGROUND

There is also archival evidence of two British Security Service investigations of Norwegians during this period. The first concerns Leonard Aspaas, a Norwegian Comintern courier who was in Shanghai between 1935 and 1937, who was also the subject of SIS reporting.[38] However, there is nothing to show that Aspaas visited Britain. The second, and more substantial file, describes the investigation of Arne Ording, a distinguished academic closely involved in DNA activities. He was an adviser both to the Norwegian government in exile during the war, and subsequently to Foreign Minister Halvard Lange.[39] He and his sister Molla attracted attention because of their close links to two known or suspected GRU agents in 1934-35. Molla had worked as a governess for one of them, Mary Martin, who was imprisoned for espionage in Finland in 1935.[40] The other, Max Hodann, was a German-born doctor and journalist with long-term international communist and Soviet intelligence contacts.[41] The Security Service intercepted Ording's mail when he lived in London in 1935,[42] and following his return to London in 1940 they warned the BBC (for whom he was broadcasting)[43] and the Foreign Office[44] about him. After making enquiries, the Foreign Office concluded that there was no action they could take unless there was positive evidence to his detriment.[45] The file on Ording

---

[38] There are detailed file notes and correspondence on KV2/1821 describing the investigation into Aspaas. These include a letter dated 3 September 1935 from SIS to Captain Liddell in MI5, quoting CX/12650/3137 of 13 June 1935, which provided details of a wide range of his contacts.

[39] Arne Ording is the subject of a two volume case file, KV 2/2560 and KV 2/2561.

[40] Letter from Security Service to Vivian, SIS, 23 April 1935, KV 2/2560.

[41] The Security Service has released five volumes of documents on Hodann, KV 2/2339 – KV 2/2343. Although they refer only to his 'possible Soviet intelligence contacts', there are references on Ording's file, for example a note from J. C. Brown, K7/D2, in May 1976, which describe Hodann as a 'known GRU agent'. So it is not clear how valid the suspicions about Hodann turned out to be.

[42] Internal note signed by KMMS, 23 April 1935, KV 2/2560.

[43] Vivian of SIS had first drawn attention to Ording's broadcasting activities in CX 40316/Vb of 8 August 1940. Subsequent letter from Frost to Sir Stephen Tallents, 14 August 1940, and reply from Clark to Frost 19 August 1940, KV/2561.

[44] Turner to Warr (FO) 7 November 1940, KV 2/2561.

[45] Ward (FO) to Turner, 11 December 1935, KV 2/2561.

remained open for more than ten years after he died in 1967. It is most likely that this ongoing work was an attempt to follow to a conclusion all the leads which had come from the investigations into Martin and Hodann. The material which has been released is not sufficient to permit any conclusive judgement about the validity of Security Service doubts about Ording. There are probably many similar cases which are unresolved, either because suspicions cannot be completely allayed, or because conclusive evidence is lacking. Since many of the later documents have been redacted, it is not known whether they concerned Ording himself or, probably more likely, whether he was merely peripheral to a wider and more intensive investigation. Whatever the truth of the matter, Ording had a distinguished career as an academic, a senior member of DNA and a government adviser. He was also considered to be very pro-British. The embassy in Oslo was in frequent contact with him and in the mid-1950s, he visited the ambassador every week for a conversation about current issues.[46]

Diplomatic reporting

Most of the detailed material describing socialist links during this period is to be found in diplomatic reporting, rather than in the archives of the labour movements. The British legation in Norway reported regularly to the Foreign Office on the activities of the labour movement, covering both serious industrial unrest and also its international links. Their reports included a detailed account of the conference of the International Transport Workers' Federation (ITWF) in Kristiania in March 1920. The legation noted that it was attended by delegates from Sweden, Germany, France, the Netherlands and Britain: listed among the British representatives was Ernest Bevin, who had already been involved in work to reconstitute the ITWF.[47] The Congress was closed to all but socialist journalists, and the legation unsuccessfully approached the Norwegian Employers' Union and the Norwegian Shipowners' Association in an attempt to find out

---

[46] Crawford to Hohler, 19 December 1953, NN1051/2, FO 371/116470.
[47] Alan Bullock, *Ernest Bevin. A biography* (Politico's, 2002), p35.

what had transpired. They had better luck with the Chief of the Secret Police, however, who reported reassuringly that he did not think anything very disquieting had occurred.[48] He noted that some of the journalists, particularly the German one, had expressed surprise at the extreme views of the Norwegian socialists and that, on the whole, the foreign element, which was in the majority, had exercised a restraining influence. In the absence of the Russians, the Dutch delegates had represented the only really Bolshevik element among the foreigners.[49]

After DNA had disaffiliated from the Comintern in 1923, the legation in Norway provided less reporting on the activities of the Norwegian labour movement. It informed the Foreign Office of a trip to Oslo by Robert Stewart, the secretary of the British Communist Party in January 1927. Stewart addressed communist meetings with the object of opposing the merger of DNA and the Social Democratic Party into one party, and argued that the most pressing question, in Britain as much as in Norway, was to prevent the Labour Party from excluding the Communist Party.[50] Later the same year it reported on moves by Olsen, the chairman of LO, to enable LO to rejoin the IFTU. These were opposed by Tranmæl and the proposal was defeated at congress by a substantial majority.[51]

This was shortly after DNA had done well enough at the October 1927 election to be able to form the first socialist government in Norway, although it lasted little more than a fortnight, in January 1928. The party at this time

---

[48] In a diary note written on the day of Bevin's funeral in April 1951, Konrad Nordahl described a dinner with Bevin in 1942 when Bevin had spoken about a meeting of the IWTF in Amsterdam, shortly before this meeting in Kristiania. He said that it was the first time that he had met any German trade unionists since the war. A photograph which showed him shaking hands with them was published in the British press and aroused great indignation – so much so that on his return to London he was obliged to slip out of Victoria Station by a side entrance to avoid the large crowd which had assembled to beat him up. Konrad Nordahl, *Dagbøker Bind 1 1950-1955* (Tiden Norsk Forlag, 1991), pp76-77.
[49] Despatch from Findley to Curzon, covering a report by the Commercial Secretary Paus, 26 March 1920, 191432, FO 371/4088.
[50] Despatch by Lindley, 17 January 1927, N349/349/30, FO 371/12567.
[51] Despatch by Lindley, 17 January 1927, N6169/349/30, FO 371/12567.

was still considerably more radical than its Scandinavian counterparts. In his valedictory despatch in 1929, Lindley observed that although the Norwegian socialists had broken with Moscow and were the objects of outrageous abuse in the local communist papers, their leaders continued to repeat the old shibboleths. They still called themselves communists and preached class war.[52] Commenting shortly afterwards on a report about a DNA proposal to change the constitution, Laurence Collier in Northern Department noted that 'it was interesting as a further illustration of the extremism of the Norwegian Socialist Party which was really semi-communist.'[53]

There is no doubt that DNA was significantly more radical throughout this period than other socialist parties in Scandinavia. But diplomatic missions overseas were not, at this time, always well equipped to provide the kind of reporting then required in London by the new Labour government. An interesting example is provided by the visit of James Maxton, the chairman of the ILP, to Oslo in March 1930 when he attended the DNA congress and addressed several DNA meetings. (At this time, as Redvaldsen notes, the ILP probably resembled DNA rather more than the latter resembled the Labour Party,[54] a reflection of the fluctuating nature as well as the fluctuating fortunes of the different factions. DNA had been in loose touch with the ILP for some time: a DNA document, surviving from 1926, describes some ILP policies, and notes that Fenner Brockway, its secretary, was in correspondence with social democrats such as Halvard Lange.[55]) Maxton spoke critically of the British Labour Party and explained how the ILP was working for a single international, which would have the power to take up the fight against capitalism internationally. He called on DNA to

---

[52] Valedictory despatch by Lindley, 2 September 1929, N4026/443/30, FO 371/14015.
[53] Minute by Collier on a letter from Gascoigne, 3 October 1929, N4612/443/30, FO 371/14015.
[54] David Aly Redvaldsen, *The British and Norwegian Labour parties in the interwar period with particular reference to 1929-1936: Electoral Prospects,* unpublished PhD Thesis, p245, footnote.
[55] Letter from Haakon Meyer in Paris to DNA, 28 August 1926, Internasjonale forbindelser 1896-1927, Daa 6, Arbeiderbevegelsens arkiv.

fight for this. When the embassy reported his visit, Collier commented that their despatch showed the now almost wholly communist character and programme of DNA.[56] It was marked to Hugh Dalton, who had been appointed parliamentary under secretary following the success of the Labour Party in the 1929 election. He noted that

> It is clear that Mr Wingfield[57] has been somewhat perturbed by the tendencies of the Norwegian Labour Party, which has indeed moved visibly to the left. But the verbiage of political manifestoes is not always to be taken *au pied de la lettre*.
>
> I wonder, in this case as in others to which I have previously called attention (eg Vienna and Warsaw) whether our Minister at Oslo, or any selected member of his staff, has any contact with the political personalities of the left. If not, it would, I think, be valuable to establish contact. Without it, political reports will lack reality. Social contacts with the court and its environs do not give a complete picture.

Seymour noted that he had mentioned this point to Wingfield, who clearly acted on the recommendation.[58] A subsequent despatch concerning the aims of the party recorded his meeting with Edvard Bull, vice chairman of the executive committee of DNA. Collier noted that Bull was an undiluted communist, although he had quarrelled with Moscow about organisational questions.[59]

In his biography of Dalton, Pimlott wrote that according to Gladwyn Jebb, during this period Dalton 'regarded his Foreign Office officials as irredeemably bourgeois in

---

[56] Despatch from Wingfield, 22 March 1930, and minute by Collier, 4 April 1930, N2159/419/30, FO 371/14816.
[57] Minister in the legation in Oslo.
[58] Minute by Dalton, 12 April 1930, note by Seymour 15 April 1930, N2159/419/30, FO 371/14816.
[59] Despatch from Wingfield, 5 June 1930, and note by Dalton 24 June 1930, N4071/419/30, FO 371/14816.

their outlook on the world'.⁶⁰ It was perhaps not surprising therefore that it was Dalton who persuaded Henderson, the foreign secretary, to distribute to permanent officials in the Foreign Office copies of *Labour and the Nation*, the policy statement adopted by Labour at its 1928 conference.⁶¹ There is no archival evidence to show that the level of interest in the policies and activities of DNA which had been shown and encouraged by Dalton, and which was reflected in some of Wingfield's later despatches, was maintained in reporting from Oslo after the Labour Party had lost power and after staff in the legation had changed. Salmon notes that Sir Cecil Dormer, Wingfield's successor, had no social contacts with members of the Labour government.⁶² Olav Riste, who interviewed Dormer after the war, recalled that 'all that Dormer could remember was dinners at the palace'.⁶³ The Leading Personalities Review for 1937 reported that Halvdan Koht, the foreign minister 'was said to be a camouflaged communist'.⁶⁴ It is difficult to see on what this judgement may have been based, and provides further evidence that the legation was not close enough to leading politicians to be able to make informed judgements about their political views during this period. Salmon notes that as late as 1939, Collier observed that apart from his formal interviews with Koht, Dormer's contacts were mainly with the king and other Norwegians whose inclinations were conspicuously pro-British.⁶⁵ (As will be seen, this situation changed significantly when he became ambassador in Oslo after the war.)

The small Norwegian legation in London was similarly only rarely involved in reporting on labour movement

---

⁶⁰ Lord Gladwyn, *The Memoirs of Lord Gladwyn* (Weidenfeld and Nicholson, 1972), p39, quoted by Ben Pimlott , *Hugh Dalton* (Harper Collins, 1995), p192.
⁶¹ Reid and Pelling, *A Short History of the Labour Party*, pp56-57.
⁶² Patrick Salmon, *Scandinavia and the Great Powers 1890-1940*, p217.
⁶³ Olav Riste, quoted in Patrick Salmon (ed.), *Britain and Norway in the Second World War* (London, 1995), p37 quoted in Salmon, *Scandinavia and the Great Powers 1890-1940* , p217.
⁶⁴ Leading Personalities Review, 7 January 1937, N371/371/30, FO 371/21087.
⁶⁵ Collier minute, 1 September 1939, N4041/64/63, FO 371/23657, quoted by Salmon, *Scandinavia and the Great Powers,* p347.

activities.[66] However, Eric Colban, the Norwegian minister in London during this period, made several attempts to encourage Koht to visit London in 1938 and 1939. These foundered on Koht's reluctance to do anything which might compromise Norwegian neutrality.[67]

Limited contacts in the early thirties: greater British interest in Sweden

In an article entitled *Nordic Socialism on the March,* Bjarne Braatoy wrote in 1935 about the progress of social democratic parties in Scandinavia. He observed that the 'unruly member of the Nordic Social Democratic Party has since the war been DNA' and that the 'entering wedge of communism had proved more disruptive in Norway than elsewhere.'[68] The thrust of his article was that DNA had made much progress along the road back to democratic socialism. This no doubt contributed to a gradual increase in contacts during this period. In 1934 Einar Gerhardsen wrote to Middleton, secretary of the Labour Party, to seek an introduction for Arne Ording to Gillies, the secretary of the International Department.[69] In the same year Haakon Lie (then running the Workers' Education Office) made his first visit to Britain on a workers' holiday, shortly after Labour had won the municipal election in London.[70] The traffic was not all one way: Gillies, secretary of the International Department from 1922 to 1944, wrote to DNA in 1938 requesting assistance for John Huddleston, who wanted to develop some contacts within the Norwegian Socialist Youth Movement.[71] He also

---

[66] See, for example, reports on TUC congresses in 1930 and 1931, and a report on trade disputes legislation in December 1930. Boks 262 H49.E8, Riksarkiv.
[67] Letter from Colban to Koht, 3 February 1938, and subsequent correspondence, Boks 71 G8E.2/38, Riksarkiv.
[68] Bjarne Braatoy, 'Nordic Socialism on the March', published in *Labour Today* (January 1935), Gillies papers on Scandinavia, Labour Party archive.
[69] Letter from Gerhardsen to Middleton, 4 July 1934, Middleton papers on Scandinavia, Labour Party archive.
[70] Haakon Lie, *Loftsrydding* (Tiden Norsk Forlag, 1980), p377.
[71] Letter from Gillies to DNA, 25 July 1938, Gillies papers, Labour Party archive.

included DNA among a list of Scandinavian and European socialist addressees in 1937 when he wrote a circular asking for details of the costs of their royal family to their national budget, as well as other details such as their liability to pay taxes and whether their wills were published.[72] However, there is no evidence that he showed much interest in Norway. Most of Gillies' energy was devoted to building up the Labour and Socialist International (LSI): his biographer notes that he consolidated his position there through an alliance with the 'Scandinavian', anti-communist, wing.[73] This did not of course include DNA.

Such contacts, however, remained quite rare. In contrast, there was a greater affinity between the labour movements in Britain and Sweden. The press attaché at the Swedish embassy in London, Thorsing, was a journalist who had worked for *Social Demokraten* and was in regular touch with Gillies. The Swedish Social Democratic Labour Party (SDLP) frequently sought to exchange information with the Labour Party on questions of policy and ideology. Dalton wrote to the SDLP to recommend a student, Brinley Thomas, who was visiting to study Swedish economic and financial policy: he noted that he hoped to visit Sweden himself later in the year. Dalton also contributed an article to *Social Demokraten* about Gustaf Møller, the Swedish minister of social affairs and former editor of *Social Demokraten,* to mark Møller's fiftieth birthday. Arthur Greenwood was invited to Gothenburg and Stockholm to lecture on housing policy: Riess went in his place. George Dallas attended the SDLP congress in Stockholm in 1936 – the first time the Labour Party had sent a representative to a congress in Scandinavia.[74]

During this period, the growth of interest in the development of social democracy in Scandinavia in general – but in Sweden in particular - was reflected in a project implemented

---

[72] Letter from Gillies, 15 February 1937 and reply from Fredrik Haskund, 14 April 1937. Gillies' papers, Labour Party archive. Gillies sent this and other replies to Dalton, but it is not clear what Dalton did with the information.
[73] Entry on William Gillies, written by Christine Collett, *Oxford Dictionary of National Biography* (Oxford University Press, 2007).
[74] Correspondence about all of these subjects is contained in the Gillies papers on Scandinavia, Labour Party archive.

by the Fabian Society to research and write a book about Sweden. *Democratic Sweden* was published by the Fabian Research Bureau in September 1938.[75] It contained contributions from socialist academics such as Hugh Gaitskell, G. D. H. Cole and Christopher Mayhew, and was very positive about the achievements of the Swedish Social Democrats.[76] In their introduction, the editors paid tribute to assistance provided by Rowland Kenney, who had given them many useful introductions. They also commented 'on the growth in interest in England – by no means confined to the Labour Party[77] – in a people who appeared unostentatiously to have rid themselves of many of the evils which had racked their more powerful neighbours.'[78]

The key participants

By the 1930s, some of those who would play a key role in the promotion of closer post-war links between the labour movements had already become involved in bilateral links. Rowland Kenney's association with Norway had started before the First World War. He came from a poor working class family and, in his early years, earned his living as a pedlar before moving to London where he ran the *Socialist Review*. He subsequently worked for the Literature Department of the ILP, where his job was to make it pay its way. This proved difficult because of interference in his work; for example, Keir Hardie insisted that a book of articles on India should be sold for 1/-,

---

[75] Margaret Cole and Charles Smith (eds), *Democratic Sweden: A Volume of studies Prepared by Members of the New Fabian Research Bureau* (Fabian Research Bureau, 1938).
[76] The Fabian Society sponsored a similar book about Norway, researched and written by a group of Labour MPs, shortly after the Second World War.
[77] There is some limited evidence of Conservative Party interest, particularly by R A Butler, in the development of social democracy in Scandinavia before the war. 'Butler visited Sweden and Denmark, accompanying Sam Courtauld at the invitation in Sweden of Wallenberg. He liked the cohesiveness of Scandinavian society, and the strength of the rural communities which he contrasted with the situation in Essex where the villages were in decline'. (E-mail from Patrick Higgins, Butler's biographer, to Patrick Salmon, 29 April 2005.)
[78] Coles and Smith, *Democratic Sweden*, Introduction p.x.

and not at 2/6d. This was effectively at a loss. So Kenney left in 1906.[79] He married a Norwegian, Asta, in Kristiania in 1911. Shortly afterwards he found work on the *Daily Herald*. The *Daily Herald* was first published as a strike sheet in January 1911 and started as a daily paper in 1912 on capital of £300. Kenney was appointed labour editor in April 1912, at a time when the paper was edited by committee, but he gradually became editor by default and worked there for a year.[80]

During the First World War, the Foreign Office sent Kenny to Norway in 1916 to study the attitude of the Norwegian public and press to war problems. His report was accepted and he returned to Norway to implement his recommendations. Since he did not wish to work in the legation or as a British official, he was appointed Reuters correspondent in Kristiania in January 1917. His job was to explain British policy, and he wrote that he mixed widely. 'In my dealings with the Norwegian press, I never made a statement that was even partly untrue. If I could not truthfully say anything good, I said nothing at all. I gave information: I did not disseminate "propaganda" in the evil sense of that much abused word' (Just over thirty years later, this effective technique was developed and exploited on a much larger scale by IRD: Adam Watson similarly commented of their work that their basic approach was to use nothing but the absolute truth.[81]) Kenney organised a system to distribute articles to the Norwegian press to supplement the news services. He was strikingly successful in this work. In February 1917, he placed three articles; by July 1917, this had risen to sixty-eight; by January 1918 he succeeded in placing 223.[82] Kenney returned to Oslo as press attaché in October 1939 and remained in Norway until after the German invasion, sometimes bypassing Dormer and writing directly to Collier to obtain support for his work.[83] (Earlier in 1939, his son Kit had

---

[79] Rowland Kenney, *Westering*. (J M Dent, 1939), p134.
[80] Ibid., pp172-173.
[81] Conversation with Adam Watson (Deputy Head of IRD 1949-1950), 3 April 2007.
[82] *Westering*, p229.
[83] See for example Kenney's letter to Collier, 4 November 1939, in which he requested more staff to enable him to fulfil his work. Collier supported this and most of his other requests. N6223/6223/30, FO 371/23676.

been appointed press attaché in Stockholm, with responsibility for Oslo, but he was transferred to Helsinki shortly after the outbreak of war.[84]) During the Second World War, Kenney worked for the Norwegian government in exile in London before returning to Oslo as the counsellor in 1945, when he was well-equipped to make use of his extensive contacts.

When Laurence Collier was posted to Northern Department of the Foreign Office in 1925, he began an association with Norway which continued in one form or another until he retired as ambassador to Oslo in 1950. Collier came from a Gladstonian Liberal family, and was given what was then a modern education at Bedales, where he noted that several of his contemporaries embraced socialism 'and that even before 1914 I began to fear that there might be no political future for Liberalism in England'.[85] His experience there made it difficult for him to understand colleagues from more traditional schools.[86] In the 1930s Collier emerged as one of the strongest opponents of appeasement, and Goldstein notes that his views estranged him from many of his colleagues, and led some of them to view him as sympathetic to the Soviet Union. That was not the case. This is revealed in some of Collier's correspondence from this period, particularly when he was debating the merits of fascism as opposed to communism with colleagues such as Osborne (minister to the Holy See). His letters provided a clear assessment of the dangers of both communism and bolshevism but emphasised his view that the immediate problem was Nazi Germany and not the Soviet Union.[87]

By the late 1930s Konrad Nordahl (later to be chairman of LO) was playing a more important part in international trade union meetings. He represented LO at an IFTU conference in London in 1936, when he was much impressed

---

[84] British Council Memorandum, SW/6/1, 1939/40, 28 March 1939 and subsequent correspondence, FO 930/9.
[85] Sir Laurence Collier, *North House,* unpublished manuscript, lent by William Collier, p222.
[86] Erik Goldstein's description of Collier, *Oxford Dictionary of National Biography* (Oxford University Press 2007).
[87] D. Lammers, 'Fascism, Communism and the Foreign Office 1937-1939', *Journal of Contemporary History* (1971). Conversation with Dr Zara Steiner, 28 November 2006.

by Largo Caballero, the president of the Spanish TUC, who painted a graphic description of Spain under Franco.[88] He attended another conference in London in the summer of 1937, which produced little concrete assistance for the Spanish trade unionists. He noted that the most well-meaning and understanding participant was Ernest Bevin, whom he met here for the first time – 'but Bevin had no military support to offer'.[89] The connection of Nordahl's family with the British labour movement went back to the nineteenth century. Nordahl's father, who worked for part of his life as a seaman, was a member of the trade union movement for many years. The first union which he joined was the British Seamens' Union, in the 1890s.[90] Nordahl continued to pursue this connection when he was awarded a Conrad Mohrs scholarship to study socialism in theory and practice. He won a place at Woodroke College in Birmingham (which had been founded by the liberal Quaker, George Cadbury) where he studied in the autumn of 1937.[91]

The TUC

As LO moved back towards the mainstream of the European labour movement towards the end of the 1930s, it attempted to build up its contacts in Britain, but without great success. Thus LO invited the TUC to attend its first national congress after it had rejoined the IFTU in 1936. However, the TUC declined, explaining that it had been agreed that only the IFTU could attend international congresses.[92] (It took Collier's post-war intervention to persuade the TUC

---

[88] Nordahl, *Minner og Meninger* (Tiden Norsk Forlag, 1967), p226.
[89] Ibid., p229.
[90] Letter from to Nordahl from John Goss, Chief of the Economic Co-operation Mission to Norway, 25 January 1950, paying tribute to Nordahl's father shortly after his death, Nordahl archive, D0001, Korrespondance, Arbeiderbevegelsens arkiv. Nordahl also mentions his father's membership of the British Seamens' Union in *Minner og meninger*, p13.
[91] *Westering*, p229.
[92] Letter from Nordahl and subsequent correspondence, 292/948/1, TUC archive.

to change this policy.⁹³) After the war, Nordahl observed that there was little meaningful contact between British and Norwegian trade unions in the 1930s, and that when Norwegian trade unionists visited the UK, their British counterparts were not prepared to treat them to so much as a cup of tea.⁹⁴

Impact of the war

However, these relationships were transformed due to the war and the need to fight a common enemy. The TUC and Labour Party responded quickly to a request for assistance from the Finns in January 1940. Citrine telegraphed Nordahl to try to arrange a meeting with the Norwegian, Swedish and Danish party and trade union movements in Stockholm to co-ordinate possible assistance to the Finns.⁹⁵ Unfortunately, Citrine was delayed in transit, and the Danes and Norwegians had left by the time he reached Stockholm.⁹⁶ However, he had a productive meeting with all of them in Copenhagen when he was on his way home the following month.⁹⁷ This co-operation helped to influence his attitude to Scandinavian labour movements: the TUC responded quickly to a Norwegian request shortly after the German invasion in April 1940. Nordahl wrote to Citrine explaining that LO had been forced to abandon its funds in Oslo. He sought financial help. Citrine replied straight away, ordering that £1,000 be sent to Nordahl from the Finnish fund and asking the Foreign Office for help to transfer the money to the Norwegians. Telegraphic instructions were sent by Cadogan (then permanent under secretary) to Mallet, the minister of the legation in Stockholm. Lord Halifax, the foreign secretary, confirmed to Citrine on 22 May that the money had been passed to the Norwegian legation in Stockholm for

---

⁹³ Despatch from Collier to Bevin, 20 March 1946, N4417/219/30, FO 371/56284. This is dealt with in more detail in Chapter Three.
⁹⁴ Nordahl, *Dagbøker Bind 1*, p386.
⁹⁵ Telegram from Citrine to Nordahl, 15 January 1940, LO arkiv, korrespondanse, LO Db 0034, Arbeiderbevegelsens arkiv.
⁹⁶ Sir Walter Citrine, *My Finnish Diary* (Penguin, 1940), p23.
⁹⁷ Ibid., p181.

onward transmission to LO.[98] The funds were repaid by the TUC to the Foreign Office a week later.

After the German invasion of Norway, a number of Norwegians who were prominent in the labour movement travelled to Sweden, seeking to find ways of continuing their resistance by other means. They included Nordahl and Haakon Lie, as well as Lars Evensen, Nordahl's deputy in LO, who arrived in Stockholm in September 1941. Dalton, by then minister responsible for economic warfare and the Special Operations Executive (SOE), asked Nordahl and Evensen to go to England because he wanted some DNA representatives to advise on facilitating the planning of operations in Norway. Evensen declined because he did not think his English was good enough. He remained in Sweden throughout the war: Lie travelled to London with Nordahl in his stead.[99] Shortly after their arrival, they met Bevin, the minister of labour, who put them in contact with John Price,[100] who was Bevin's political secretary in the Transport and General Workers Union (TGWU).[101] As they got to know each other better, Bevin arranged for Price to give them weekly political briefings on significant developments.[102] Their relationship became close enough that, in 1943, Nordahl travelled to Iceland with Price to meet Icelandic labour movement representatives.[103] This had been proposed by Trygve Lie, the Norwegian foreign minister, who suggested that Price should

---

[98] Internal TUC correspondence and letters between Citrine and Halifax, May 1940, 292/948/1, TUC Archive, Warwick University. Nordahl also describes this request in his book *Med LO mot Friheten* (Tiden Norsk Forlag,1969), p29, although there are several differences in his account. He says that the sum given was only £100, and the dates do not match those given in the papers in the TUC archive. This is of little significance: what is more important is the speed with which the TUC responded to the Norwegian request.
[99] Conversation with Haakon Lie, 5 July 2005.
[100] Price, who was a Norwegian speaker, had worked at the Labour and Socialist International headquarters before the war. At this time he was secretary of the Political Department of the TGWU. After the war, he worked for the ILO in Geneva.
[101] Konrad Nordahl, *Med LO mot friheten* (Tiden Norsk Forlag, 1969), p87.
[102] Conversation with Haakon Lie, 14 December 2004.
[103] Nordahl, *Med LO mot friheten*, p126.

accompany Nordahl so as to make it clear that the visit had no ulterior motive.[104]

During the war, many others who were also to play a significant role in developing relations in the post-war period were moved into jobs which provided them with relevant experience and the opportunity to develop closer links. Thus Collier, who had been head of Northern Department since 1932, was appointed minister and later ambassador (in 1942) to the Norwegian government in exile. Rowland Kenney, after initially working in the Ministry of Information, was appointed an adviser to the Norwegian government.[105] Olav Bratteli, the first post-war Norwegian labour attaché in Britain, worked for the Norwegian Seamens' Union in London. While their focus was on contributing to the war effort, there were also frequent opportunities for formal and informal contacts to discuss political issues and to begin to plan for reconstruction once occupied Europe had been liberated – and to develop relationships which they would be able to put to good use once they had returned home after the war was over. During the later part of the war, contact between members of the LSI was maintained through a small committee of refugees in London. In March 1945, this committee passed a resolution calling for the earliest possible re-establishment of a Socialist International.[106] There were also significant improvements in and the rejuvenation of the organisation at Labour Party head office: Middleton was replaced as party secretary by Morgan Phillips in 1944. Gillies was finally persuaded to resign from the International Department in the same year. He was replaced by Denis Healey in 1945.

Tranmæl's Visit to London in 1942

The close co-operation which developed during this period occasionally provided some notable opportunities for one

---

[104] Letter from Bevin to Eden, 14 July 1943, N4113/4113/15, FO 371/36827.
[105] Cadogan to Monckton, 5 September 1941, N4893/4805/30, FO 371/29452.
[106] Denis Healey, 'The International Socialist Conference 1946-1950', *International Affairs*, (July 1950), p364.

side to serve the interests of the other. In October 1942, Ernest Bell (international secretary of the TUC) informed Sir Walter Citrine of an approach which Nordahl had made to John Price. Nordahl was concerned that Martin Tranmæl, though doing good work in Stockholm, was very cynical of the Allied war effort. He wanted to arrange for Tranmæl to visit Britain to see the extent of the work done there. However, Tranmæl had refused an invitation from LO to visit and had made it clear that nor would he accept an invitation backed by the British government. Nordahl thought that he might accept an invitation from the TUC, and asked if they would be prepared to offer one, making clear that they would not need to meet any of the costs. Price had added that Trygve Lie had emphasised that the Norwegian government also wanted Tranmæl to visit Britain. Citrine obligingly asked Bell to draft an invitation from him to Tranmæl, phrasing it so that it <u>looked</u> like a TUC invitation.[107] (This would have avoided the need to consult anyone else about what he wished to do.) Tranmæl accepted the invitation.[108] He had an extensive tour which included meetings with Attlee in the War Cabinet, Noel Baker, Henderson, Huysmans (the former secretary of the LSI), members of the Norwegian and British labour movements, many exiled European socialists and also trips to a wide range of factories producing war material. In his biography of Tranmæl, Haakon Lie concluded that the visit had made a very positive impression on him.[109]

During the war, Norwegian socialist politicians did not only work closely with their British counterparts. Some of their relationships with Conservative politicians were equally intimate and productive, in particular that between Eden and Trygve Lie, who got on much better than Lie subsequently did with Ernest Bevin.[110] Lie and Eden played tennis together quite frequently and sometimes confided in each other to a remarkable degree. After Lie's visit to Moscow in November 1944, when Molotov confronted him with an unexpected

---

[107] Bell to Citrine, 6 October 1942, 292/948/1, TUC archive.
[108] A facsimile of the carefully worded invitation is to be found in Haakon Lie, *Martin Tranmæl. Veiviseren* (Tiden Norsk Forlag, 1991), p321.
[109] Lie, *Martin Tranmæl. Veiviseren,* pp320-323.
[110] Conversation with Haakon Lie, 14 December 2004.

demand to share sovereignty of Svalbard, Lie stopped in Stockholm on the way back to London. He briefed Jens Chr. Hauge, the leader of the Norwegian resistance, on Molotov's demand, adding that he wanted to discuss the problem with Eden before he spoke to any of his Norwegian government colleagues.[111] His intention to take this unusual step is borne out by a report from the British ambassador in Moscow on 20 November 1944,[112] who had been told of Lie's intentions by the Norwegian ambassador, Andvord.[113] Eden noted in his diary that he had met Lie on 24 November: 'Lie came, he was in good form and worth hearing on Moscow. He maintains that it is possible to work with the Bear and that they want to work with us. Though he doesn't minimise the difficulties'.[114] Informing Churchill of some of the subsequent exchanges with the Soviet government early the following year, Eden noted that Lie was most anxious that the Soviet government should not become aware that he had been keeping Eden aware of these developments.[115]

Despite the lack of material covering the pre-war period in the DNA archive, the picture which emerges from other sources, relating to links between the two parties and their respective labour movements, is quite consistent. For a significant period after 1918, DNA was either so radical, or was considered to be so radical, that the mainstream of the British labour movement had little wish to collaborate with it. There were better prospects for co-operation between DNA and more extreme factions within the Labour Party, particularly once Maxton had been elected chairman of the ILP. However, there is no evidence to show that these links amounted to very much, and anyway, such significance as

---

[111] Conversation with Haakon Lie, 14 December 2004.
[112] Letter from Sir A C Kerr to Eden, marked Top Secret, Private and Personal, 20 November 1944. This letter, reference N8107/8107/G, is contained in the Avon papers, reference AP SCA 44/19.
[113] Rolf Andvord was the Norwegian ambassador in Moscow from 1942-1946. He served later as the ambassador in Paris (1948-1958) and in Madrid (1958-1961). He was also Secretary General in the Norwegian Ministry of Foreign Affairs from 1946-1948.
[114] Eden, diary note, 24 November 1944, AP 20/1/24, Avon papers.
[115] Letter from Eden to Churchill, 19 January 1945, PM/49/39, Reference SCA/45/3, Avon papers.

they might have had would have dwindled further once the ILP disaffiliated from the Labour Party in 1932.

Newly discovered documents – particularly those relating to the arrest and deportation of Zachariassen, reveal the extent to which Norwegian Bolsheviks or their supporters were involved in helping the incipient revolutionary movement in Britain during the early post-war period. These documents, and the material on Arne Ording, also provide an indication of the measures which were already being put in place by the British authorities, both in Britain and overseas, to counter both Bolshevik and possible espionage activity. While it is not clear to what extent the security authorities kept the Foreign Office aware of their investigations, it is reasonable to assume that these episodes would have added to a general distrust of the Norwegian left, thereby contributing to the arms length relationship during this period.

As moderate tendencies in DNA grew stronger in the 1930s, both the party and LO affiliated themselves again to the LSI and the IFTU. However, their attempts to build up their links with their British counterparts initially met with little success, partly perhaps because it may have taken time for residual suspicions and uncertainties to be dispelled. A more compelling reason, though, was that by then the Labour Party was much more interested in developments in Sweden and what had already been achieved there. So were the Fabians. Thus little progress was made. It was the outbreak of war, and the German invasion of Norway, which led to the increasingly close mutual understanding and co-operation on all levels between Britain and Norway, including their labour movements. This laid the basis for the much more effective collaboration which was to be achieved in the post-war period.

3 The development of a uniquely close relationship: 1945-1948

After the victory of the British Labour Party at the general election, the Party received the following telegram from Einar Gerhardsen, sent in the name of DNA:

> Your brilliant victory is greeted with enthusiasm by the Labour Party in Norway. It is our firm belief that this victory is the beginning of a bright future for the British people and for democracy and socialism all over the world. We look forward to strengthening the friendly collaboration between the Norwegian and British people towards this aim.[116]

This prompted the following reply:

> The British Parliamentary Labour Party on the eve of the new Parliament sends greetings to Norwegian socialists and hopes each may play a worthy part in the reconstruction of their countries.[117]

Both parties won resounding victories at general elections. The support enjoyed by their respective labour movements was also correspondingly strong. The TUC had a membership of over 6,650,000 members, while its Norwegian equivalent, LO, had a membership of nearly 400,000 out of a population of just under 3,000,000. This chapter will examine how the

---

[116] Telegram from Einar Gerhardsen to the Labour Party, 27 July 1945, DNA Internasjonalt utvalg, D Da4, Arbeiderbevegelsens arkiv.
[117] Telegram from Mr Carol Johnson, secretary of the Parliamentary Labour Party, DNA Internasjonalt utvalg, D Da4, Arbeiderbevegelsens arkiv.

3 THE DEVELOPMENT OF A UNIQUELY CLOSE RELATIONSHIP: 1945-1948

links established during the war were maintained and developed after members of the Norwegian government in exile had returned to Norway.

However, in the immediate aftermath of the war they were not extensively used. Given the relative paucity of communications before the war, it is not surprising that it took time to develop new methods of maintaining contact which suited both sides. This was not always straightforward. For example, the minutes of a DNA Central Committee meeting in July 1945 show that the British Labour Party was not at first included in the list of foreign parties to be invited to the first post-war national conference. The initial list included only the Nordic parties: the British were added later.[118] The British visitors were Harold Laski, the chairman of the National Executive of the British Labour Party, and Morgan Phillips, secretary of the party. This was the first time ever that a DNA conference had been attended by delegates from the British Labour Party and they were given a warm welcome. It was an important visit to a significant event – the conference at which DNA members debated and agreed their strategy for the forthcoming election. The delegates also discussed the complex question of whether they should have a joint list with the Norwegian Communist Party (Norges Kommunistisk Parti (NKP)). Laski (who during the war had himself been interested in the possibility of an accommodation between the Labour Party and the Communist Party) gave a speech in which he emphasised the importance of socialist reconstruction. He also thanked the Norwegians for Narvik, 'because it had enabled Britain to get rid of the Chamberlain government, which is the worst that Britain has had.'[119] A senior member of DNA told Rowland Kenney that it was the best congress that he had attended in over thirty years.[120]

However, post-war austerity - and equally importantly some travel restrictions - kept the number of exchanges and

---

[118] Minutes of DNA Central Committee 23 July 1945, DNA Sentralstyre møteboker A Ac, Ardeiderbevegelsens arkiv.
[119] DNA Landsmøteprotokoll 1945, Arbeiderbevegelsens bibliotek.
[120] Despatch from Collier to Bevin, 13 September 1945, N12515/203/30, FO 371/47521.

3 THE DEVELOPMENT OF A UNIQUELY CLOSE RELATIONSHIP: 1945-1948

contacts at a fairly low level during the next few months. Thus when Haakon Lie visited London in early March 1946 to discuss Spain with members of the Labour Party, he travelled on a flight secured for him by the British ambassador, acting on a request from the Norwegian Foreign Ministry.[121] Similarly when Mary Sutherland, Chief Woman Officer of the Labour Party, wished to attend the conference of Social Democratic Women in Oslo in August 1946, she sought Foreign Office assistance in facilitating air travel because other commitments prevented her from travelling by sea.[122] These travel problems continued well into the following year. In his contribution to the 1947 embassy annual review, John Inman, the labour attaché, commented that 'connexions with Britain have, unfortunately, been hindered by exchange and transport difficulties and – on the British side – by lack of funds'.[123]

In the aftermath of the war, it was scarcely surprising that Britain would maintain close military, economic and diplomatic links with Norway. Norway, after all, would have been considered to be just about Britain's most loyal European ally. Military links continued to be developed; Britain sold much equipment to Norway at reduced prices and Norway contributed forces to the occupation of Germany from 1947. Despite their war-ravaged economies, the two countries continued to trade extensively with each other. Diplomatic links were equally close. However, Collier did not think this sufficient. As Norway maintained an independent foreign policy and developed its policy of bridgebuilding, keeping its distance between both the main power blocs, he looked for other means to maintain British influence and to help to link Norway more closely to its former allies.

---

[121] Collier to Bevin, 28 February 1946, SC 46/1, FO 800/500.
[122] Letter from M.E. Sutherland to Bevin, 29 June 1946, N8601/365/30, FO 371/56291.
[123] Comment by Inman, acting labour attaché, Oslo annual review for 1947, 15 March 1948, N3433/3433/30, FO 371/71505.

Collier's despatch to Bevin of March 1946 recommends the development of links between the labour movements

Collier realised the importance of taking concrete steps to encourage the development of closer relations between the two parties and their respective labour organisations. In a detailed and carefully argued despatch, he wrote to Bevin in March 1946 to outline the need to encourage a better understanding of British policy among DNA members, and to explain why he thought this important. He described the fragmentation of the opposition and – with uncanny prescience - predicted that the dominance of the position of DNA was unlikely to be challenged for quite some time:

> The Labour Party has confidence in its own abilities and a great sense of responsibility, and there is reason to think that its strength in the country is on the increase rather than the other way around. The latest figures for the membership of the party are the highest ever recorded. The trade unions, which in the years before the war had already become very strong in Norway, also show a tendency to a further increase in membership since the liberation. The trade union movement has a strong central organisation, the unions are closely consulted on all measures connected with the government's economic policy, and take a positive and active part in reconstruction.[124]

He therefore concluded that in relations between Britain and Norway, the attitude of the Norwegian labour movement should be considered a major factor.

Collier further pointed out that this was important because the Norwegian labour movement probably resembled the British labour movement both in spirit and policy more closely than any other labour movement in Europe. However, the problem was that among the rank and file of the Norwegian labour movement, and certain of its leading personalities, the picture of Britain which existed was

---

[124] Collier to Bevin, 20 March 1946, N4417/219/30, FO 371/56284.

largely coloured by the socialist propaganda of past years; Britain was regarded as an imperialist power abroad, and at home as a country characterised by aristocracy on the one hand, and slums on the other. Collier explained that comparatively little was known of those democratic and socially progressive aspects of the British community which were becoming more prominent, such as the development of social services, interwar re-housing efforts, and the British trade union and labour movements. He highlighted a striking contrast between the lack of knowledge about Britain with a widespread impression that Russia was the true workers' state, and the country which should receive the sympathy and support of Norwegian workers. He believed that such an impression existed throughout much wider sections of the population than the comparatively limited number of members of the NKP. He also complained that while the DNA newspaper *Arbeiderbladet* was involved in frequent and bitter exchanges with the NKP on internal policy, it was also printing articles by Torolf Elster, one of its chief contributors, which invariably supported the Russian as opposed to the British thesis in any disputed question of foreign affairs.

Turning to his recommendations for some possible solutions, Collier explained that among the DNA leadership, and no doubt among the rank and file as well, there was a section which was much more aware of the actual conditions in Britain.

> This group is largely comprised of Norwegians who have been in Britain or in the United States during the war and it tends to be more internationally minded and less provincial in outlook than the average Labour supporter. This section, which is very influential in the Norwegian Labour movement, wishes to see the development of relations with Britain in all possible ways, through the exchange of information to the general and trade union press, the exchange of delegations of educational and trade union organisations belonging to the Labour movement, as well as the increase of facilities for the study of British social and labour developments and the expansion of contacts between Norwegians and British people who are involved in such matters. These people want to see

closer connections between the Norwegian and British Labour movements both because they want to develop united labour action on an international basis, but also because they want to set up a focus of interest which would counter the inclination towards Russia which might otherwise exist in the Norwegian working class.[125]

The key Norwegian participants

Collier did not identify any of those in this more internationally minded group who had been in Britain and the United States during the war. However, it is not difficult to work out who they were. The two most prominent Norwegians among the leadership who met this description were Haakon Lie and Konrad Nordahl. Lie was elected secretary of DNA at the party conference in September 1945, and held this position until 1969. Nordahl had been acting chairman of LO since before the war, and was substantively confirmed in 1946.

Unlike Healey, Haakon Lie had never been a member of the Communist Party. But as a young teenager, he had followed the events of the Russian Revolution with keen interest; at that time, he thought that the war for peace was more important than the war against poverty. He first began to be disillusioned with communism when he visited Moscow during the winter of 1933 and met an old friend, Rosa Marthinsen, a member of DNA who had married a Russian engineer whom she had met while a member of a party delegation visiting the Soviet Union. She had given up her Norwegian citizenship to protect him, but was now living in dreadfully straitened circumstances and wished to return home. Lie tried to obtain assistance for her through the Norwegian embassy and later through LO's legal section in Oslo, but without success. Although she was able to keep in touch with him for a while, Marthinsen subsequently disappeared. It was during this winter that three million Russians died of hunger. These personal experiences made

---

[125] Collier to Bevin, 20 March 1946, N4417/219/30, FO 371/56284.

3 THE DEVELOPMENT OF A UNIQUELY CLOSE RELATIONSHIP: 1945-1948

a deep impression on Lie: they marked the beginning of his detestation of communism.[126]

The Russian embassy became aware of Lie's developing views at a fairly early stage, before the German invasion of Norway. Viktor A. Plotnikov, the Russian plenipotentiary in Oslo, sent a report to Deputy Foreign Minister Solomon A. Lozovski in December 1939, describing Lie as a Trotskyist and outlining the work which he was doing to help support Finland during the Soviet-Finnish war.[127] Some years later, shortly after Bevin had made his Western Union speech in January 1948, Lie had a meeting with Mikhail F. Cherkasov, who reported on their exchanges to Moscow. Deputy Foreign Minister Valerian A. Zorin wrote to Sergei A. Afanasiev, the ambassador, reprimanding Cherkasov for his failure to refute 'rude and brazen' comments by Lie about Scandinavian military links, and his support for the Bevin plan for Western Union. Zorin instructed that, in future, no one from the embassy was to have any contact with Lie.[128]

Lie in particular, but also other members of DNA, were frequent visitors to Britain both to attend international socialist conferences (discussed in a later chapter on the Socialist International) and for bilateral exchanges - for example, visits to discuss Spain, which will also be examined later. They also met their British Labour Party colleagues regularly at conferences elsewhere in Europe. They therefore had many opportunities to maintain their contacts and for informal - and if necessary discreet - exchanges. Lie thought that this might have been the most important feature of international socialist co-operation during this period.[129]

Apart from the DNA members described by Collier, there was also scope for officials to play an important role. These included labour attachés. In London the first Norwegian representative was Olav Bratteli, who worked for the Norwegian

---

[126] Conversations with Haakon Lie on 5 and 18 July 2005.
[127] Letter from Plotnikov to Lozovsky, 17 December 1939, Sven Holtsmark (ed.), *Norge og Sovietunionen 1917-1955. En utenrikspolitisk dokumentasjon.* (Cappelens Forlag, 1995), p272.
[128] Letter from Zorin to Afanasev, 9 March 1948, *Ibid,* p417.
[129] Conversation with Haakon Lie 18 July 2005

Seamens' Union in London during the war.[130] He took up his post in early 1947. He developed a close relationship with Denis Healey, and with a range of other political contacts, both MPs and trade unionists, whom Lie had also recommended to him in an introductory letter.[131] Bratteli was quite frequently asked to represent DNA at socialist conferences or other important events when no one could be sent from Oslo. When Bratteli was not available, Anders Buraas, the *Arbeiderbladet* correspondent in London, would be asked to take his place. *Arbeiderbladet* had decided to open a London office after the war because 'there was such intense interest in Norway in the social and political changes which were taking place in Britain'.[132] Buraas also had a good relationship with Healey. Healey gave him an hour-long and detailed briefing on the national and international political situation every Monday morning, from early in 1947 until his departure from London in June 1949. When Buraas asked why he had been singled out for such privileged treatment (for Healey had told him that no other journalist received such briefings), Healey replied simply that 'Scandinavia is important to us'.[133]

With the exception of Olav Bratteli, the Norwegian embassy in London was not especially involved in work to develop links between the labour movements, although Eric Colban's successor, Per Prebensen, who arrived as ambassador in 1946, occasionally made use of some of Bratteli's contacts to resolve issues or to obtain information. Prebensen built on the extensive links developed by Colban and established a range of effective contacts with ministers and officials both within the Foreign Office and across Whitehall. He was probably closest to McNeil, though Bevin also occasionally confided in him. In December 1947, when Prebensen asked him for an explanation for the breakdown of the Foreign Ministers' Conference, Bevin spoke about the Russian demands for war compensation from Germany and

---

[130] Olav was the younger brother of Trygve Bratteli, minister of finance and later prime minister.
[131] Letter from Haakon Lie to Olav Bratteli, 26 February 1947, Lie arkiv, D Da 15, Arebiderbevegelsens arkiv.
[132] Conversation with Anders Buraas, 13 August 2005.
[133] Letter from Anders Buraas, 11 August 2005.

their continuing requirements for a share in current German production. He said that he would explain the background to him not as a foreign minister, but 'as friend to friend'. He explained that at both the Tehran and Yalta summits, Roosevelt had given the Russians to expect too much by way of compensation from Germany. The main reason for this, especially at Yalta, was that Roosevelt was willing to make major concessions to Stalin to encourage him to go to war against Japan. At that time the Americans did not have an atomic bomb, and Roosevelt's military experts had told him that the war against Japan would last another eighteen months after the collapse of Germany. During the Potsdam conference, when the Russians had still not joined the war against Japan, the Americans revealed to Stalin that they had the atomic bomb, so the war against Japan would be much shorter. Stalin then almost immediately said that Russia would be prepared to go to war against Japan – and the Americans once again left the Russians with the impression that they could expect significant compensation from Germany, which they remained determined to obtain.[134]

The key British participants

As with the Norwegian side, both party members and officials played a key role. The process was facilitated by the removal of the long-serving secretary of the international department of the Labour Party, William Gillies, who finally left his position in January 1945. Curiously for one in his position, Gillies (who was described by Arthur Creech Jones, the minister for colonies in Attlee's post-war government, as the 'least social socialist whom he had ever met'[135]) was not considered by some of his colleagues to be interested in developing closer relations with other socialist parties.[136] He was replaced by Denis Healey, who in November 1945 was selected for the job in which he served until the end of 1951. He considered his main tasks to be to rebuild

---

[134] Prebensen to UD, 24 December 1947, Boks 25.4/13, Bind XII, Riksarkiv.
[135] Haakon Lie, *Krigstid* (Tiden Norsk Forlag, 1982), p206.
[136] Ibid., p210.

relationships between the Labour Party and sister socialist parties in Europe, and to help in re-establishing the Socialist International.[137]

Healey joined the Communist Party when an undergraduate at Oxford University in the summer of 1937: his main reason for doing so was less an attraction to communist ideology than the fact that the Communist Party was the only party which at that time stood unambiguously against Hitler and fascism.[138] Healey noted that many politically active undergraduates at Oxford joined the Communist Party during that period for the same reason. An exception was Christopher Mayhew, who remained a socialist and who in 1948, as a junior minister in the Foreign Office, was to play a prominent role in the work of IRD. Although the situation changed with the Soviet attack on Finland, Healey did not leave the Communist Party until after the fall of France some months later, in the summer of 1940.[139]

The relationship between Lie and Healey was crucial to the steady development of closer links between the two parties.[140] Healey achieved a great deal during his time in the international department, on the most slender of resources. When he began working there, his only assistants were a young sixteen-year-old and a secretary, Chris Howie, who had been working for Healey's predecessors since the end of the First World War and who, as an early Fabian, had known George Bernard Shaw. By the time Healey left in 1951, he had acquired one deputy and a specialist on colonial

---

[137] Denis Healey, *Healey's Eye* (Jonathan Cape, 1980), p21.
[138] Interview with Andrew Whitehead 13 December 1991, when Healey discussed his membership of the Communist Party, CP/HIST/01/01, Labour Party archive Manchester.
[139] Denis Healey, *The Time of my Life*, p46.
[140] Healey maintained his connections with Norway after he stepped down as Secretary of the International Department of the Labour Party and was elected to Parliament in February 1952. When *Arbeiderbladet* had to close its London office to save money after the departure of Jacob Sverdrup in 1952 and following the opening of an office in Washington, Buraas, then foreign editor, invited Healey/ to write a weekly column for the paper. He produced over 700 articles during the next twelve years before he stopped on becoming Secretary of State for Defence in 1964. Conversation with Anders Buraas, 15 August 2005.

affairs.¹⁴¹ It is a reflection of Healey's energy and effectiveness that he was able to achieve as much as he did during this period with such a small staff, particularly since he was travelling a great deal.

There were several other key participants on the British side. The background of the ambassador, Sir Laurence Collier, was earlier considered in some detail in Chapter Two. Among the others were Rowland Kenney and his son Kit. It is unusual for a father and son to serve together in an embassy. However, Rowland Kenney's background was in any case unusual and his connections with Norway were very strong. During the war, while acting as a consultant for the Norwegian government, he travelled to North America to give a lecture tour about the Norwegian war effort.¹⁴² He was appointed counsellor in the embassy in Oslo in 1945, and was also responsible for labour affairs. After leaving Oslo in 1946, he worked in the Foreign Office Research Department and retained close connections with members of the Norwegian government, including Prime Minister Einar Gerhardsen and Foreign Minister Halvard Lange.¹⁴³ He sought a meeting with Attlee in March 1947 before a visit to Oslo, because he planned to meet both of them again in the course of researching another book.¹⁴⁴ The Foreign Office commented that 'he had a special position in Norway', and recommended that Attlee find time for him.¹⁴⁵

Kenney's son, Kit arrived in Oslo in early 1946 to work as the press attaché. Kit Kenney already knew Haakon Lie: they had first met by chance on a train in Finland in late 1939, shortly after the beginning of the Winter War

---

¹⁴¹ Denis Healey, *Healey's Eye,* p21.
¹⁴² Letter from Kenney to Warner, September 1942, seeking permission to make this trip on behalf of the Norwegian government, Boks 11244, 40.6/33, Riksarkiv.
¹⁴³ Lange had spent some time in England before the Second World War, working in London for a pacifist organisation. In 1927, he studied at the LSE under Laski. Undated Norwegian Information Bureau bulletin, N1967/1345/30, FO 371/56302.
¹⁴⁴ In 1946, Kenney had published *The Northern Tangle* (J. M. Dent), a history of the countries of Scandinavia and their problems in the post-war world.
¹⁴⁵ Letters from Kenney to Attlee, March 1947 and from Halford to Addis, 10 Downing Street, 3 April 1947, N4067/66/30, FO 371/66020.

between Finland and the Soviet Union. Lie was evaluating a Finnish request for assistance, while Kenney did not reveal to Lie what he was doing there.[146] At that time, he was actually working as a press attaché in the British embassy in Stockholm.[147] Kenney, who also had some experience as a journalist, had spent part of the war working in the Political Warfare Executive (PWE) which was responsible for dealing with 'black' propaganda. During that period he had run a number of courses for intelligence officers who were later to work in Norway.[148] In early 1944 he was involved in planning for the Normandy invasion insofar as it affected Norway, and in resolving propaganda and information planning issues with the Norwegian High Command. This job required tact and skill because Norwegian relations with PWE were not always harmonious. The Norwegian government considered propaganda and political warfare in Norway to be an internal Norwegian affair and was reluctant to allow PWE any independence in the way it discharged its responsibilities there.[149]

Shortly after his arrival in Oslo in 1945, Kit Kenney secured agreement to enlarge the press section and arranged for John Inman (with whom he had worked in PWE) to be transferred from the Ministry of Information in London to work as a press reader in the embassy.[150] After the departure of Rowland Kenney, Inman was appointed acting labour attaché, a job which he held until early 1949.[151] Inman did not come from the Ministry of Labour and was not a part of the cadre of labour attachés which Bevin wanted to build up during this period. His background, based on wartime propaganda work, had not given him any particular experience for this job. When he left Oslo, he returned to London to obtain a position in the Colonial Office.[152] Nonetheless, despite his

---

[146] Conversation with Haakon Lie, 5 July 2005.
[147] A Ministry of Information Publicity Division Planning Section paper of 2 September 1939 noted that a press attaché, Mr K Kenney, had been appointed to cover Stockholm and Oslo, FO 930/9.
[148] David Garnett, *The Secret History of PWE* (St Ermin's Press, 2002), p339.
[149] Various papers in FO 898/242.
[150] Collier to FO, 9 August 1945, N10104/150/30, FO 371/47504.
[151] Kenney to Western European Information Department, 11 July 1946, P/1300, FO930/414.
[152] Inman to Tracey, 292/948/2, TUC Archive, Warwick University.

lack of labour experience, he established himself quickly, developed a wide network of contacts and was able to play a useful role, especially after the establishment of IRD in January 1948. Haakon Lie described him as 'a member of the family' and he was sometimes used to pass sensitive messages from Healey to Lie which the former did not wish to entrust to open communications or even to official Foreign Office channels.[153] Both Kenney and Inman travelled widely through Norway. The contacts which they made helped to consolidate links with provincial labour movements, and their reporting provided useful insights into the political situation outside Oslo. For example, Kenney reported in June 1946 the NKP's enthusiastic promotion of anti-British propaganda in northern Norway, portraying the British as dishonourable and claiming (plausibly but inaccurately) that they had irresponsibly destroyed captured German materials which might have been of benefit to Norwegians.[154] After his departure in 1948, Kenney was awarded an OBE for his work in Oslo.

Some Labour MPs also established a reputation for their interest in and closeness to Norway. Prominent among them was William Warbey[155] who had worked as an information officer for the Norwegian government in exile. He was elected to Parliament in 1945 and frequently visited Norway, first shortly after the war as a guest of the Norwegian government.[156] One particularly significant trip took place in April 1948, when he accompanied a group of mainly left-wing Labour MPs, on a trip arranged by the Fabian Society, to gather material for a book about post-war Norway. (This will be examined in more detail later in the chapter.) Lie

---

[153] Conversation with Haakon Lie, 14 December 2004.
[154] Report by Kenney on a visit to Nordland and South Troms, 30 May – 8 June 1946, N8433/528/30, FO 371/56292.
[155] Warbey was always to the left of the Labour Party, but moved further in that direction from the late 1950s onwards, when he adopted an extreme left-wing line which led him to write and publish *Vietnam, the Truth*. In his diaries describing this period, when the Labour government had a majority of only three, Richard Crossman described Warbey as 'the only dangerous, erratic man who could lose Labour their majority.' *Diaries of a Cabinet Minister Volume One* (Hamilton, 1975), p322.
[156] Note in UD files concerning details of the trip made by Warbey and his wife at government expense, Boks 11268, 40.6/13, Riksarkiv.

3 THE DEVELOPMENT OF A UNIQUELY CLOSE RELATIONSHIP: 1945-1948

recommended Warbey to Bratteli: he had also encouraged contact with Patrick Gordon Walker.[157] However, in the post-war period, Gordon Walker was not as deeply involved in Norwegian affairs as Warbey, largely because he was to be distracted by other business, particularly after he was appointed a junior minister in the Commonwealth Office.

In the period after it was re-established in Norway, the British embassy made effective use of existing wartime contacts to maintain and extend its links with those members of DNA and LO who had been in London during the war and who subsequently joined the government. Rowland Kenney also took advantage of his Labour Party background to build up links with other members of DNA, particularly the prime minister, Gerhardsen, who had remained in Norway during the war before being transported to Sachsenhausen concentration camp. In early 1946, Kenney reported to Collier a discussion with Gerhardsen on foreign affairs. Gerhardsen said that he thought that the next few months would be a transition period which would decide whether the nations of the world would work for peace or quarrel among themselves, and that during this period it would be best if the Norwegian people attended to their own affairs and did not argue about world issues. He maintained that it would certainly be of no benefit to Norway or to its people if it became involved in serious argument. Kenney commented:

> We had further talk about this and I mentioned the dangers of the Norwegians becoming indifferent and psychologically isolated and ignoring their responsibilities as world citizens. To this, Gerhardsen remarked that he had referred to this 'transition period' but I doubt whether he realised the full extent of the danger. In fact, I fear that he is himself too self-centred as a Norwegian, and has not yet had the time and experience to enable him to develop an international outlook.[158]

---

[157] Letter from Lie to Olav Bratteli, 26 February 1947, Lie arkiv, D Da 15, Arbeiderbevegelsens arkiv.
[158] Minute by Rowland Kenney to Collier, 30 January 1946, N2083/1345/30, FO 490/005.

Reporting of this nature clearly helped to shape Collier's views. Some of the concerns expressed here, as well as the wording, are to be found in his subsequent policy recommendations to Bevin, which are described below.

During this period, the Foreign Office began to express concern about the dangers of the growing influence of communism in Norway. As early as July 1945, Christopher Warner, head of Northern Department, wrote to Collier to ask for comments on a report from the American embassy in Stockholm, which he thought unduly belittled the prospects of NKP in Norway. Collier's reply pointed out the extent to which Norwegians respected Soviet achievements during the war and their contribution to the liberation of Norway, though he balanced these observations by recalling how badly the NKP had behaved in Norway up until the time when Germany had invaded the Soviet Union.[159]

Collier's recommendations for developing closer trade union contacts

In his despatch to Bevin, Collier made two specific recommendations. He said that LO had invited the TUC to attend its annual congress in May 1946. Nordahl, the chairman of LO, had made clear that this was not merely a pro-forma invitation. He had emphasised that the presence of a British delegation would be greatly appreciated. Furthermore, Collier knew that LO would welcome an invitation to the annual congress of the TUC in the autumn and that Norwegian unions were generally keen to exchange visits with their British counterparts at their annual conferences. Collier concluded that it would be in the interests of the British government for such invitations to be accepted. He hoped that the TUC could be encouraged to respond favourably.[160]

---

[159] Warner's letter to Collier of 6 July 1945, Collier's letter to Warner of 24 July 1945. These papers are contained in a file of Oslo embassy correspondence in the National Archives, 337/104, and do not have a fuller reference.
[160] Collier to Bevin, 20 March 1946, N4417/219/30, FO 371/56284.

3 THE DEVELOPMENT OF A UNIQUELY CLOSE RELATIONSHIP: 1945-1948

Shrewdly, Collier did not point out that acceptance of this invitation would require the TUC to change its policy. Nor did he mention, as he would surely have known, that LO had sent its invitation to the TUC in January 1946 but had not yet received a reply. LO had invited the TUC to attend its own congress on more than one occasion before the war, but the TUC had always declined. Its policy then was that only the International Federation of Trade Unions (IFTU) could attend such international congresses.[161]

Shortly after Collier had sent his despatch to Bevin, Inman wrote in March to Ernest Bell, international secretary of the TUC, asking for assistance in developing relations between the British and Norwegian labour movements. He explained that he wished to promote this by encouraging the exchange of delegations to conferences, through study visits and by exchanging information. He also sought assistance in enabling LO to acquire a better understanding of the relatively more complicated TUC structure. He offered in return to help facilitate visits by TUC delegations to Norway by arranging meetings with leading figures in the Norwegian labour movements, thereby also enabling TUC officials to study local conditions. In his reply, Bell provided the information and the literature which Inman had requested, and a regular correspondence developed thereafter.[162]

After some hesitation about how to respond to Collier's suggestion, Northern Department drafted a letter for Bevin to send in late April to Sir Walter Citrine, general secretary of the TUC. The letter laid out the background and explained why Bevin hoped that the TUC would be able to accept the invitation to attend LO's congress, invite LO to attend its own congress and also encourage further similar exchanges.[163] Citrine replied that the TUC had decided to accept the invitation to attend the LO congress. They would send Luke Fawcett, the general secretary of the Amalgamated Union of Building Trade Workers. He added though that it would be difficult for the TUC to invite LO to attend their congress in

---

[161] Citrine letter, 20 June 1938, 292/948/1, TUC Archive.
[162] Inman to Bell and subsequent correspondence, 292/948/1, TUC Archive.
[163] Bevin to Citrine, 23 April 1946, N4417/219/30, FO 371/56284.

October, because they would then be obliged to invite quite a number of other national trade union organisations. They wished to avoid this complication.

After the LO congress, Fawcett wrote a report recording that it had been attended by representatives from France, the USA, Denmark, Sweden, Finland and Switzerland and had been addressed on the first day by the Norwegian prime minister, Gerhardsen. Vincent Tewson, the assistant general secretary of the TUC, then informed Bevin that the TUC had decided after all to invite LO as an observer to its October congress.[164] Tewson wrote to Nordahl on the same day to extend the invitation, referring in positive terms to the reception which Fawcett had been given in Oslo.[165]

Collier's recommendation for a visit by a British MP

In his despatch, Collier had further recommended to Bevin that an MP in the confidence of the government, but without an official position, should be invited to Norway to give some private talks to Norwegian Labour Party leaders on the situation in Britain and the aims of British policy abroad. He had reason to believe (and had therefore presumably discussed it with some of those party leaders beforehand) that it would be possible to organise such meetings.

The implementation of this recommendation, which was accepted, created a problem in London. Someone in the Foreign Office (it is not clear who) decided that Warbey, because of his long experience of Norway, would be a suitable choice. By this time, though, Warbey was acquiring a reputation for strong left-wing and pro-Russian views. This did not appear to have been appreciated at all levels in the Foreign Office, or at least by whoever authorised the invitation to him. So Warbey was invited. He accepted, adding the caveat that he could offer no assurances as to what he might say on Spain, on which he held strong anti-Franco views. When the Foreign Office informed the embassy of their selection of Warbey to fulfil this mission and of his comments on Spain,

---

[164] Tewson to Bevin, 22 May 1946, 292/948/1, TUC Archive.
[165] Tewson to Nordahl, 22 May 1946, LO arkiv, D Db 0014, Arbeiderbevegelsens arkiv.

they replied that this issue was now of no consequence. The Norwegian government's and DNA's policy on Spain had been fixed. However, they pointed out that Warbey was becoming well-known for his left wing views and asked whether his general attitude was now such that a visit by him would indeed help to meet the objective of countering pro-Soviet bias. In response Christopher Warner, by now assistant under secretary dealing with Soviet and Eastern European matters, commented that it would be unfortunate if a persistent critic of the secretary of state should visit Norway with Foreign Office approval. The minister of state, McNeil, agreed that it was a matter of some delicacy. He said that he wanted to talk to Warbey before deciding whether or not he should go.[166]

Before a decision was taken, Collier wrote to Robin Hankey,[167] who had replaced Warner as head of Northern Department, enclosing what he described as a sensitive minute from Inman which commented adversely on Fawcett's visit in May to the LO congress and which also questioned Warbey's suitability to visit Norway under Foreign Office auspices. (In this letter, Collier commented that Inman was now the chief contact with Labour circles following the departure of Rowland Kenney, and recommended his work, saying that he knew what he was talking about.) Inman wrote that Fawcett was a most knowledgeable interlocutor on trade union administration and the area of his expertise but that, when compared with the generally young and progressive Norwegian trade unionists, he came across as elderly and old-fashioned. This was clearly apparent during the LO conference. He was not able to talk about political issues, either domestic or foreign, he was ill at ease with foreigners and he had snubbed several Norwegians who tried to talk to him, including Tranmæl, prominent member of DNA and the edi-

---

[166] Correspondence and minuting on N6354/219/30, FO 371/56284.
[167] Hankey had just completed a short posting in Warsaw. Rothwell asserts that this experience did more than anything to form his attitude to wider policy-making during the Cold War: he was aware of how difficult it was to persuade liberals and social democrats of the aims and nature of communism. V. Rothwell, 'Robin Hankey', in J. Zametica (ed.), *British officials and British foreign policy 1945-50* (Leicester University Press, 1990), pp156-189.

tor of *Arbeiderbladet*. Although Fawcett gave a good speech to the congress, he made a decidedly bad impression. (Not surprisingly, the Foreign Office did not pass these comments back to the TUC. Presumably as a result, later the same year Fawcett also represented the TUC at the triennial congress of the Swedish TUC in Stockholm.[168]) On Warbey, Inman commented that he knew him well: he was one of the few British politicians of any colour with any knowledge of Norway, even if he was sometimes a foolish, uncritical admirer of it. He did not think that it would do Britain any good to have him making speeches which might strengthen pro-Russian feelings and which would be critical of Britain. In view of this advice, McNeil decided that Warbey should not go and chose Adam McKinlay, the MP for Dumbarton, instead.[169]

Members of DNA would have been well aware of Warbey's views on foreign policy at that time.[170] However, there is no indication that they found him an undesirable interlocutor as a result of this, either then or later. On the contrary, his opinions would have struck quite a wide resonance among those DNA MPs who were committed to the policy of bridge-building and maintaining a distance between the Soviet Union on the one hand, and the United States and Britain on the other. Furthermore it was only shortly afterwards, in February 1947, that the committed anti-communist Haakon Lie recommended him to Olav Bratteli.[171] Warbey continued to visit Norway regularly until he temporarily lost his seat as an MP at the 1950 election. In the event, perhaps because of the passage of time, the invitation to McKinlay does not appear to have been pursued.

Instead, probably at the instigation of the British embassy, DNA itself decided to invite a group of Labour MPs to visit Norway. Haakon Lie and Åke Ording (secretary of the DNA Storting Group and a member of the central comm-

---

[168] Healey to Mayhew, 4 December 1946, N15638/15638/63, FO 371/56245.
[169] Collier to Hankey, 16 May 1946, enclosing a minute by Inman, 14 May 1946. Minute by Hankey, 6 June 1946, and letter to Collier, 13 June 1946, N6470/219/30, FO 371/56284.
[170] Arne Ording, *Dagbøker 24 July 1945 - 4 April 1949* (Universitetsforlaget, 2003), p88.
[171] Lie to Bratteli, 26 February 1947, Lie arkiv, D Da 15, Arbeiderbevegelsens arkiv.

ittee) told Kit Kenney in June 1946 that they would like to see a visit to Norway in October by a group of MPs including Warbey, Christopher Mayhew, Hugh Gaitskell and Patrick Gordon Walker (then a member of the Labour Party Foreign Affairs Committee). Collier reported this to the Foreign Office with a recommendation that it be pursued. Hankey replied that that there would be problems with a delegation comprising members from just one party. He suggested instead that DNA should invite the delegation and look after all their costs in Norway. He also pointed out that since Gaitskell had just been made Minister of Fuel and Power, he would not be eligible for an invitation.[172] Not surprisingly, in view of these difficulties, the Embassy did not pursue this idea further.

However, Haakon Lie found another solution. On 14 October he wrote to Carol Johnson, the secretary of the Parliamentary Labour Party (PLP), inviting between two and four members of the Labour Party to visit Norway for a fortnight, travel separately around the country and address local Labour Party organisations. He said that these local organisations would wish to hear about British reconstruction and social progress, and the work of the Labour government. He wanted the visit to take place as soon as possible. Three MPs, Harold Neal, Jean Mann, and Stephen Swingler visited Norway for two weeks in November and travelled separately to different parts of the country.[173] The visits were successful, and were still the cause of favourable comments when Inman went a few months later to some of the provinces they had visited.[174] In view of the concern shown earlier over the choice of Warbey to visit Norway, it is worth noting that only a few months earlier, in March 1946, Swingler had been one of a group of half a dozen Labour MPs who were the sternest and most outspoken critics of Bevin's foreign policy. Bevin had been obliged to confront these critics at a stormy meeting of the Parliamentary Labour Party,

---

[172] Collier to Hankey, 26 June 1946, Hankey to Collier, 12 August 1946, N8221/219/30, FO 371/56284.
[173] Lie to Johnson, 15 October 1946, DNA Internasjonalt utvalg, D Da 10, Arbeiderbevegelsens arkiv.
[174] Collier to Bevin, 18 June 1947, N7187/66/30, FO 371/66072.

where he won a vote by a convincing majority.[175] Given the views which he held on Bevin's policies at that time, it is not surprising that in a separate report which he sent to Mayhew, Swingler commented on the depth of interest he had found expressed in Norway in the programme of the British Labour government: he added that he had received a great deal of criticism of British foreign policy, particularly on Spain. He noted that there was very strong sympathy in Norway towards the Spanish Republican movement and commented that DNA was carrying out a campaign for relief and assistance to Spanish socialists.[176] Lie had earlier written to Philip Noel Baker, inviting him to visit Norway, and adding significantly that it might be useful if the British Labour Party were to become aware of some of the problems now facing DNA in Norway.[177] There is no record to show that this invitation was followed up, which probably explains why Lie chose to invite a delegation from the PLP instead.

Collier reported that the visit of these MPs had been a great success. In addition to meetings with Lange and DNA members in the Storting, the group made separate trips to a large number of provincial centres and addressed up to ten meetings each, almost all of which were well attended. He added:

> This is the first occasion on which a group of British speakers on British political and social affairs has been able to devote sufficient time (and stamina) to establishing touch with the rank and file of the labour movement throughout southern Norway, and it is abundantly evident that the results have justified both the efforts of the visitors and the embassy and the Foreign Office to bring the visit about.... As a means of influencing the Norwegian popular outlook on British policy this visit will, I think, prove more important than all the previous visits by British lecturers and personalities, and there is some irony in the

---

[175] Article in the Observer of 13 March 1946, Ambassaden i London: Politiske Meldinger, Boks 25.4/13, Bind VII, Riksarkiv.
[176] Swingler to Mayhew, 19 December 1946, N16389/528/30, FO 371/56292.
[177] Lie to Noel Baker, 12 July 1946, DNA Internasjonalt utvalg, D Da10, Arbeiderbevegelsens arkiv.

fact that the expenses attending so successful an effort of national propaganda have been borne entirely by the Norwegian and British Labour Parties. I cannot emphasise too strongly that visits of this kind are of cardinal importance in fostering good relations between Britain and Norway and in promoting a real understanding among Norwegians of British aims and policies, and that British interests would be well served by stimulating further visits by British delegations.[178]

Noting how widely the group had travelled, Hankey commented that perhaps a number of relatively low-level visits like this would be better than a few ministerial ones. He marked the papers to Mayhew, and suggested that Collier's despatch should be shown to Healey. Mayhew agreed and arranged it.[179]

Other contacts between the parties and labour organisations

Not all the exchanges which took place during this period were arranged through diplomatic or party channels. Notwithstanding the travel restrictions, there were a few others. A delegation from the Postal and Telegraph Union visited Norway in October 1945. Jarman, the chairman of the British Seamens' Union, also went to Norway in February 1946. In both cases the embassy was unaware of the incoming delegations until after they had left, when they read about them in the Norwegian press. The embassy wrote to Northern Department on 9 April 1946, asking for assistance which might help to provide them with some forewarning of incoming visits: they also wrote in similar terms to Morgan Phillips. The Foreign Office thought the lifting of travel restrictions might make this difficult but undertook to do what it could.[180] There were also visits in the other direction, to Britain. Several journalists from Østfold including Reff,

---

[178] Collier to Bevin, 5 December 1946, N16155/219/30, FO 371/56286.
[179] Ibid.
[180] Wardrop to Allen, 9 April 1946, Allen to Wardrop, 12 May 1946, N4930/219/30, FO 371/56284.

3 THE DEVELOPMENT OF A UNIQUELY CLOSE RELATIONSHIP: 1945-1948

the secretary of the provincial DNA newspaper *Fredrikstad Demokraten,* had visited the UK in late 1945.[181]

In early 1946, Kit Kenney arranged for a visit to Britain by twelve members of the Norwegian Iron and Metal Workers' Union, the largest and most influential Norwegian union with a membership at that time of 44,000. The group had representatives from iron and rolling mills, heavy electrical and automobile industries. The main aim of the visit by this delegation was to develop contacts and to study conditions in the British engineering trades, with particular reference to the assessment of Joint Production Committees, which had been developed in Britain during the war.[182] The arrangements for such a large group, with a fairly detailed itinerary, were complex and nearly collapsed. While the visit, once it finally took place, was generally considered a success, there was some criticism of the programme. This was attributed by the embassy to the failure of the TUC to honour a commitment to arrange a series of factory visits.[183] It was not surprising that no subsequent attempt was made to repeat it on anything like such a scale. Smaller groups were much easier to organise. A few months later, a group of three Norwegian trade unionists were invited by the Durham Miners' Union to attend the celebrations of their gala in July 1946. This was arranged through an invitation sent by the local office of the British Council to the local representative in Newcastle of the Norwegian Seamens' Union. They were shown low-cost housing provided for miners, and the free accommodation provided for retired miners. The British Council played a part in organising this visit.[184] In return, a group of Durham miners spent a fortnight in Norway during

---

[181] Collier to Bevin, 18 June 1947, N7187/66/30, FO 371/66072.
[182] Nordahl to Citrine, 25 January 1946, LO korrespondense, Dd 0014, Arbeiderbevegelsens arkiv.
[183] Minute by Kenney recording a conversation with Olson, Chairman of the Iron and Metalworkers' Union, 29 June 1946, N9082/365/30, FO 371/56291.
[184] LO report, August 1946, LO arkiv, D Db 0014, Arbeiderbevegelsens arkiv.

the summer of the following year, invited by the Norwegian General Workers' Union.[185]

The LO representative to the TUC Congress in Brighton in October 1946 was Arthur Ruud, from the Norwegian Telegraph and Telephone Union. He did not finish his very full eight-page report until 21 January 1947, noting that this was due to pressure of work, but he provided twenty-five copies of the report for circulating among his colleagues. He wrote that the only other foreign representatives present at the congress had been from the USSR, USA, Canada, Czechoslovakia and from the World Federation of Trade Unions (WFTU), which at that time was becoming increasingly Moscow-oriented. He commented that Citrine had drawn attention to this in his speech and Ruud himself advised that LO take care in its handling of this issue to avoid the prospect of splitting the international trade union movement – something which did indeed happen a couple of years later.[186]

In August 1946, Inman wrote again to Bell. He said that he would shortly be travelling to London and wanted a meeting to discuss how co-operation between the British and Norwegian labour movements could be better developed. As background to the topics he wanted to raise, he attached a memorandum entitled 'British Influence and the Norwegian Labour Movement'. The text of the main part of this letter, which he described as an analysis of the current position, was exactly the same as that which had been used by Collier in his earlier despatch of 20 March to Bevin. However, in his conclusions Inman painted a slightly gloomier picture, asserting that it would require time and sustained effort to bring about the improvement in the attitudes towards Britain by the Norwegians, which were being sought to promote British interests. He predicted that it would require the removal of some deep-rooted habits of thought, perhaps by causing the younger generation to think along different lines, rather than by trying to change the views of the older

---

[185] Collier to Bevin, Oslo embassy annual review for 1947, 15 March 1948, N3433/3433/30, FO 371/71505.
[186] Ruud report, 21 January 1947, LO arkiv, Dd 0027, Arbeiderbevegelsens arkiv.

generation.[187] In December, Bell wrote to Healey, providing a summary of the trade union exchanges which had taken place during the year, and outlining plans for future exchanges of visits by delegations from both countries in order to maintain the momentum which he believed had been created during the last few months.[188] (In view of Bevin's earlier exchange of correspondence with Citrine about attendance at conferences, it is not clear why Bell wrote to the Labour Party, rather than to the Foreign Office.) Healey passed this information on to Christopher Mayhew, the Foreign Office parliamentary under secretary, on 4 December, but appears to have taken no further action on it.[189]

A comparison with Sweden

Work was also done elsewhere in Scandinavia to improve contacts between British and local labour movements. Several attempts were made in Sweden to develop closer links, but they did not get very far. Both sides showed reluctance. Aunesluoma quotes the views of Sven Andersson, the secretary of the Swedish Social Democratic Party. According to a report from Lamming, the long-serving labour attaché in the embassy in Stockholm in February 1946, Andersson was genuinely interested in creating some kind of anti-communist bloc from the social democratic and social democratic-controlled trade union movements in Scandinavia. This Scandinavian bloc would eventually then form a common front with its Western European counterparts, especially in Belgium, Holland and Britain.[190] Lamming had spoken to Andersson when seeking his opinions on a contentious article in *Pravda* which had criticised the formation of a Nordic bloc under Swedish influence. Both Hankey and Thomas Brimelow (who later became permanent under secretary) commented approvingly on Lamming's report, but the ideas

---

[187] Inman to Bell, 15 August 1946, 292/948/2, TUC Archive.
[188] Bell to Healey, 2 December 1946, 292/948/2, TUC Archive.
[189] Healey to Mayhew, 4 December 1946, N15638/15638/63, FO 371/56245.
[190] Juhana Aunesluoma, *Britain, Sweden and the Cold War, 1945-54*(Palgrave Macmillan, 2003), quoting from the report by G.N.Lamming, FO 371/56222, p13.

were not developed further.[191] The reason became apparent soon afterwards when Jerram, the ambassador in Stockholm, reported the views of Lamming that while Andersson and many of his colleagues would like much closer contact with the British labour movement and the West, they would have cold feet if such contact were to be on a scale involving Sweden as a nation, and not merely the SPD as such. Jerram commented that this furnished additional proof of Swedish intentions to do nothing which might lead the Russians to believe that they were oriented towards a western bloc, and that Swedish social democrats were most anxious to avoid exciting Russian suspicions.[192]

In October 1946 McNeil, the Minister of State, suggested to Bevin that in order to combat communist infiltration into Sweden, contacts between the TUC and the Swedish TUC should be strengthened, with a view to enhancing the prestige of Swedish social democrats. He proposed that the TUC should invite some Swedish trade unionists to visit the UK. Bevin broached these ideas with Tewson, whose reply was discouraging. He wrote that he was not against the idea in principle, but thought it was the turn of the TUC to send some representatives to Sweden because some Swedish trade unionists had recently visited the UK. However, this would be difficult to arrange owing to the unwillingness of the majority of trade union representatives to go there. He would bear in mind the need to strengthen the association with Sweden, but doubted whether any action could be taken at present.[193] At the request of Jerram, the Foreign Office took up this reply, emphasising the importance which it attached to the subject. Tewson explained that the TUC would have problems in financing travel to Sweden, and that in any case only a small number of British trade unions had affiliations or associations with Swedish trade unions. McNeil tried again the following spring, emphasising to Tewson the importance of promoting exchanges, especially

---

[191] Minuting by Hankey and Brimelow,17 March 1946, N3398/29/63, FO 371/56222.
[192] Jerram to Hankey, 20 April 1946, N5810/2844/42, FO 371/56966.
[193] McAlpine minute, 27 January 1947, N15778/10499/30, FO 371/56995.

with the Iron and Metal Workers' Union.[194] Tewson's reply was no more helpful. He pointed out that the TUC General Council thought they had done well by Sweden: they were also inundated with other requests for assistance, for example from Czechoslovakia.[195] Other attempts to arrange visits similarly came to nothing, usually because of organisational complexities and a lack of enthusiasm among potential host unions in Britain.

Although there were more contacts between Britain and Norway during this period than there may have been with Sweden, despite the efforts of those involved on both sides, there is little evidence that these exchanges increased to the extent that they were able to go very far towards achieving the goals which had been set out by Collier in his earlier despatch to Bevin in March 1946. Delegates from the TUC and LO attended the national conferences of each other. However, on the British side the delegates tended to be people who were experts in their own field, but who lacked international experience and the capacity to build on the contacts which they were establishing. There were also some exchanges of delegations to study conditions and working practices. Their importance should not be underestimated as both sides had much which they could learn from each other. But while they clearly helped, they were not extensive enough to be capable of achieving Collier's objectives. This was partly because the structure of the two organisations was too different to enable them to interact with each other effectively. In July 2005, Haakon Lie commented that organisational differences, as well as a lack of common goals, prevented the two sides from cooperating together effectively. While they were cordial and closer than they had been before the war, the links between the TUC and LO never came anywhere near matching the level which was achieved by the British Labour Party and DNA because they did not have enough common interests.[196] Perhaps too the TUC during this period was simply insufficiently internationally minded compared with LO, and its priorities lay elsewhere.

---

[194] McNeil to Tewson, 27 March 1947, N3350/3350/42, FO 371/66514.
[195] Tewson to McNeil, 22 May 1947, N4264/3350/42, FO 371/66514.
[196] Conversation with Haakon Lie, 18 July 2005.

3 THE DEVELOPMENT OF A UNIQUELY CLOSE RELATIONSHIP: 1945-1948

Links between the British embassy and both labour parties

Shortly before he had written to Bell at the TUC, Inman contacted Hughes, the acting general secretary of the Fabian Society, with another idea to develop links between the labour movements. He wanted to find a British journalist, or perhaps a Labour MP, willing to write articles about social and economic developments in Britain, and about the British labour movement. The articles could then be sent to LO, which would translate them into Norwegian and publish them in a variety of Norwegian trade union magazines. Hughes forwarded this request to Denis Healey, asking him to reply. There does not appear to have been any outcome from this proposal, although Francis Noel Baker MP (son of Philip Noel Baker MP, who had longstanding connections with Norway and who, after the war, had been a junior Minister in the Foreign Office) was approached a few months later by Haakon Lie with a request to write some articles, an offer which was not taken up.

After contact with Healey had been established, Inman wrote to him again in August 1946, when he also wrote to Bell at the TUC. He provided a copy of the same enclosure which he had sent to Bell, drawing heavily on the text of Collier's earlier despatch to Bevin. He explained that he would be visiting London towards the end of August, and that he wanted to meet Healey and Morgan Phillips to discuss the development of connections between the British and Norwegian labour movements. The international department replied that Healey would be abroad during Inman's visit, but that they would try to arrange a meeting with Phillips if he was available.[197] Material in the Labour Party archives in Manchester shows that Inman and Healey subsequently maintained a fairly regular correspondence, and that Inman provided some useful information to Healey on developments and personalities in DNA.

As their relationship developed, Healey began to trust Inman with some sensitive tasks. For example, after Bevin

---

[197] Correspondence with Norway, Healey papers, LP/ID Box 4, International Department file, Labour Party archive, Manchester.

had made his Western Union speech to Parliament in January 1948, Haakon Lie wrote to Healey to ask whether he could provide any information on the thinking behind Bevin's speech. Healey replied that he was unable to do so in writing (though he enclosed a classified briefing document which had been prepared for Bevin), but that he would arrange for Lie to be briefed in more detail by someone in Oslo. He arranged for Inman to perform this task.[198] (No evidence has been found to show whether the ambassador or the Foreign Office was aware of what Healey had done. No report of it has survived in the archives.) This represents an interesting example of the pragmatic flexibility which was shown by members of both parties at significant moments during this period. It is not clear exactly when Inman briefed Lie. Arne Ording noted in his diary on 1 February that he had attended a Fabian meeting that day, at which Lie, Aase Lionæs and Torolf Elster among others had also participated, when Inman gave a presentation on Bevin's speech, so Inman's briefing would presumably have taken place before then.[199] Shortly afterwards, on 3 February 1948, Collier reported an editorial in *Arbeiderbladet* which in his assessment marked a considerable change in the attitudes of the DNA leadership towards co-operation between Eastern and Western Europe, and which included a statement that 'continued neutrality may lead to disaster'.[200] It is likely that this editorial would have been influenced by the briefing provided through Inman by Healey.

In their discussions with Kenney after their return from the Clacton conference in May 1946, Lie and Åke Ording also told him that they were concerned to ensure that the embassy found a way to counter the anti-British propaganda which was being circulated by the Communists in Norway. Collier commented that in view of the reorganisation of *Friheten*, the Communist Party newspaper, under a new and more competent editor, the embassy could not view with complacency

---

[198] Haakon Lie, *Skjebneår 1945-50* (Tiden Norsk Forlag, 1985), pp241-242 and conversation with Lie, 18 July 2005.
[199] Arne Ording, *Dagbøker 24 July – 4 April 1949. Bind 1*, p355.
[200] Collier to Bevin, 3 February 1948, N 1586/34/G30, FO 371/71485.

the prospect of an intensified and probably more intelligently directed stream of propaganda. He added that

> it might be pointed out to Lie and Ording that DNA should first set its own house in order, in view of the attitude of the notorious Elster in *Arbeiderbladet*.

He noted that Lie had helpfully suggested that one of the best means of countering the propaganda would be to issue a small volume of the collected speeches of Bevin: Kenney was looking into this.[201]

Collier missed few opportunities to find even small ways of enhancing relations between the two Labour parties. For example, he sent a telegram on 29 August 1947 noting that on 31 August, DNA would be celebrating its sixtieth jubilee. He suggested that the Labour Party should send a message of greeting, timed to arrive on 30 August. Morgan Phillips duly provided an appropriate message, which the Foreign Office forwarded to the embassy in Oslo.[202] In a subsequent despatch, Collier reported that he had attended a ceremony in Frogner Park in central Oslo, with 30,000 participants, which marked the anniversary and that Inman had delivered the message from Phillips to Haakon Lie. The text was published in *Arbeiderbladet* a couple of days later.[203]

The influence of the Norwegian and British Labour parties on their respective governments: the position of Healey

It is worth considering the extent to which the two parties were seen to be exercising influence over the development of foreign policy during this period. Their organisations and power structures were not the same. On the Norwegian side, DNA exercised significant influence on the foreign policy of the Norwegian government. The international committee of DNA which was appointed in October 1945 consisted of

---

[201] Collier to Hankey, 21 June 1946, N8221/219/30, FO 371/56284.
[202] Collier to FO, 29 August 1947, FO to Collier, 30 August 1947, N10075/10075/30, FO 371 66075.
[203] Collier to Bevin, 10 September 1947, N10828/10828/30, FO 371/66075.

3 THE DEVELOPMENT OF A UNIQUELY CLOSE RELATIONSHIP: 1945-1948

Haakon Lie as chairman, Finn Moe, Halvard Lange, Trygve Lie, Martin Tranmæl, Arne Ording, John Sanness, Aase Lionæs and Konrad Nordahl. Almost all of them had spent the war years in London and they included the Foreign Minister and his successor, the chairman of LO and the editor of *Arbeiderbladet*. This committee met regularly and reported to the Central Committee of the party, on which several of them also sat and which was chaired by the Prime Minister, Gerhardsen

The political structure in Britain was different. The Norwegians may not have immediately understood that the international department of the British Labour Party, and indeed the leadership of the party itself, would not have been able to have the same input or to call on the same degree of ministerial involvement and support. For example, when in 1945 Laski, the party chairman, argued that the new Labour government had been elected with as clear an expectation of radical change in foreign as in domestic policy, and repeated this assertion when attending a conference in Paris, he was neither a member of the government nor even of Parliament. For these comments he earned a stiff rebuke from Attlee, who told him that he had no right whatsoever to speak on behalf of the Government, and that foreign affairs were in the capable hands of Ernest Bevin.[204] Attlee's relations with Laski had often been uneasy.[205] In his autobiography, Healey wrote that he was responsible to the international subcommittee of the Labour Party's national executive, but that the subcommittee was not a very effective body. Its political members were nearly all Cabinet ministers, who had little time or inclination to read the papers which he submitted, and the trade union members were generally not of the first

---

[204] Alan Bullock, *Ernest Bevin, a biography* (Politico's, 2002), pp399-400, quoting from Francis Williams, *A Prime Minister Remembers* (London, 1961), p169.

[205] After the Blackpool party conference in May 1945, when a section of the Labour Party wished to get rid of Attlee, Laski wrote to him to inform him of the widespread feeling in the party that "the continuance of your leadership of the Party is a grave handicap to our hopes of victory in the coming election" and called on him to resign. This prompted Attlee's celebrated laconic reply: "Dear Laski, Thank you for your letter, contents of which have been noted". Quoted by Bullock in his biography of Bevin, p 384, from Francis Williams, *A Prime Minister Remembers,* p 7.

3 THE DEVELOPMENT OF A UNIQUELY CLOSE RELATIONSHIP: 1945-1948

rank either. Furthermore, the subcommittee only met for an hour or two once a month.[206] But the Norwegians gradually began to appreciate the differences in the power structure. As will be considered in more detail in Chapter Six on Spain, Haakon Lie noted in March 1946 after a frustrating visit which had not produced the progress which he sought, that

> on foreign policy matters, we must take into account that the British Labour Party leadership has little or no influence on the daily work of the government.[207]

At this time, it was insufficiently clear to him that neither the Labour Party itself nor the Foreign Office had reason to alter their position on Spain. Nonetheless, the Labour Party shortly afterwards demonstrated that it was quite capable of delivering high-level ministerial participation for representational purposes at international socialist events when the agenda was important enough. Thus at the international conference of socialist parties at Clacton in May 1946, the British participants included Bevin, Hugh Dalton (Chancellor of the Exchequer and Chairman of the international sub-committee of the NEC), Laski, Philip Noel-Baker (Minister of State at the Foreign Office) and Manny Shinwell (Minister for Fuel and Power), as well as Phillips and Healey. In February 1948, the *Times* reported that the Prime Minister and other ministers had been present at the meeting of the national executive of the Labour Party which approved a long statement on the party's attitude to the European Recovery Programme, which had been prepared for the conference of fourteen European socialist parties to be held in London on 21-22 March – a demonstration of their interest in this subject, which Healey was closely involved with.[208]

Moreover, as Healey developed a closer relationship with Bevin, so his influence grew. He became increasingly well-connected and well-informed. On 11 November 1946, the

---

[206] Denis Healey, *The Time of my Life*, p77.
[207] Haakon Lie, Rapport om Spania-spørsmålet fra besøk i London 4-8 mars 1946, Lie arkiv, Dc 0004, Arbeiderbevegelsens arkiv.
[208] Article in the *Times*, 28 February 1948, DNA Internasjonalt utvalg, Dc 0005, Arbeiderbevegelsens arkiv.

permanent under secretary in the Foreign Office, Sir Orme Sargent, wrote a circular to all heads of departments and under secretaries concerning contact with Healey. He set out the arrangements, agreed with Bevin, by which he should be regularly briefed on confidential matters. He emphasised Bevin's concern that Healey should be kept as fully informed as possible. In setting out the procedures, he made clear that only information from secret sources should not be passed to him, meaning presumably that he should be excluded from seeing reports from the intelligence and security agencies. Sargent also emphasised the reciprocal nature of the arrangement by adding that there were also times when the Labour Party might be able to assist the Foreign Office with the reception of foreign visitors or – perhaps more significantly – in taking action with their contacts in socialist parties abroad. (This was a facility which the Foreign Office subsequently used fairly frequently, not least once IRD had been established.[209]) This arrangement was to be kept confidential and not mentioned to anyone outside the Foreign Office.[210]

In his autobiography, Healey wrote that Bevin gave him a pretty free run of the Foreign Office. He made many friends among its officials.[211] He contributed to the development of policy and also kept the Foreign Office informed about the development of Labour Party thinking. For example, in February 1948, he wrote to McNeil enclosing a final version of a memorandum by the Labour Party (which he himself had written) on European co-operation within the framework of the European Recovery Programme, seeking Foreign Office comments. This paper was to be used at the Selsdon Park conference of European socialist parties which were due to meet in March to discuss the Marshall plan.

---

[209] However, the Foreign Office also occasionally considered using the Labour Party to deal with problems within Britain. Thus in June 1947, Hankey minuted to Mayhew about his concern over the extent of the influence of WFTU bulletins. He wanted to get the *Daily Herald* to publish articles making fun of the WFTU anti-British propaganda campaign. Since this could not be arranged through News Department, he wondered whether Healey could help, and asked Mayhew to consider this possibility. Hankey minute, 27 June 1947, UNE/471/33/96, FO 371/67613.
[210] Sargent, Foreign Office internal circular, 11 November 1946, N14905/G, FO 371/56705.
[211] Healey, *The Time of my Life,* p107.

Healey emphasised that the practical value of the conference would lie in the agreement it could produce on a programme for increased co-operation.[212] He had already produced a draft which had been discussed a few days earlier at a meeting which he attended in the Foreign Office, chaired by McNeil, whose other participants had included Treasury and Board of Trade representatives, as well as Morgan Phillips. He undertook to amend his paper in the light of the official views expressed during the meeting, thereby ensuring that Labour Party policy fully reflected government policy.[213] The final version of the paper was circulated quite widely at under secretary level and attracted positive comments.[214] As Healey became more experienced and better informed about foreign policy issues, so he became more authoritative and confident enough to make recommendations to the Foreign Office about organisational and personnel weaknesses which he discovered within the Foreign Office or in embassies abroad. Thus in March 1949, after a visit to Athens to examine the position of Svolos and the Greek Socialist Party, he wrote a report to Bevin on this subject in which,[215] in suggesting remedial action, he also commented that the British embassy in Athens should contain at least one individual of standing who combined a strong personality and diplomatic ability with some training in economic and social questions and administrative experience.[216] Following an idea recently implemented by Kennan in the State Department, it was Healey who was among the first to recommend that the Foreign Office should have a Planning Staff, an idea which was subsequently adopted.[217]

---

[212] Healey to Mayhew, 21 January 1948, UE1952/243B, FO 371/68943.
[213] Minute by J.V. Rob recording this meeting, UE1928/243/53, FO 371/68943.
[214] Healey to McNeil,19 February 1948, UR 131/131/98, FO 371/71808.
[215] Healey to Bevin, 8 March 1949, R3463/1054/19, FO 371/78452.
[216] Healey had sent his draft report to McNeil first, saying that he had some difficulty in finding suitable words to suggest the inadequacy of the embassy staff at that time. McNeil replied that he thought that Healey's report was a very good memorandum indeed, so Healey forwarded it to Bevin three days later. Healey to McNeil 4 March 1949, McNeil to Healey, 5 March 1949, R2755/1054/19, FO 371/78452.
[217] Minute by W. Hayter, 30 November 1948, W7836/7836/50, FO 371/70272.

Sargent's minute about Healey was one of the outcomes of a meeting chaired by Christopher Mayhew on 5 November 1946, which discussed relations between the Foreign Office, the Labour Party and the TUC. The meeting found it harder to think of a way of dealing with the TUC. It agreed that an officer should be appointed to the Foreign Office who should specialise in labour relations and act as a link for labour attachés abroad. It also decided that labour attachés should keep in touch with international federations, so that the Foreign Office would be kept as fully informed as possible about attempts by communists to penetrate or misuse them. A circular was to be sent to heads of missions defining the responsibilities of labour attachés in this regard.[218] A subsequent minute by Gore-Booth identified three significant organisations as communist-run or communist-penetrated – the World Federation of Trade Unions (WFTU), the World Federation of Democratic Youth (WFDY) and the World International Democratic Federation (WIDF).[219]

British embassy contacts with provincial labour movements

In the summer of 1947, Inman made two visits to provincial parts of Norway. In early June he went to Østfold, and visited Sarpsborg, Fredrikstad and Halden, where he called on the offices of DNA newspapers in each town. He reported that he found attitudes to be provincial and mentally isolated, and added that he was struck by the amount of influence which could be exercised by Anders Buraas, the *Arbeiderbladet* correspondent in London. He pointed out that reports from Buraas were circulated throughout the country to the Labour press by the Arbeidernes Pressekontor and observed that his interpretations of British developments were not always as satisfactory as they might be. In his covering despatch, Collier expressed concerns about the reporting of Buraas (whom he noted also wrote for the Swedish paper *Morgontidningen*, which was the Swedish

---

[218] Minute by Hankey, 8 November 1946, UNE33/33/96, FO 371/67613.
[219] Minute by P.H. Gore-Booth, 28 April 1947, UNE 294/33/96, FO 371/67613.

equivalent of *Arbeiderbladet*), though he accepted that News Department considered that Buraas was well regarded in Fleet Street.[220] (Collier may not have realised that reports from Buraas were also sent to the Swedish equivalent of Arbeidernes Pressekontor and that his reporting therefore actually reached the whole of the Scandinavian peninsular.[221]) Subsequent Foreign Office minuting referred to concerns raised by Kenney that Norwegian correspondents in London obtained their information from the British press service and were not in touch with leading personalities in Britain. The Foreign Office News Department agreed to do something about this, but it is not clear what steps it took.[222]

In a further report, Inman reported on another trip which he had made to Røros, Trondheim, Løkken, Kristiansund and Aalesund. His main aims were to investigate the extent of the use of British press material and to contact leaders in local labour movements so as to ascertain their general attitudes to the UK. He commented again on the provincialism which he found. However, he also observed that the labour movement, with its nationwide centralised organisation and rather definite philosophy, was a strong factor in unifying the country and breaking the widespread provincialism and separateness in remote areas, which were still to some extent cut off. In his covering despatch, Collier concluded that the most serious obstacle to the adoption of a more pro-British attitude by Norwegian public opinion lay in the ignorant and in some respects prejudiced views prevalent in the Norwegian labour movement, particularly in the usually self-sufficient and mentally isolated provincial centres. He considered that there was

1. a case for a journal
2. a case for establishing Anglo-Norse societies in the provinces
3. a case for re-establishing consular representatives.[223]

---

[220] Collier to Bevin, 18 June 1947, N7187/66/30, FO 371/66072.
[221] Letter from Anders Buraas, 25 July 2005.
[222] News Department minute to Warr, 9 July 1947, N7187/66/30, FO 371/66020.
[223] Collier to Bevin, 25 July 1947, N9045/66/30, FO 371/66072.

The Foreign Office did not reply to these recommendations. In the prevailing financial circumstances, it is not surprising that there was little enthusiasm for such projects, which would have cost more, with unpredictable benefits. Nonetheless, the embassy in Oslo returned to the idea of a journal later.

Although by now, in the face of the lack of enthusiasm of the TUC, the embassy had probably lost some of the impetus in its drive to promote closer links between the two labour movements, it continued to provide reporting and guidance which was aimed at that end. In March 1948, Collier submitted a twelve-page report by Inman to the Foreign Office, which described in considerable detail the structure and organisation of the trade union system in Norway, and the nature of its very close relationship with DNA.[224]

Healey's visit to Oslo: October 1947

Since Haakon Lie made frequent visits to London on DNA business and occasionally addressed local meetings by Labour Party invitation, he met Healey regularly. They also kept in contact through correspondence, exchanging ideas and materials, such as Healey's pamphlet *Cards on the Table*, in which – mainly at the initiative of Bevin – he forcefully described growing Russian involvement in Eastern Europe. He attacked the way in which Russia's 'attempt to destroy Britain's freedom of initiative was double-edged', arguing that the Soviet Union represented the biggest danger to Britain, while America had to be encouraged to give up her desire for isolationism. Healey cleared the draft with McNeil and also sought Foreign Office assistance in amending and verifying some of the statistics which it contained, for example on displaced persons.[225] Not surprisingly, it proved

---

[224] Collier to Hankey, 6 March 1948, FO 211/748 (It should be noted that this report has been filed in the wrong series: FO 211 is a series containing correspondence from the British embassy in Copenhagen... However, FO 211/748 contains a large quantity of political reporting from the embassy in Oslo in 1948.)

[225] Exchange of letters between Healey and McNeil 21, 24 and 28 April 1947, Healey Papers ID/LP, Box 11, Labour Party archive.

controversial.[226] Kenney discussed with Lie the possibility of having the pamphlet published in a Norwegian version. Lie supported the idea, as did colleagues in DNA. In a letter to Healey in September 1947, Kenney made clear the great importance which the British embassy attached to the circulation of *Cards on the Table* among the Norwegian labour movement.[227] Lie translated it into Norwegian himself and disseminated it widely.[228]

Although he was in frequent touch with Lie, Healey (whose responsibilities were wide- ranging) paid only one visit to Norway during this period, in October 1947. The background to this trip and the reasons for it deserve examination, not least for the extent to which the embassy was involved in obtaining Healey's invitation and then co-ordinating the arrangements for his visit. Kenney had been concerned to learn that the Norwegian Students' Association had invited Konni Zilliacus, a left-wing Labour MP who was very critical of Bevin, to address it.[229] Kenney contacted Skodvin, the chairman of the association, to ask why they had not invited a speaker who was more representative of the British Labour Party. Skodvin replied that if Kenney could suggest such a person, the association would be delighted to invite him. Kenney therefore arranged for Healey to spend a long weekend in Oslo. His programme was arranged by Kenney, Inman and Haakon Lie. He

---

[226] Healey's views caused considerable concern and opposition among the left wing of the Labour Party, who wished to maintain their distance from the United States. This group had earlier published a pamphlet of their own, entitled *Keep Left*, criticising Bevin for a 'dangerous dependence' on the United States. *Cards on the Table*, a response to this, was also the subject of heated debate at meetings of the National Executive during the party conference at Margate later that year – a further reflection of the divided opinions which it provoked among a wide range of the party leadership. It was also of significance because it marked a further stage in Healey's changing attitude towards the Soviet Union. Reed and Williams *Denis Healey* (Sidgwick and Jackson, 1971), p62.
[227] Kenney to Healey,10 September 1947, Healey papers, ID/LP Box 11, Labour Party archive.
[228] Haakon Lie, *Skjebneår,* p192.
[229] Zilliacus and Collier both went to Bedales school in the early 1900s. Thereafter, their paths diverged quite considerably. Zilliacus had co-authored *Keep Left* with Crossman, Foot and Mikardo. In May 1949, he was one of only six Labour MPs to vote against the signature of the North Atlantic Treaty, for which he was promptly expelled from the Labour Party.

addressed the students' union, the DNA group in the Storting, the Norwegian parliament and the Central Committee of DNA. During his meeting with the Storting DNA group, he answered questions for more than two hours, which in the view of the *Arbeiderbladet* parliamentary correspondent was quite unique. Wardrop, the chargé d'affaires, commented that Healey's visit had been very effective.[230]

This chapter has already examined several examples of contacts between the embassy and both parties, which involved it passing information and performing tasks on behalf of both. However, Kenney's involvement in facilitating a visit of a purely political nature demonstrates how, during this period, embassy staff frequently blurred the boundaries between diplomatic and party political work, to the extent that the two often became indistinguishable.

Nils Morten Udgaard speculates that this visit, together with one a fortnight later by Kurt Schumacher, the leader of the West German social democrats, was probably encouraged by the DNA leadership for propaganda purposes, in order to prepare the rank and file and its parliamentarians for choosing sides on the 'bridgebuilding' issue, at a time when it knew full well that opinion within the party remained sharply divided.[231] This may well have been a supplementary reason, but the impetus for it came from the need perceived by Kenney (and no doubt Haakon Lie) to ensure that the views of Zilliacus were put into their proper context by Healey. Healey's visit would certainly have helped to achieve this objective. Zilliacus was a good speaker, but he was not as effective and forceful as Healey.

Concerns about the influence of Buraas, the London correspondent of *Arbeiderbladet*

It is worth examining the concerns expressed by the embassy about the influence of Buraas, the *Arbeiderbladet* correspondent, to see how well founded they were. By the

---

[230] Wardrop to Bevin, 22 November 1947, covering Kenney's account of Healey's visit, N13645/4718/30, FO 371/66061.
[231] Nils Morten Udgaard, *Great Power Politics and Norwegian Foreign Policy* (Universitetsforlaget, 1973), p235.

end of 1946, a total of forty DNA newspapers were published in Norway, compared with forty-four in 1940. This included *Arbeiderbladet* itself, published in Oslo. These newspapers achieved a total readership of around 352,000, compared with around 220,000 in 1940, which represented an increase of about 57%. By the end of 1949, the readership figure had fallen slightly to 345,000. This figure still represented twenty-two per cent of the total newspaper readership in Norway.[232] Since articles written by Buraas, containing what the embassy considered to be unfavourable comments, were reprinted in all these provincial newspapers, they were reaching the very audience which the embassy wanted to influence more positively. Buraas himself noted that the embassy complained to the Norwegian Foreign Ministry about his reporting. Arne Ording, then working as an adviser to Foreign Minister Halvard Lange, recorded that Kenney had also complained to him about Buraas because of his negative reporting and because he was getting mixed up with the wrong people.[233] Warner considered Buraas to be a fellow traveller. When making recommendations to the Foreign Office on work in Norway following the establishment of IRD (see Chapter Five), Collier suggested the need to influence Norwegian correspondents abroad, especially those in London. IRD commented that they had doubts about the orthodoxy of Buraas and Thorstad, another Norwegian journalist based in London. Warner noted that it was because they were fellow travellers that Oslo had recommended influencing them. However, after discussion with News Department and Kenney, Woolwych (Western European Information Department) concluded that they were agreed that there was not very much amiss with the messages of the Norwegian correspondents in London and that what little there was arose chiefly from personal defects or inexperience in the correspondents themselves. Woolwych

---

[232] DNA Beretninger 1945-1950, Arbeiderbevegelsens bibliotek.
[233] Arne Ording, *Dagbøker 24 July 1945 – 4 April 1949 Bind 1*, p276.

undertook to discuss the matter further with Lehmkuhl, the press attaché in the Norwegian embassy.[234]

Buraas gives an explanation for his behaviour in his unpublished memoirs:

> I did not have much competition before *Morgenbladet* sent Birger Kildal over. He was as blue as I was red. We alternated on Norwegian radio broadcasts. This was fine, because Birger was uncritical of everything English, while I found in particular their foreign policy hard to accept. The Foreign Office arranged daily briefings for us foreign correspondents. Birger swallowed things quickly, and became the Ministry's favourite. My own reporting became so investigative that the embassy in Oslo raised some objections with the Norwegian Foreign Office.
>
> The Foreign Office spokesman had teeth like a cow-catcher on a train (*'som kufanger på et lokomotiv'*) and at times I thought that he treated us in the way in which Goebbels' spokesman would have done in Berlin during the war. We were briefed on what the Foreign Office wanted us to write. After a while, Kildal was sent an assistant called Erik Egeland. Above all, Erik was an artist, and he reacted violently to being dictated to in this way, which he thought went much further than the instructions given to British journalists during their daily meetings, which included much more nuanced briefings. Erik quickly went home. What made me so critical? Above all, that Britain always attributed hidden motives to the Soviet Union. In our case, I thought that the Soviet Union had helped us to secure the victory over Hitler, and had in particular striven for the liberation of Finnmark. Because of that, I thought that one should show the Russians a little indulgence when their foreign policy showed a lack of respect. And it did not make things any better that the British

---

[234] Minuting between members of IRD and Warner based on Collier's letter to Warner of 12 March 1948, PR97/G, FO 1110/3, No reference to this was found in the Riksarkiv among any of the papers submitted by Lehmkuhl to UD during this period. These documents were released under the Freedom of Information Act.

followed the Americans unquestioningly in all important matters....

But then came the coup in Czechoslovakia and we all got a wake up call.... And so did the Norwegian Foreign Office in Oslo, which had been implementing its bridge-building policy, applauded as much by *Arbeiderbladet* as it had been by the non-socialist press.[235]

Buraas later commented: 'damn the News Department of the Foreign Office: they had been right all along'.[236] Not surprisingly, no evidence has been discovered of any subsequent complaints by the British about material written by the *Arbeiderbladet* correspondent in London.

Links between DNA and the labour attaché in London

Although Olav Bratteli did not often send copies of his official reports to DNA, he maintained a regular informal correspondence with Haakon Lie, and often sent him material unofficially. For example, Lie wrote to Bratteli in September 1948 to say that he was going to produce a Norwegian copy of the book by Allan Flanders on the British trade union movement, on behalf of the Workers' Information Association. He needed some information on TUC policies since the war, and asked Bratteli to send him a copy of their latest annual report and other documents. In reply, Bratteli provided a series of reports which he had written for the Ministry of Social Affairs on wages policy in Britain, as well as the report from a major union meeting in March which had discussed the government's policy on wages, prices and services and a range of other background materials.[237] It was presumably easier for Lie to obtain this sort of material from Bratteli than from the Labour Party, although he sought information from them on a fairly regular basis as well.

---

[235] Unpublished memoirs of Anders Buraas, 1998, Buraas arkiv, Arbeiderbevegelsens arkiv.
[236] Letter from Buraas, 13 August 2005.
[237] Lie to Bratteli 9 September 1948, Bratteli to Lie 24 September 1948, TUC London Boks, 652 76.1/b, Riksarkiv.

Fabian Society interest in Norway

Before the war, the Fabian Society had shown much interest in the achievements of the Social Democratic party in Sweden, and by contrast little interest in Norway. This changed after the war. In April 1948, the international secretary of the society, Anne Whyte, organised a study visit by three Labour MPs, Warbey, Palmer and Champion. The results of their research were published in 1949 in a book entitled *Look to Norway,* printed at Fabian Society expense in Norway to save costs. Collier, who knew that Warbey was not highly regarded in the Foreign Office at this time, allowed himself some critical and candid comments in the letter which he wrote to Hankey about the visit of the delegation:

> Warbey is not a man whom I would choose for liaison work abroad, but he kept comparatively quiet on foreign affairs while he was here.... I have yet to meet any British Labour MPs in Norway who can be regarded as really first class value from our point of view, but this lot seem to have done rather more good than harm on balance.[238]

In a minute which Collier forwarded to Hankey with his letter, Inman commented that the group would produce a report which should increase knowledge of the Norwegian labour movement in Britain and further improve links.[239] He added

> I have the impression that these links have been greatly strengthened by the very good delegations which the Norwegian labour movement have sent to the numerous international conferences which have been held recently in connection with the Marshall Plan.

He added enviously that he only wished that the British labour movement could be persuaded to attach something of

---

[238] Collier to Hankey, 28 April 1948, N5150/174/30, FO 371/71489.
[239] Despite Collier's reservations about Warbey, the book received favourable reviews: G. A. Gathorne Hardy wrote that it was probably the best study of conditions in Norway available in English. *International Affairs,* (July 1951), pp380-381.

the same importance to its international connections as did the Norwegians.[240]

The Marshall plan: initial reactions and Lie's proposal to Healey

The economic and political significance of the Marshall plan is well known: the details need not be rehearsed here. However, the reactions of Lie and Healey to the original proposal by Marshall, and their collaboration in launching the initiative for the Selsdon Park conference, merit some study. Marshall made his speech at Harvard while accepting an honorary economics degree in June 1947. It was largely ignored by the American press and most international correspondents: even when it was picked up, its significance was downplayed by many. Haakon Lie was attending a COMISCO conference in Zurich, and noted that the speech was not mentioned at all during the three days which the meeting lasted.[241] Healey was initially not impressed and described Marshall's speech as 'mere waffling aloud'.[242] However, Bevin happened to hear a broadcast by the BBC correspondent in Washington, Leonard Miall,[243] who had been briefed beforehand on the speech's potential significance by Dean Acheson, then under secretary of state and who immediately grasped its importance.[244] It was Bevin's reaction to the opportunity represented by the speech which was key to the developments which followed, especially following the Russian decision to boycott the plan. As Bullock explains, Bevin saw that a Russian boycott would have serious consequences. It would

---

[240] Minute by Inman, 26 April 1948, N5150/174/30, FO 371/71489.
[241] Haakon Lie, *Skjebneår*, p201.
[242] Kenneth O Morgan, *Labour People* (Oxford University Press, 1987), p153.
[243] Obituary of Leonard Miall, *The Times*, 26 February 2005.
[244] In a broadcast that evening. Miall described Marshall's statement as 'an exceptionally important speech', which 'propounded a totally new, continental approach to the problem of Europe's economic crisis'. The British embassy in Washington chose to report the text to London by diplomatic bag, rather than by telegram and it was fortuitous that Bevin happened to hear the broadcast. Years later, Acheson commented that 'it was a good thing that Miall did not lose his voice that night'. (Miall's obituary)

make it impossible to include Eastern European countries such as Poland and Czechoslovakia (thereby hardening the division of Europe) but Bevin also realised that it might also make it difficult for other countries – such as France with its large communist party, or Norway, which was potentially exposed to Russian pressure – to take part in the operation. This could impair, or perhaps prevent, the European response which Marshall had made the premise of American aid.[245] In the event, the Scandinavian countries accepted the invitation to take part in the Paris conference, but stipulated that they would not be drawn into any political bloc as Norway maintained its policy of neutrality expressed through 'bridgebuilding'. Throughout the rest of the year, the proposals were developed and further details were gradually worked out in the face of strengthening opposition from Russia and (under Russian pressure) from Eastern Europe, whose socialist parties used the opportunity of the Antwerp conference of European socialist parties, in late November 1947, to make a strong attack on the plan.

Lie decided that it was time for the democratic socialist parties to take the offensive. He discussed the idea privately with Healey who supported it. They agreed that at the next meeting of COMISCO in London in January 1948, Lie would propose a conference of European socialist parties to discuss (and support) the Marshall plan.[246] The Danish and Swedish Labour parties, consulted beforehand, declined to associate themselves with this proposal and so Lie made it on behalf of the Norwegians alone. He asked that the conference be convened by the British Labour Party, in London, later that year.[247] Healey went ahead with this only after he had received assurances that Labour Party representatives in government would provide, unofficially, sufficient political backing and guidance to justify the expectations which he foresaw that such a conference would raise. Mayhew consulted Bevin on this

---

[245] Alan Bullock, *Ernest Bevin. A biography,* p553.
[246] Conversation with Haakon Lie, 18 July 2005.
[247] Report by Lie on the first meeting of COMISCO in London, 10 January 1948, Lie arkiv, Internasjonale forbindelser, Dc 0005, Arbeiderbevegelsens arkiv.

point and obtained his consent.[248] The conference took place at Selsdon Park in Surrey in March 1948 and provided a forum for a constructive debate on the Marshall plan by participants from Western European parties alone.

Western Union: the involvement of Healey and Lie

Mention has already been made of the exchanges between Lie and Healey after Bevin's Western Union speech in the House of Commons on 22 January 1948, which led Healey to arrange Inman's briefing of Lie. Mayhew's description of his contribution to Bevin's speech is worth noting. Following the breakdown of the Council of Foreign Ministers in December 1947, Bevin had presented a paper to Cabinet on the Spiritual Unity of the West – i.e. including the United States, and not just Western Europe alone. This was approved, and Bevin was shortly thereafter expected to make an important statement on the subject in Parliament. However, the speech which he drafted said little that was new and made no mention of any Western defence union. Mayhew wrote that when shown the draft on the day before it was due to be delivered, he was shocked by its emptiness, vast length, unoriginality and lack of style. He redrafted it completely, drawing on the Cabinet paper and making the crucial demand for a defence union of France and the Benelux countries. He cleared it with senior Foreign Office officials the following morning and showed it to Bevin, who accepted it with only minor amendments. It was not only Haakon Lie who sought more information about the proposal: many British embassies would also have wanted more background because there had been insufficient time to brief them in advance.[249]

The reporting which the Norwegian Foreign Ministry received on reactions to Bevin's speech did not always reach it through orthodox channels. On 30 January 1948, the Norwegian embassy in Copenhagen sent the Foreign Ministry

---

[248] Healey to Mayhew, 21 January 1948, and subsequent minuting, UE1952/243/53, FO 371/68943.

[249] Mayhew describes his role in drafting Bevin's speech in his autobiography *Time to Explain* (Hutchinson, 1987), pp112-113. He gives more detail in his diaries, extracts of which are contained in his papers in the Liddel Hart archive, box 5/2.

a copy of a restricted telegram from the British embassy in Oslo to the Foreign Office, which as a result of a mistake by the Danish post was delivered to the Norwegian embassy in Copenhagen rather than the British one. (The envelope had only been addressed to HM Embassy Copenhagen.) The telegram reported press coverage in Norway of Bevin's speech. It noted that *Morgenbladet* and *Nasjonen* contrasted Bevin's serious tone with the apparent complacency of the Norwegian Foreign Ministry, and exhorted the government to reconsider the situation against the possibility of Norway being invited to join the Western Union. The telegram was marked to both Ording and Lange, whose marginal comments showed that they had studied it carefully.[250]

Soon after Bevin's speech, in early February, Healey learned that there was going to be a meeting of the executive committee of DNA, in preparation for the meeting of Scandinavian socialist parties in Stockholm on 7 and 8 February, which was going to discuss Western Union. Without referring to what he had already arranged for Inman to do, he asked the Foreign Office to send a telegram to Oslo, asking them to meet Haakon Lie in order to dispel any doubts and difficulties which he might have with this subject.[251] The embassy replied on 2 February that Lie expected to be able to carry the executive, and that efforts were being made to procure a statement of the Labour Party's adherence to Western Union. However, Lie was not sure whether he would be able to achieve success at quite this stage. He was even less sure that the Swedes would be prepared to be accommodating. The Foreign Office noted that Healey had been informed and was very pleased with this outcome.[252] This is a most interesting example of co-operation between the two parties, in pursuit of a Foreign Office objective, at a time when a significant part

---

[250] Letter from the Norwegian embassy in Copenhagen to UD, enclosing the telegram, Boks 25.4/13, Bind XIII, Riksarkiv.
[251] FO telegram to Oslo, 29 January, N1336/34/30, FO 371/71485. Hankey copied this telegram to Stockholm, because Healey had wondered whether Jerram might be able to take the same action with the Swedish socialists. There is no evidence to show that this recommendation was acted upon in Sweden.
[252] Oslo telegram to Foreign Office, 2 February 1948, Mackenzie Johnston minute, 3 February 1948, N1294/34/30, FO 371/71485.

of DNA – as well as the Swedes – were reluctant to accept the ideas expressed in Bevin's speech.

These exchanges also provide two very different examples of the way in which sensitive business was transacted between the two parties. In the first, Healey avoided using senior diplomats to provide a briefing for Lie on Bevin's thinking, presumably because he felt that he could go further if he used an informal channel less closely linked to the formal Foreign Office structure. In the second, he chose to use the Foreign Office for the transmission and receipt of messages concerning DNA business, both because speed and confidentiality were important, but also because it was an objective which the Foreign Office supported.

Members of the embassy also used the Foreign Office as a means of transmitting sensitive correspondence to Healey by secure means. In a letter to Hankey in March 1948, Collier quoted freely from correspondence which had been sent by Kenney to Warner a few days earlier. Kenney had asked Warner to pass this letter to Healey. Collier's letter put forward for consideration some proposals to invite Norway to join Western Union, once France and Benelux were signed up, without approaching Sweden or Denmark at the same time. Although the text of Kenney's letter is not available, the context of Collier's comments suggests that it was describing aspects of these ideas to Healey and therefore keeping the Labour Party informed of some significant developments. (By passing it through a senior diplomat such as Warner, Kenney would also have ensured that the Foreign Office remained aware of what the Labour Party was working on.) In an intriguing postscript, Collier noted that events had moved on recently. He thought there might be a case for inviting Norway to join the Western Union straight away, without waiting for the joining formalities for France and Benelux to be completed. He noted that 'the head of the Norwegian Intelligence Service[253] had suggested this to his contact in the Embassy' and proposed that Lange should be sounded out about the possibility by Bevin when the latter

---

[253] Vilhelm Evang

saw him in Paris a few days later.[254] In the event, nothing came of this idea.

Collier had earlier sent a despatch to Bevin commenting on a report in *Arbeiderbladet* which noted that the executive committee had passed a positive resolution on Western Union 'which was the result of the efforts of Haakon Lie and his friends'. He also noted Lange's dissatisfaction with a speech by the Swedish Foreign Minister, Undén.[255] Shortly afterwards, Jerram wrote to Sargent from Stockholm to describe a conversation with Vougt, the Swedish Minister of Defence, who had regretted Undén's speech and the fact that the Swedish government was so far out of touch with British thinking. He asked whether it might be possible to get some British social democrats over to Sweden to meet their Swedish counterparts, mentioning as possible candidates Noel Baker and Dalton, the latter because he was currently unemployed.[256] Jerram replied that he had been thinking of inviting the Minister of State, McNeil, to visit Sweden on holiday: such a trip could enable him to go to Norway and Denmark as well. Vougt agreed that it would be much better to invite British social democrats to Sweden than to send Swedish social democrats to Britain. This would have a wider impact. He undertook to raise the idea with Undén: perhaps not surprisingly in view of Undén's views at that time, there is no evidence to show that this idea was taken any further.[257]

In his despatch to Bevin, Collier added that Lange had observed that it was possible that Norway might have to act on its own in Scandinavia, without Swedish or Danish support, a comment which attracted some attention in the Foreign Office. Hankey asked that both Healey and Warner be shown this report. It was considered a useful step in the right direction, though there was of course still a long way to

---

[254] Collier to Hankey, 8 March 1948, N3154/637/63G, FO 371/71450.
[255] Collier to Bevin, 5 February 1948, N1524/34/30, FO 371/71485.
[256] Dalton had been Chancellor of the Exchequer, but was forced to resign in 1947 after budget details were leaked to a journalist. He returned to office later in 1948 when he was appointed Chancellor of the Duchy of Lancaster.
[257] Jerram to Sargent, 11 February 1948, FO 211/749 (British embassy Copenhagen file containing correspondence on Western Union.)

3 THE DEVELOPMENT OF A UNIQUELY CLOSE RELATIONSHIP: 1945-1948

go. At the official level, Norway remained publicly cautious in its approach to this subject. Reflecting this, the *Sunday Times* noted for example that in a speech to the Storting on 18 February 1948, Lange had strongly advocated co-operation in the Marshall Plan, but had totally ignored Bevin's plan for a Western European Union.[258] Privately, though, opinions continued to change, especially after the coup in Czechoslovakia. Commenting on a visit to Norway in early 1948, the BBC programme editor for Norway, Martin, noted optimistically that while Swedish and Danish reactions to the Bevin plan had come as a cold douche, there was no longer any pretence of neutrality in Norway and that Gerhardsen, the assistant editor of *Arbeiderbladet* (and brother of the Prime Minister) had agreed to print BBC programmes. 'We will be bound to sooner or later, and we might as well start now'.[259]

Given the shared background during the wartime years of many of the key figures in the two parties, and their common interests, it is perhaps not surprising to see the extent to which their relations grew closer and more productive during this period. This shared wartime background was of course lacking in Sweden, and it is interesting to speculate on the extent to which this may have contributed to the lack of correspondingly close relations between the respective Labour parties - and consequent policy differences. The case studies of work involving IRD, Spain and the Socialist International, which are considered in more detail in later chapters, will provide a clearer idea of the extent of contacts and discussions between the parties on individual issues and demonstrate how they functioned in different areas where they did not necessarily share the same interests as they had in countering the spread of communist influence.

Despite sustained encouragement from both ambassador Collier and at the highest level in London, relations between the TUC and LO never developed the same degree of effectiveness as the links between the two parties. The TUC was never as internationally minded as LO, and its

---

[258] Article by Ralph Hewins, Stockholm, *Sunday Times*, 19 February 1948, N1285/34/G30, FO 371/71485.
[259] Report on a visit to Norway, 14 February to 17 March, by A. Martin, BBC programme organiser, N3800/34/30, FO 371/71485.

international department was certainly not as effectively staffed. In correspondence with Bevin and McNeill, Tewson more than once referred to a lack of interest among his members in developing foreign contacts. Furthermore, by the end of 1947, developments in Eastern Europe and problems within the WFTU were absorbing more of the TUC's limited capacity for engagement in international affairs. However, while the embassy may have been disappointed by the relative lack of interest shown by the TUC, there are no indications that this view was shared by Nordahl or any of his colleagues in LO.

The most striking aspect of this period was the extent to which both the Foreign Office and senior staff in the British embassy in Oslo were involved in encouraging and facilitating the development of contacts between the two parties. Healey, who developed an increasingly close relationship with Bevin, played a key role in this process, but it was ambassador Collier who had first identified the importance of these links as early as March 1946. An illuminating example of the close involvement of the embassy can be seen in the way in which Kit Kenney arranged for the visit to Oslo by Healey in October 1947, as a means of counteracting the impact made by Zilliacus a few weeks earlier. It is thus possible to identify a triangular relationship, in which the two Labour parties, and the Foreign Office and its representatives in Oslo, all had significant influence on each other. Healey's relationship with the Foreign Office, and embassy relations with DNA, were so close that their interests were sometimes indistinguishable.

From the Norwegian side, there is nothing to show that the Foreign Ministry tried to take advantage of the links between the two Labour parties to pursue any particular policy or advantage. There are certainly informative documents, often written by the labour attaché in the Norwegian embassy in London, to be found in DNA files which report on significant British topics such as nationalisation, elections, party conferences and so on. These documents were copied to DNA by the Norwegian Foreign Ministry. These would have helped the leadership of DNA to be well-informed on important developments in Britain. (No such Foreign Office papers, apart from a few very general background papers on Russia which appear to have originated in IRD, are to be found in the British Labour Party archive in Manchester.) But beyond that, there is no evidence to demonstrate that the Foreign Ministry may have considered the development of a strategy for promoting closer and more effective contacts between the labour movements in the two countries. There is no evidence, either, in British archives that the subject was ever officially discussed.

4 Information Research Department

'Do good by stealth, and blush to find it fame.' [260]

The background to the establishment of IRD has already been carefully and thoroughly examined in a number of publications by the FCO historians, Richard Aldrich and Andrew Defty.[261] It is not intended to replicate their work here. This chapter aims to provide an overview of the origins and structure of IRD and the links which it developed, through the Labour Party, with labour movements in those other countries where it was working against the spread of communist influence. This will provide a context which should better facilitate an understanding of its work in Norway, which will be analysed in Chapter Five and Chapter Eight. It highlights certain new material which has been discovered in the course of the research for this book, which throws additional light on the links between IRD and the Labour Party and work done by the Labour Party to assist IRD.

The chapter also examines the way in which IRD worked in three countries – France, Italy and Burma – which were considered to be of key importance due to their vulnerability to communist influence and penetration. It assesses the means by which IRD sought to make use of links between the labour movements to achieve some of its objectives, and identifies several of the obstacles which prevented their

---

[260] Alexander Pope on *Paradise Lost*. Quoted by Adam Watson, 3 April 2007.
[261] Historians, Library and Records Department, FCO, 'Origins and Establishment of the Foreign Office Information Research Department 1946-48' (August, 1995); Richard J. Aldrich, *The Hidden Hand: Britain, America and Cold War Secret Intelligence* (John Murray, 2001); Andrew Defty, *Britain, America and Anti-Communist Propaganda 1945-53* (Routledge, 2004).

effective exploitation. Its generally limited success there contrasts with the greater effectiveness of the links with the Norwegians, which will be studied in greater detail in subsequent chapters. Finally, the chapter considers why the Russians, who would have been aware of the existence of IRD and its purpose almost from the outset, appear to have made no attempt to frustrate any of its work.

The origins of IRD: Warner's paper of 1946

The first major attempt to counter Soviet propaganda was an outcome of a meeting of senior officials in March 1946, whose purpose was to brief Sir Maurice Peterson, ambassador-designate to Moscow. After a discussion of the aims underlying Soviet expansion in the Middle East, the meeting considered possible means to counter the spread of communism. The permanent under secretary, Sir Orme Sargent, requested that a paper should be drafted on this subject, commenting that it was important that the aims of British counter-propaganda should be clearly defined.[262] Within a fortnight Christopher Warner, formerly head of Northern Department and now the assistant under secretary dealing with Soviet Affairs, produced a paper entitled 'The Soviet campaign against this country and our response to it'.[263] The paper was considered and endorsed by the first meeting of the Russia Committee. This committee was established in April 1946 following a recommendation from Frank Roberts, counsellor in Moscow, who suggested the creation of a group within the Foreign Office to study Soviet activities and co-ordinate a global response. The conclusion of Warner's paper was that

> The Soviet government makes co-ordinated use of military, economic, propaganda and political weapons and also of the communist 'religion'. It is submitted, therefore, that we must at once organise and co-ordinate our defences

---

[262] Minutes of the briefing meeting for Sir Maurice Peterson, 18 March 1946, N5572/605/38G, FO 371/56832.
[263] Minute by Warner, 2 April 1946, N7905/140/38, FO 371/56786.

against all these and that we should not stop short of a defensive-offensive.[264]

The paper was endorsed by Bevin and by Attlee.

Shortly after this, Sargent sent a circular letter to heads of missions abroad to brief them on this policy development. He enclosed a slightly shortened copy of Warner's paper, noting that although it had not yet been approved by the Cabinet, a summary had been circulated with the approval of Attlee to those British ministers who had taken part in recent discussions with the Dominions' Prime Ministers. He sought comments and suggestions on how the policy might be put into effect in the country to which heads of missions were accredited.[265] It was read with interest by Collier in Oslo, who replied to Sargent that the letter was welcome because he had been wondering how he should counter the Russian campaign, against the British government and everything else British, which was proceeding in Norway as everywhere else. Building on some of the ideas which he had expressed in an earlier despatch, when he had first begun to emphasise the importance of building links with the Norwegian labour movement,[266] Collier observed that there was no immediate danger of the Norwegian government coming under Soviet control or direct influence. The Norwegian police and intelligence services were keeping a close watch on the activities of the Norwegian Communist Party (NKP) and the Soviet embassy in Oslo, and the authorities needed no encouragement in that respect. He judged that the question was almost exclusively one of propaganda to the public, where there was certainly a great deal to be done. He referred to a recent report from Kenney which had contained some detailed recommendations on the methods by which propaganda

---

[264] Russia Committee meeting, 28 May 1946, N7079/5169/G38, FO 371/56885 quoted by Defty, *Britain, America and Anti-Communist Propaganda*, p38.
[265] Circular letter from Sargent to heads of mission abroad, 21 June 1946, N7905/140/G, FO 371/56784. Sargent initially decided that his letter should not go to posts in the Americas because of the danger of loss in transit, or of subsequent leaks.
[266] Collier to Bevin, 20 March 1946, N4417/219/30, FO 371/56284.

could reach the rank and file of the Norwegian Labour Party (DNA), as well as the Norwegian public in general.[267]

Collier observed that while the government and DNA were on bad terms with the NKP, there was considerable communist influence in some of the trade unions. The labour press, including *Arbeiderbladet,* was also full of talk of friendship with Russia, presenting Russian policy in the most favourable light possible, while British policy was often criticised on the old anti-imperialist grounds. In discussing the sort of propaganda which he thought could make an impact on the average Norwegian labour voter, Collier stressed the importance of emphasising the moral issue involved in the ongoing struggle against the domination of Europe, and perhaps the world, by a power which preached and practised the doctrine that the Soviet system was above such morality. He thought that it was important to counteract Soviet propaganda by measures designed to show Britain in a positive light. This could best be achieved by extending the programme to exchange visits, particularly by members of the labour movement and trade union delegations – a proposal to which he attached great importance and which he often encouraged. Commenting on the problems of arranging travel between Britain and Norway in the immediate interwar period, he put forward the somewhat unrealistic suggestion that the Admiralty might be willing to provide the embassy with one of their small ships, which they were selling off at low prices, to use to transport any government guests who needed to be carried across the North Sea.[268] In his reply Hankey, head of Northern Department, not surprisingly politely discouraged Collier from thinking that such a source of low-cost transport might be available, though he thought that the Navy might be able to help occasionally.[269] This idea was not pursued.

It did not, however, prove possible to translate the proposals contained in Warner's paper into a global policy. Sir Ivone

---

[267] Kenney's report was not found in the archives and does not appear to have been transferred there.
[268] Collier to Sargent, 26 July 1946, N9817/140/G, FO 371/56786. These papers were released under the Freedom of Information Act.
[269] Hankey to Collier, 29 August 1946, N9817/140/G, FO 371/56786.

Kirkpatrick chaired a committee which produced recommendations for preparing a propaganda campaign, but some of his proposals were linked with a more dangerous plan for subversion[270] and Bevin commented that the proposed measures were too negative. He wanted to see something which would project the more positive aspects of the new Britain.[271] He was eventually persuaded to agree to the launch of a propaganda offensive in Persia, as a result of concerns expressed by the British embassy in Tehran about the growing influence of the communist Tudeh party, which was inciting violence against the Anglo-Iranian Oil Company. He insisted that the campaign should be positive and not make excessive attacks on communism. It was, Defty notes, 'the first example of the more active offensive-defensive strategy for responding to Soviet propaganda involving the co-ordination of covert and overt propaganda'.[272] However, Bevin declined to endorse a proposal to extend the campaign to the whole of the Middle East, commenting 'I am not going to commit myself to the whole of Kirkpatrick's scheme in order to tackle Persia... The more I study it, the less I like it'.[273] He added: 'I am quite sure that the putting over of the positive results of the British attitude will be a better corrective'.[274] In time, however, Bevin began to adopt a tougher line towards this issue, following the creation of a series of communist governments in Eastern Europe in late 1946. In July 1947 he agreed that the British response to communist propaganda attacks should after all be extended to the rest of the Middle East.[275]

Although Bevin did not authorise action on a wider scale during this period, Aldrich notes that there was a great deal of slippage and that Sargent, together with McNeil and Mayhew, had clearly decided just to carry on with what they

---

[270] Defty, *Britain, American and Anti-Communist Propaganda* p42.
[271] P449, FO 930/488, quoted by FCO Historians, 'Origins and Establishment of Foreign Office Information Research Department', p3.
[272] Defty, *Britain, America and Anti-Communist Propaganda,* p43.
[273] Minuting on Tehran telegram of 26 May 1948, FO 930/488, quoted by FCO Historians, 'Origins and Establishment of Foreign Office Information Research Department', p3.
[274] Minuting on N6092G, Mayhew archive, Establishment of IRD, Box 4.2, Liddell Hart archive.
[275] Defty, *Britain, America and Anti-Communist Propaganda,* p45.

could get away with.²⁷⁶ The Russia Committee considered several requests for support from European posts, including France and Italy, where the extent of communist propaganda caused particular concern. It is clear that work was done to combat this propaganda during the French election campaign. Defty notes that 'when discussing such intervention, the question of ministerial approval was rarely mentioned although the Committee was apparently aware of the limitations imposed by Bevin'.²⁷⁷ It is not clear to what extent, if at all, McNeil and Mayhew may have been consulted about such specific issues.

The main domestic political factor which constrained Bevin during this period was the left wing of the Labour Party, which advocated a return to a greater degree of socialism in the government's foreign policy. The *Keep Left* group considered that Britain had become dangerously dependent on the United States, and advocated the creation of a Third Force to hold the balance of power between the two major blocs. Their views were challenged in a pamphlet entitled *Cards on the Table* written by Healey in 1947 shortly before the party conference in Margate, where it was fiercely attacked.²⁷⁸ Bullock considers that *Cards on the Table* in part reflected, in part stimulated, a shift in the mood of the Labour Party.²⁷⁹ Further steps were undertaken to encourage this by a meeting in the Foreign Office in November 1947 which considered the question of relations between the Foreign Office, the Labour Party and the TUC. It was agreed that information should be exchanged between Mayhew and Healey: this would be additional to the briefings already authorised by Sargent in November 1946.) It was hoped that Mayhew would receive useful indications about public opinion in return and that a useful two-way traffic would

---

[276] Aldrich, *The Hidden Hand*, p129.
[277] Defty, *Britain, American and Anti-Communist Propaganda*, p44.
[278] Denis Healey, *The Time of my Life*, p105.
[279] Alan Bullock, *Ernest Bevin. A biography* (Politico's, 2002), p538.
Although Dalton was one of those who commissioned Healey's pamphlet and subsequently approved it, he was slow to acknowledge his responsibility at a meeting of the NEC at Margate, a fact noted by Healey in his autobiography.

develop.[280] During this meeting, McNeil pointed out that it was harder to secure any similar contact with the TUC. The subsequent discussion led to the decision to appoint an adviser to the Foreign Office who would specialise in labour relations and liaise with labour attachés abroad.

Three further issues contributed to the change in attitude towards the Soviet Union during this period. The first, in September 1947, was the establishment by the Soviet Union, together with eight other European communist parties, of the Communist Information Bureau, or Cominform. Defty observes that this did more to undermine left-wing sympathies in Europe than any of the measures implemented by the British and American governments.[281] Soon afterwards, in December, the Council of Foreign Ministers broke up, principally over its failure to reach agreement over the German problem, after three weeks of meetings which had found little common ground and where Soviet stubbornness had caused considerable frustration. The third issue was the effect of the continuing Soviet attacks at the UN, which the British delegation was not equipped to refute. Returning from New York on the *Queen Elizabeth* and unaware of the initiative taken by Sargent which had led to Warner's paper eighteen months earlier, Mayhew wrote Bevin a long memorandum entitled 'Third Force Propaganda'. This was prepared on the assumption that the meeting of the Council of Foreign Ministers would end in deadlock, and he urged that the time had come for a change in policy towards the Soviet Union.[282] Mayhew's ideas envisaged the concept of a Third Force 'which would comprise all democratic elements which were anti-communist as well as genuinely progressive and reformist'.[283] Bevin was now more disposed to accept the arguments which Mayhew put forward, and asked for further work on them. The result, a paper prepared in final form by Warner, drew more on some of his original arguments from his 1946 paper than it did on

---

[280] Minutes of a meeting with McNeil, Mayhew, Sargent, Warner, Caccia, Hankey and others on 5 November 1947, UNE33/33/96, FO 371/67613.
[281] Defty, *Britain, America and Anti-Communist Propaganda*, p50.
[282] Mayhew minute to Bevin, 17 October 1947, IRD Box 4.2, Mayhew archive.
[283] Mayhew to Bevin, IRD Box 4.2, Mayhew archive.

Mayhew's Third Force concepts.[284] The resulting papers were put to Cabinet by Bevin in January 1948 in a memorandum entitled 'Future Foreign Publicity Policy', and endorsed.[285] It was this decision which led to the establishment of IRD very shortly afterwards.

Mayhew's work in SOE promoting co-operation with communist organisations

In view of the significance of Mayhew's involvement in the establishment and early work of IRD, it is interesting to note the extent to which, during the war, he had been attempting to work with communist organisations rather than against them. Mayhew spent part of the war in SOE, where for a time he was Dalton's private secretary. He described in a series of letters to his family how, while in the planning section, he attempted to develop links with left-wing parties in Europe, with whom contact was very limited. His idea did not initially find much favour. However, in early 1941 Mayhew attempted to build some links with the Fourth International, which unlike the Third International or Comintern, was strongly anti-Nazi and which he described as 'a decrepit anti-Stalinist Trotskyist organisation', with some branches in France, Spain and Mexico. Mayhew drafted a paper suggesting that the French branch, although weak, might be usefully employed in subversive activities. In addition, if subsidised and controlled by SOE, the French branch might also provide a means of supporting certain other elements such as the Republicans in Spain, without provoking political problems for the Foreign Office. SOE was impressed and asked him to develop these ideas. However, they foundered on objections from SIS, which was already using a part of the Fourth International for its espionage work in France. Shortly afterwards, Germany invaded Russia, the Comintern became an ally, and co-operation with the anti-Stalinists was no longer possible. Mayhew then played a

---

[284] FCO historians 'Origins and Establishment of Foreign Office Information Research Department', p5.
[285] Bevin memorandum to Cabinet, 4 January 1948, PR 1/1/913G, FO 1110/1.

part in briefing Colonel Guinness, head of the SOE Planning Section, who was sent to Moscow to explore the possibilities of helping the Comintern in Europe to organise anti-Nazi sabotage and subversion. This did not get off to a good start: a bad air crash wrecked the first expedition to drop communist agents and there were also political problems . Later, Mayhew also provided advice on the potential for SOE activities in the Caucasus, where he suggested that support should be given to the communist parties in the region.[286]

Foreign Office briefing on the new department

News of the Cabinet endorsement of Bevin's paper of future publicity policy, and a description of the initial aims of the new department, were sent out to posts in circular telegram No 6 in late January 1948.[287] This invited comments and suggestions from heads of mission on methods of implementing the policy in the country to which they were accredited. Collier's reply is examined in Chapter Five: those from Rome, Paris and Rangoon will be considered later in this chapter. Ralph Murray was appointed head of the new department, and in early February he sought approval for a staff of ten.[288] Many of those selected had worked in the Political Warfare Executive (PWE) during the war. By August, when Murray wrote his first report, his staff had increased to sixteen, although this was three short of the approved establishment of nineteen. Murray's report was critical of the limited

---

[286] Mayhew wrote an account of his time in SOE based on letters which he had sent to his stepmother during the war. These letters, known within his family as the Budget, were then circulated to other members of his family. (Conversation with Lady Cicely Mayhew, 14 August 2006.) The letter on which much of the account here is based was written on 17 March 1942: the account itself is in Box 3.1, Mayhew archive.
[287] Circular telegram of 23 January 1948, PR 1/1/913G, FO 1110/1
[288] Murray minute, 11 February 1948, XS03/954/5/48G, FO 366/2759.
Since some savings had been identified elsewhere, the initial staffing costs of the new department were expected to be £3,500, although the Foreign Office obtained approval from the Treasury for an additional £150,000 to cover anticipated operational expenditure.

amount which he felt he had achieved, and he asked for more staff, some of whom needed to be specialists.[289]

Mayhew's role as the link with the Labour Party

From the beginning, much of IRD's product was sent to Healey at the Labour Party, who arranged distribution to a limited number of addressees.[290] Mayhew, used by the Foreign Office as an intermediary, played an active role in encouraging Labour Party involvement in the work of IRD. Warner suggested to Mayhew the production of a series of Speaker's Notes, which could be supplied on demand to ministers and friendly Labour MPs to help them combat Communist-inspired opposition at Labour Party and trade union meetings. This was discussed with McNeil, who disliked the idea of talking points, but who agreed that IRD should prepare a stock of personal letters from Mayhew, making just these points.[291] A later minute by Warner in June, after a complaint about the problems of getting ministers to make anti-communist statements in Parliament, showed that he had persuaded Mayhew to agree that all IRD papers be sent to all Cabinet ministers. These ministers were also to be asked to use them in speeches whenever possible. Mayhew accordingly wrote to Bevin, who did not support the proposal and would only agree to a limited circulation to ministers on a personal basis.[292]

Mayhew also attempted to encourage the expansion of TUC activities to provide greater assistance with anti-communist propaganda abroad. In June 1948, he promoted the idea of an international edition of *Freedom First*, a trade union publication produced by Herbert Tracey. As will be

---

[289] Murray minute to Warner, August 1948, XS03/95H/10/48G, FO 371/2759. Some of the material in this minute has been redacted, so it is not clear precisely how many additional staff Murray was requesting.
[290] FCO Historians, 'Origins and Establishment of Foreign Office Information Research Department', p12.
[291] Warner minute, 24 March 1948, and subsequent correspondence, PR 142/142/913, FO 1110/41.
[292] Warner minute, 16 June 1948, Mayhew minute to Bevin, 6 July 1948, PR445/142/913G, FO 1110/41. Mayhew's minute of 6 July is also contained in the Mayhew archive, IRD, Box 4/1/1.

demonstrated later, this project came to nothing.²⁹³ In March 1949 he commissioned some work reviewing trade union activities in support of foreign policy, noting that 'they simply don't seem any good at it at all.' This resulted in a paper which was submitted to Bevin in May. It recommended that the TUC should assist anti-communist groups abroad by supporting them with reciprocal visits, providing them information and a counter-propaganda service for foreign trade unionists, and assisting them in securing the publication of suitable books in foreign countries. Mayhew hoped that the TUC's withdrawal from the communist-dominated World Federation of Trade Unions (WFTU) would make it easier for the TUC to play the sort of role which he envisaged.²⁹⁴ However, there is little evidence to show that this subsequently proved possible to any significant degree.

In the light of his experience of Soviet attacks at the UN in the autumn of 1947, Mayhew was also keen to use IRD material to make some counter attacks. He did so most effectively in his speech on the use of forced labour by the Soviet Union at the eighth session of the Economic and Social Council on 15 February 1949. He had already spoken at the previous UN General Assembly at which he had presented part of the evidence of the existence of mass forced labour in the Soviet Union. On this occasion he also provided details of the use of forced labour spreading beyond the boundaries of the Soviet Union, mentioning examples in Czechoslovakia, Bulgaria and the Soviet zone of Germany.²⁹⁵

There is some further evidence which demonstrates how far the Foreign Office was prepared to go in supporting the use of the Labour Party as a tool of political influence. A telegram was sent to Rome in early 1948, describing the visit of Phillips and Healey to assist with strengthening the moderate wing of the socialist movement. It noted that this visit was a Labour Party matter, but nonetheless asked Mallet

---

[293] The origins of this project are described in FO1110/11, beginning with a minute from Mayhew to Warner, 3 June 1948, PR517/1/913G. The details are examined in more detail in Chapter Five.
[294] Minutes by Mayhew, 18 March and 7 May 1949, PR 1217/69/913G, FO 1110/258.
[295] Note written by Norman Reddaway, August 1996, IRD, Box 4/1/1, Mayhew archive.

to arrange accommodation, book flights and advance funds if required, as well as provide a briefing.[296] Shortly afterwards, in an internal minute, Henniker noted that Bevin had approved the use of an RAF aircraft to take Phillips and Griffiths from Vienna to Frankfurt when they were on their way to Paris. He wished to ensure that it did not become known that the Foreign Office had arranged their journeys, and that the details did not appear in Foreign Office accounts. Sir Orme Sargent knew nothing of this, and had to be briefed.[297]

IRD articles published by Labour MPs

As IRD continued to grow in size and experience, it developed new methods to disseminate its material. Some of these also required co-operation from the Labour Party. Recently released documents show that in January 1950, Murray wrote to an unnamed contact about an earlier discussion concerning articles written by MPs. He outlined carefully how his contact might approach this subject. It is reproduced in full because it shows the caution with which IRD approached this sensitive subject:

> We have had several articles from various people, but you very kindly agreed to advise me on subjects for a number of others. You said that, if you thought the proposed subject fitted the writers in question, you might drop a hint to them that they would probably be approached by a journalist who traffics in articles, for an article; you would hope that, if so approached, they would, in the general interest, agree to write; if they were in any difficulty as to the material, you would find it from your own resources. (You would then get us to turn out some facts if necessary.) On hearing from you that you had spoken to one or more of the authors, we would get our article-buying friend to make a suitable approach.
>
> I am now sending briefs of articles by seven proposed writers. As soon as you have spoken to any of the proposed

---

[296] FO telegram 599 to Rome, 11 March 1948, FO 800/494.
[297] Minute from Henniker to Halford, 5 June 1948, FO 800/494.

authors, will you please let me know, and I will put the rest of the scheme into action. The briefs are long for your eye, but they only represent the shape of the articles as we see them: they are not intended to be anything like mandatory of course, and could not be presented to the writers in question, they would merely form the basis of an approach by the article buyer.

A subsequent letter from Wilkinson to the same unnamed addressee showed that Roy Jenkins MP had agreed to write one of these articles. It provided an outline of the proposed article, which was entitled 'Soviet Sharp Practices Exposed: How Yugoslavia was Exploited'. It was based on a speech by the Yugoslav Dr Josa Vilfan at the UN General Assembly in October 1949. A subsequent letter from Wilkinson to Healey in early February discussed the agreement of the Rev. Gordon Lang, the Labour MP for Stalybridge and Hyde, to write an article which had been proposed to him on 'Marxist Dogma Self-Destroyed'. The letter also provided some additional briefing material for him.[298] There is no indication which other Labour MPs also agreed to write these proposed articles.

IRD use of Labour Party links in Italy: the 1948 election

Sir Victor Mallet, the ambassador in Rome, was among the first to reply to the circular telegram announcing the establishment of IRD. Concerned by the threat posed by the Italian Communist Party (PCI) at the forthcoming April elections, he reported that he had already given the highest priority to the communist menace in the embassy's work, and that he

---

[298] Murray letters, 3 January 1950 (PR 1/1), Wilkinson letter 28 January 1950 (PR 1/11) and Wilkinson letter to Healey, 3 February 1950 (PR 1/18), FO1110/278. These documents have been released under the Freedom of Information Act. Although the identity of the addressee in the first two letters has been redacted, the index of Foreign Office documents in the National Archives for 1950 contains the following entry for Denis Healey: 'Use of IRD material: PR 1/1–11-18-23.' It may therefore reasonably be assumed that Healey was the addressee of all this correspondence. Given his close involvement in almost all other aspects of the dissemination of IRD material through the Labour Party, it would be most surprising if he were not.

chaired a small committee which met regularly to co-ordinate it.[299] Considering the means of disseminating anti-communist propaganda likely to be most successful in Italy, he noted that the task would be greatly facilitated by the existence of a strong anti-communist press. He also thought that it would be possible to work through the party organisations of the political parties, adding that the embassy had already been asked for anti-communist material by the Christian Democrat party.[300] Finally, referring to the Popular Front alliance between the PCI and the Italian Socialist Party (PSI), led by Nenni,[301] he stressed the valuable contribution which he considered the Labour Party could make to the new policy.

Mallet explained that what the anti-communist forces in Italy wanted more than anything else was some definite expression of disapproval by the British Labour Party of the policy of close collaboration with the communists. This policy had culminated in the decision to fight the election on a single list. 'A forthright declaration by the Labour Party in this sense within the next few weeks might do more in a short time to ensure the success of your policy in countering communism in this country than could be expected over years by the adoption of long-term measures such as those envisaged in your circular telegram No 6'.[302] When he did not immediately receive the reply he sought, he repeated his views in even stronger terms: 'I have not the slightest doubt that the immediate and burning need is for open condemnation by spokesmen of the government and the British Labour Party of

---

[299] Defty asserts that there is evidence to show that the Americans had already begun work to provide support to anti-communist forces in Italy in late 1947. See Defty, *Britain, American and Anti-Communist Propaganda*, p47. Aldrich cites evidence showing that, in 1945 and 1946, the American Federation of Labour was already giving $200,000 to anti-communist groups in Italy. Aldrich, *The Hidden Hand*, p137.
[300] Mallet subsequently reported that the Christian Democrats had asked for material on living conditions in Russia and the satellites, wanting particularly photographs and statistics. He explained that these conditions were a major point in their electoral programme, especially in the south of Italy. Telegram of 1 March, PR 25/1/913G, FO 1110/1.
[301] When the war ended, the Italian socialists were united in a single party, the PSIUP. This split into two following the Rome Congress in January 1947, when the PSI (under Nenni and Basso) and the PSLI (under Saragat) were formed.
[302] Rome telegram, 24 February 1948, PR24/1/913G, FO 1110/1.

Nenni's disastrous collaboration with the communists. This is the only important influence which we can hope to exercise before the elections...'³⁰³ Despite the urgency expressed by Mallet, it took the Foreign Office some time to respond to his proposals. This was due to their preparations to sign the Benelux treaties and their preparations for the conference of European socialist parties to discuss the Marshall plan. A separate draft was prepared concerning the Labour Party's condemnation of Nenni's policy. However, Bevin could not broadcast it on the BBC overseas service until after Easter, on 4 April.³⁰⁴

In view of the significance attached to the Italian election by both governments, it is not surprising that the Foreign Office authorised contact between the British and American embassies in Rome. The British embassy reported to IRD the extent to which the Americans were publicising the economic assistance they were providing, as well as the similarity of much of their approach to anti-communist propaganda at that time. (Reporting from the embassy in Washington reflected the concerns of the American ambassador in Rome about the outcome of the election; he expected that the communists and Nenni socialists could win as much as forty per cent of the vote between them.³⁰⁵) The British embassy also reported information obtained from 'top secret sources' that the OSS ³⁰⁶ was active, operating on its own responsibility and not necessarily with the knowledge of the American embassy. Ward reported that a number of newspapers such as the independent right-wing *Il Tempo* were receiving large financial subventions from the OSS. He added that the OSS was also giving money to the *Voluntari Civili* and the *Armata Italiana Liberta,* which he described as semi-secret right-wing paramilitary formations of the

---

³⁰³ Rome telegram, 7 March 1948, PR46/1/913G, FO 1110/2.
³⁰⁴ Warner minute, 11 March 1948, Murray minute, 19 March 1948, PR75/1/913G, FO1110/3.
³⁰⁵ Washington telegram, 14 February 1948, Z/1319/93/22G, FO 371/73156.
³⁰⁶ The OSS was abolished by President Truman in October 1945, and the CIA had been created by the National Security Act in September 1947. The reference to the OSS here was therefore presumably inaccurate, as the organisation involved would have been the CIA.

type which the Foreign Office had instructed the embassy to avoid. He sought Foreign Office approval to co-ordinate their work with the Americans to avoid duplication or crossed lines. Warner's reply, cleared with Mayhew, authorised an exchange of information, emphasising that it was important to avoid any arrangement which 'might tie our hands'. Raising a concern which was quite frequently reflected in IRD correspondence during this period, he wrote that he was by no means confident that American official publicity (and still more the OSS) would not commit some costly blunder. Moreover, the British approach to social problems was often quite different from the American one, and should be seen to be so.[307]

The Christian Democrats won the election. The results gave the two socialist parties each about seven per cent of the vote, which was little more than half of what the combined party had polled in the previous election of 1946. Responsibility for the PSI's failure was universally attributed to its electoral alliance with the communists. Nenni and Basso lost their party positions at the Genoa congress of the PSI in June 1948. While the newly formed IRD did not play a crucial role in influencing the electoral outcome, it certainly made a worthwhile and wide-ranging contribution. Thus, almost all of the IRD papers provided to the embassy were passed to the Christian Democrats for electoral propaganda purposes. In addition, articles by Healey (among others) were replayed in the Italian press and a broadcast by Healey was reprinted quite widely in the metropolitan and provincial press.[308] The American contribution was considerably greater: Aldrich quotes evidence showing that 'the $600 million of aid authorised by the Marshall plan to Italy and France was supplemented by $10 million of "unvouchered funds" fed by the CIA and other covert methods to pay for anti-communist propaganda and for bribes to aid the Christian Democrats and other non-communist

---

[307] Ward telegram, 20 March 1948 and Warner reply, 14 April 1948, PR 93/1/913G, FO 1110/3. The references to OSS in this jacket were released following a request under the Freedom of Information Act.

[308] Telegram from Stewart, information officer in Rome, 24 April 1948, PR 237/57/913G, FO 1110/26.

parties'.[309] It is not surprising that Defty concludes that American support, both covert and overt, was more decisive than the campaign run by IRD.[310] The situation in Norway was different, for neither before the 1949 nor the 1953 election was there any serious concern that the communists would do especially well. However, as will be demonstrated in Chapter Five, IRD provided material intended for use by DNA in planning and executing its election campaigns.

Occasionally, Northern Department tried to supplement IRD's work by making proposals for work against the communists. Rothwell quotes an example: Hankey suggested enlisting TUC support to work against the communist leaders of the trade unions in France and Italy, especially the latter. This would have been a complex task, because the CGIL (TUC equivalent in Italy) was under exclusive communist control. Gee, a seconded officer from the Ministry of Labour who had been brought in as the labour adviser to facilitate liaison between the two departments, strongly criticised the proposal, since he considered that the end did not justify the means, and it was not taken further.[311]

The split in the Italian socialist movement made it difficult for IRD to exploit effectively the Labour Party links in Italy. During the next two years, the Labour Party and COMISCO spent considerable time and energy trying to find ways to persuade the parties to unite as a social democratic movement. This was no straightforward matter. Moreover, the Italian Prime Minister, De Gasperi, complained to Mallet about alleged interference by the Labour Party in the affairs of the PSLI under Saragat.[312]

In general, Healey's close links with the Foreign Office did not create a conflict of interest with his position in the Labour Party, because the policies the government and party were pursuing were generally close or identical. However,

---

[309] Aldrich, *The Hidden Hand,* p138.
[310] Defty, *Britain, America and Anti-Communist Propaganda,* p107.
[311] Victor Rothwell, 'Robin Hankey' in Zametica (ed.), *British Officials and British Foreign Policy* (Leicester University Press, 1990), pp172-173.
[312] In a personal and private letter to Ivo Mallet in London, Victor Mallet wrote that De Gasperi's secretary alleged that Healey was responsible for putting pressure on the Saragat socialists. V. Mallet to I. Mallet, 26 May 1949, Z3908/1018/22, FO 371/79299.

De Gasperi's complaint led to one significant exception in December 1949, when Healey was due to address the Italian Socialist Unification Conference in Florence. The Foreign Office was concerned about what Healey might say, for they believed that neither the Labour Party nor the Italian Socialists really understood each other. Healey had already clashed with Saragat, while statements by the Italians showed that they did not appreciate the difference of views between the British government and the Labour Party on the question of unification of the Italian Socialist Party. So the Foreign Office asked Mayhew to speak to Healey before he left, and to advise caution. However, Healey paid no heed. He told Mayhew that he needed to reply to Saragat's charges against the Labour Party, and subsequently did so in an outspoken speech which upset many Italian Socialists. Mallet sent a very critical telegram from Rome about the impact of Healey's intervention, and Mayhew noted 'that instead of walking a delicate tightrope, Healey had jumped straight into the abyss, lacking restraint in his references to Saragat'.[313] Bevin marked these papers to Dalton. Healey wrote at length to Mayhew to defend himself, alleging that he had been misquoted. The outcome appears to have been a compromise. Bevin summoned him for a ticking off on 22 December, and decided that no further action should be taken. [314] Healey's account of this meeting (at which no officials were present) notes that the subject was only briefly discussed, and that Bevin said to him that he would 'tell Mallet to stop whining'.[315] It is not clear whether this happened, because in mid-January 1950, Western Department sent a personal letter to Mallet relating what had happened in London over the issue. It concluded 'the Secretary of State then had a talk with Healey. No record of the conversation was made, but the Secretary of State said that no further action was required, and I fancy that he remonstrated with

---

[313] These papers are all contained on Z8071/1018/22, FO 371/79301.
[314] Healey's letter to Mayhew and the reference to his meeting with Bevin are contained on Z8346/1018/22, FO 371/79301.
[315] Denis Healey, *The Time of My Life*, p105.

Healey'.[316] It is possible that Bevin wisely decided that there was nothing to be gained from further action.

Although greater co-operation between the socialist parties was achieved shortly before the elections in 1951, the issue of their unity was still contentious. Many socialists did not support the new coalition. With some foresight, Western Department commented that Italian socialism had been, and would remain for the foreseeable future, a broken reed. [317] However, Italy remained a country to which IRD attached the highest priority. Despite the lack of socialist unity and other local problems, they were at least able to develop a satisfactory system for circulating their product throughout the country. In his report for the first seven months of 1949, Murray noted that in Italy it had been possible to achieve some considerable publicity for many of the articles which IRD was now producing, and that he hoped to increase output considerably in the near future. An article by Tewson, the general secretary of the TUC, had 'achieved really splendid publicity recently'.[318] His report for the later part of 1949 concluded that although nothing notable had been published in the latter part of the year, the usage rate in Italy was 'not unsatisfactory'. Echoing a problem which must concern anyone dealing with propaganda, Murray concluded that his report might be complacent. 'It is extremely difficult for us to judge what the effect of our work is in the various countries and what we might be doing there, if we were really alive to countries' differing needs and the different markets for our wares. We are still working, indeed, too much in the dark'. [319] Although usage rates declined a little in 1950, prompting Watson to wonder whether Rome might have reached its

---

[316] I. Mallet to Sir Victor Mallet, 13 January 1950, WT1016/1, FO 371/89638.
[317] Minuting on Rome despatch of 26 July 1951 on the Italian socialists, WT1015/7, FO 371/96226. Healey noted that it took until the arrival of Craxi before they were able to become a force in Italian politics again. Healey, *The Time of My Life*, p92.
[318] 'Progress report on the work of IRD up to 31 July 1949', Murray to Warner, 13 August 1949, PR 2919/112/G, FO 1110/277.
[319] 'Report on the work of IRD 1 August to 31 December 1949', Murray to Warner, 15 February 1950, PR 110/5/G, FO 1110/359.

limit,³²⁰ they had increased to a record level in early 1951. In March, fifteen IRD articles were placed in forty-three papers, seven IRD second rights articles in nineteen papers and eleven other anti-communist articles were published in eighteen papers. IRD wrote to Pilcher, the information officer, to congratulate him.³²¹

IRD work in France: initial stages

A number of posts – Paris among them – did not respond directly to circular telegram No 6, and Warner had to send a reminder. His telegram also sought additional detailed information from posts on the strength, organisation and activities of communist parties in their territories.³²² It took some time to work out a satisfactory means of proceeding in France. Harvey, the ambassador, commented that the directive, as far as France was concerned, would need some modification before any discussion of its means of implementation. He shrewdly pointed out that in dealing with communism, it was essential to expose concrete and reliable facts about its practices, without becoming involved in arguments about its principles. He did not wish British officials to become publicly involved, although he thought that they might provide material to public figures who could make use of it. However, he did not at this stage provide any specific proposals.³²³ Murray challenged the view that IRD could not publish in France any anti-communist or anti-Soviet themes. He arranged a meeting with the information officer, Tennant, to discuss ways of developing IRD work. They agreed that the embassy should be asked to produce a local directive and discussed a range of possible actions, such as providing background material to embassy contacts, a specialised weekly publication and a joint distribution venture with an existing feature agency. In addition– no doubt with wartime experience from PWE in mind – the

---

[320] Comment by Watson on letter from Pilcher, information officer in Rome, 17 April 1950, PR55/16/G, FO 1110/324.
[321] IRD letter to Pilcher, 21 May 1951, PR 77/13, FO 1110/428.
[322] Warner telegram, 4 March 1948, PR 40/1/913G, FO 1110/2.
[323] Harvey to Warner, 9 March 1948, PR 60/1/913G, FO 1110/3.

use of 'Black Radio' (a form of covert propaganda), rumours and special operations against the communist propaganda machine were suggested. A number of these ideas were not followed up because of their cost or impracticality.[324]

After this meeting, Harvey wrote to Warner to emphasise that he was not in favour of covert activities in France, except perhaps in the matter of rumours - provided that they had been carefully worked out and thought through. He also thought it increasingly important to clear, at a suitably high level in the French government, the nature of the anti-communist campaign which was being launched. Although he did not think it necessary to go as far as collaboration with the French on this project, he sought permission to inform the Foreign Minister about these planned activities.[325] After consulting with Kirkpatrick, Warner informed Harvey that it was agreed that covert activities should not be undertaken in France but that the Foreign Office did not wish to inform the French government about the new policy.[326] Harvey found it difficult to accept this ruling, and challenged it several times before the policy was finally changed, and the French officially informed, towards the end of the year. These exchanges from Harvey provide an interesting contrast to the reactions in Oslo. Collier, for example, quickly produced a series of suggestions – welcomed by Warner – which attempted to exploit the sort of service which IRD was intended to offer. Haakon Lie, the secretary of DNA, would rewrite IRD's first major

---

[324] Minute recording a meeting attended by Murray, Tennant, Warner and Woolwych, 22 March 1948. PR111/1/913G, FO 1110/3. Part of this document was released following a request under the Freedom of Information Act. Examples of the sorts of rumours which might have been used by IRD, suggested by posts in France, included one that Molotov might resign as a result of Russian fear of anti-communist maquis in Poland and Czechoslovakia, and that his resignation or liquidation would result in a new and conciliatory attitude by the Soviet Union towards the West, and a further suggestion that Molotov would be replaced by Litvinov. Murray commented that the decision not to undertake covert work in France meant that such proposals could not be acted upon: he hoped that Tennant would not find IRD's attitude pusillanimous. Letters from Whiteley-Smith 22 April and from Tennant 4 May 1948, Murray's reply 24 May 1948. PR 264/1/913G and PR 304/1/913G, FO 1110/8.
[325] Harvey to Warner, 7 April 1948, PR 312/1/913G, FO 1110/9.
[326] Warner minute to Kirkpatrick, 30 April, letter to Harvey, 10 May 1948, PR 312/1/913G, FO 1110/9.

paper, entitled 'The Real Conditions in Soviet Russia', and publish it in *Arbeiderbladet* under his name.

Murray occasionally came up with some very imaginative ideas for developing IRD work in France. For example, he wrote to Tennant to say that he was considering putting forward a formal submission that IRD might buy or take an influential interest in one or more important French newspapers. He had been told that one of the large French papers was in financial difficulties, and 'that efforts might be made from undesirable quarters to nobble it. It looks as though we may soon have francs to burn and one of the bigger British private interests in France might possibly provide cover.' He thought that such an investment might be worthwhile; it should produce a well-informed paper which would take an independent line on political issues – as long as its connection with IRD remained secret. Murray realised that such a proposition was rather heretical, but he sought Tennant's opinion nevertheless.[327] Tennant replied, bluntly, that he did not like the idea. Most French newspapers were on the rocks and it would be a waste of money to finance any of them. He thought that it would be hard to maintain editorial control, and even harder to keep the arrangement secret. He concluded that it would be cheaper and more profitable to get what was wanted into the French press without financing it, rather than financing it and being extremely uncertain of the results.[328] Even if Tennant had supported the idea, it is likely that Murray's suggestion would have fallen foul of the subsequent ruling, made by Warner and Kirkpatrick, that no covert work was to be undertaken in France.

Little scope for the use of Labour Party links in France

In a letter to Warner in May 1948, Harvey described how the embassy in Paris was implementing the new policy. He stressed the importance of material received from Labour Party or trade union sources in the embassy's work to reach

---

[327] Murray to Tennant, 12 April 1948, PR 164/1/G, FO 1110/4. This jacket was released under the Freedom of Information Act.
[328] Tennant to Murray, 23 April 1948, PR267/1/913G, FO 1110/8. This document was released under the Freedom of Information Act.

the most important targets in the French labour movement. Articles which showed how work was being carried out against communists in Britain could be used in France, as they would show that Britain had a similar problem and was dealing resolutely with it. This would justify the British attitude towards communism elsewhere. He noted that the information officer in Lyons had made admirable use of an article by Healey, recently published in the *Listener*, and asked for more of the same.[329]

Although rumours circulated occasionally about British support for the French Socialist Party, the Section Française de l'Internationale Ouvrière (SFIO),[330] there is little evidence of a close or productive working relationship between the two parties during this period. One major reason was the state of the SFIO under Blum. Writing about their national conference in July 1948, Davies, the labour attaché, reported that membership had dropped by 30,000 in 1947 and by a further 50,000 in 1948 and that the party was nearly bankrupt. The embassy observed 'that it would be an illusion to suppose that the French Socialist Party holds a position in France closely corresponding to that of the British Labour Party. Not only are the parliamentary positions of the two parties vastly different in strength, but even in matters of policy and doctrine there are divergences'. Davies added that Phillips and Laski, who had attended the conference, had been nonplussed by the failure of the SFIO to face realities. He had arranged for Brutelle, the secretary of the SFIO, to meet Phillips: he had confirmed their worst fears. Brutelle said that he could not depend on local officials, and branches were little more than discussion groups. Very few members were prepared to undertake propaganda or recruiting work. When Phillips suggested the possibility of arranging exchanges between local branches of the two parties, Brutelle replied that it would take him several months before he could provide the names of French sections as he would need to visit them first. Mayhew commented that the report was 'full of

---

[329] Harvey to Warner, 13 May 1948, PR 334/1/913G, FO 1110/9.
[330] Whitney-Smith to Murray, 7 December 1948, PR 1216/137/913G, FO 1110/38.

warnings for us over here'.[331] The situation did not improve after Mollet replaced Blum, and Harvey reported in August 1949 that membership of the SFIO had fallen by a further 100,000 and that its support was increasingly white collar rather than industrial.[332] In these circumstances, it is not surprising that there is no significant evidence in IRD papers during this period of any attempts to use Labour Party links for propaganda purposes in France.

IRD therefore had to look elsewhere for its support. However, the results were not altogether satisfactory. Tennant reported in November 1948 that they were issuing IRD papers to a range of journalists on the major French newspapers, but that the scale of their operation was insufficient to have had any real effect on public opinion.[333] Later in 1949, following the briefing of the French government about the activities of IRD, arrangements were made for an official from the French Foreign Ministry to visit London for a week of discussions. The official, van Leetham, had been given responsibility for organising a department which was in some respects comparable to IRD.[334] In his report on IRD work for the first part of 1949, Murray noted that France was a difficult territory to work in. Although there had been some improvement in the provinces, there had been none as far as the metropolitan press was concerned. He observed that even the Codex (the report on forced labour in the Soviet Union) which had achieved considerable publicity in practically every other country, was given little space in French newspapers. Murray, however, added wryly that this was largely because it was competing with the final day of the Tour de France.[335]

Further dissatisfaction was expressed by Murray after a conference of provincial information officers in October 1949, when Tennant estimated that the most suitable type

---

[331] Despatch from Paris, signed by Clarke in the absence of Harvey, 16 July 1948, Z5832/6/17, FO 371/72948.
[332] Harvey despatch on the SFIO conference, 2 August 1949, Z5329/1019/17, FO 371/79055.
[333] Tennant to Murray, 20 November 1948, PR 1181/57/913G, FO 1110/30.
[334] Murray to Harvey, 28 July 1949, PR2079/109/G, FO 1110/276.
[335] Murray to Warner, report on the work of IRD up to 31 July 1949, 14 August 1949, PR 2919/112/G, FO 1110/277.

of material for France would be one high-grade article to be supplied every four to six weeks. While acknowledging that France remained a difficult country to work in, and that the political situation made anti-communist work difficult, Murray minuted that this was a terrible admission of defeat. He noted too that little use was made of other IRD material either. He thought that this represented a poor contrast with the progress which had been made in Italy, the other country which was both difficult and of highest priority to IRD.[336] He expressed doubts about the value of any of IRD's normal material as far as its use in France was concerned.

However, there were occasional and unexpected successes. In November 1949 Rousset, the editor of an influential left-wing newspaper *Franc Tireur,* made extensive use of IRD material on the Codex and published a series of critical articles on the use of forced labour. (This was the 'discovery', translation, presentation and publicity of the Forced Labour Codex of the Soviet Union. It was prepared for use at the Economic and Social Council of the UN in Geneva and achieved quite considerable worldwide publicity.[337]) Rousset's articles were extensively replayed and commented on in the French press. A communist paper, *Les Lettres Françaises,* denounced the original articles as being based on fraudulent documents. Rousset sued for libel. Discreetly assisted with evidence provided by IRD, he won his case. The proceedings were widely publicised.[338]

Gradually, progress was made in arranging for a wider distribution of IRD material. By June 1950, following a visit to Paris, Murray commented that while editorial work was largely ineffective, the basic work of circulating IRD material was satisfactory and should be continued.[339] The range of outlets used was also extended. By the middle of 1951, material was being circulated through a number of agencies

---

[336] Comments by Murray on the report of a conference of provincial information officers in France, 24-25 October 1949, PR 3395/39/G, FO 1110/229.
[337] Report on the work of IRD up to 31 July 1949, 13 August 1949, PR2919/112/G, FO1110/277.
[338] Murray, report on the work of IRD from August to December 1949, PR 110/5/G, FO 1110/359.
[339] Minute by Murray, 7 June 1950, PR 123/1/G, FO 1110/364.

and organisations, including the French Foreign Ministry.[340] An arrangement was reached at the Quai d'Orsay: material would be passed to Laloy, who would be responsible for arranging its publication if he saw fit.[341] Together with CIA, IRD was also involved in assisting the French to set up an anti-communist organisation, Paix et Liberté, with some semi-official sponsorship. During this period, the French government also closed down the Paris headquarters of several communist front organisations including the World Federation of Trade Unions and the World Federation of Democratic Youth.[342] These represented significant achievements: while IRD was not of course directly responsible for them, it made a useful contribution.

IRD work in Burma: Labour Party support

There was considerable concern in the Foreign Office that Burma, which had become independent at the beginning of 1948, would prove susceptible to communist influence. Although the communist party had only won six seats (out of 250) in the 1947 election, it was thought that its influence was far greater than this number suggested. Burmese communists were known to be in touch with foreign communist parties: these foreign influences were considered to have encouraged them to stage an unsuccessful coup to remove the socialist government in March 1948.[343] Shortly afterwards, the embassy replied to circular telegram No. 6 with a suggestion to strengthen the links with the socialist government by requesting that the British Labour Party establish direct contact with the Socialist Party and trade unions in Burma. Bowker, the ambassador, also recommended the supply of cheap, simple literature to popular bookshops, and encouraged the idea of a social democratic bookshop.[344] IRD responded positively to these ideas, asking

---

[340] Marchant, information officer, to Peck, 7 July 1951, PR 90/47/G, FO 1110/438.
[341] Marchant to Murray, 13 April 1950, PR 16/13/G, FO 1110/290.
[342] Aldrich, *The Hidden Hand*, p140.
[343] Foreign Office Research Department, paper for the War Office British Intelligence Survey, 22 September 1948, FO 370/1685.
[344] Rangoon telegram, 18 March 1948, PR 82/1/913G, FO 1110/3.

for further details about how a social democratic bookshop might be encouraged and for details of the organisations in Burma with whom the Labour Party might get in touch.[345]

Once this information had been collected, Mayhew wrote to Healey to ask him about links between the Labour Party and the Burmese Socialist Party. He mentioned that he was encouraging the Inter Parliamentary Union (IPU) to send a delegation to Burma, and hoped that one or two really good Labour and trade union MPs might be in the delegation.[346] (This latter idea did not come to fruition as Mayhew had hoped.) Mannell, Healey's assistant, replied in his absence that Healey had met U Kyam Nyein, the Home Secretary and leading member of the party and some other senior Burmese socialists who had visited London in 1947. This group was on the circulation list for party literature: Healey was also in touch with the Burmese Socialist Party's unofficial representative in London.[347] Contact between the TUC and its Burmese equivalent, TUC (B), was, however, at best fairly loose. However, Gee, the Foreign Office labour adviser, took steps to try to improve contacts and to provide materials through the British director of labour, Baker, who was working for the Burmese Ministry of Labour.[348] Pilcher from IRD and a colleague from South East Asian Department met Healey, who provided them with a selection of Labour Party publications suitable for use in Burma, which was sent to the information officer in Rangoon. It was also agreed that Morgan Phillips would send a message of greetings and goodwill to U Ba Swe of the Burmese Socialist Party, and that the Labour Party would also present a gift of suitable books to the party.[349] Healey later wrote to Mayhew to describe the assistance which the Labour Party had provided and would be willing to offer in future. He added that he thought that the real answer would be to have someone in the embassy who was *persona grata* with the Burmese socialists, and whom they could naturally regard as a confidant.[350] However,

---

[345] Rangoon telegram, 6 April 1948, PR 82/1/913G, FO 1110/3.
[346] Mayhew to Healey, 1 June 1948, PR 220/1/913G, FO 1110/6.
[347] Mennell to Mayhew, 3 June 1948, PR 220/1/913G, FO 1110/6.
[348] Minute by Gee, 20 May 1948, PR 220/1/913G, FO 1110/6.
[349] FO telegram to Rangoon, 22 June 1948, PR 220/1/913G, FO 1110/6.
[350] Healey to Mayhew, 16 June 1948, PR545/1/913G, FO 1110/11.

it took more than two years before it was possible to post a labour attaché to Rangoon

Later in 1948 Adam Watson, the new deputy in IRD, reported on a meeting he had attended, arranged by Healey with two visiting Burmese ministers. They had spoken about how the communists were surprisingly efficient in delivering their literature to Burma, and commented on the difficulty of obtaining corresponding British material. This led Healey to reconsider the idea of trying to establish a socialist bookshop, which IRD supported. At this time, it was not possible to find a way of making good anti-communist material commercially available at a price which ordinary Burmese might afford. Although further work was done, it was not immediately possible to produce a satisfactory result.[351] It is worth noting that when George Orwell was subsequently consulted about ways of furthering IRD objectives in Burma (where he served in the Indian Imperial Police between 1922 and 1928), he emphasised the importance of written material, saying that one plane load of leaflets would probably do more good than six months of broadcasting.[352]

Other IRD work in Burma

A regional information office was set up in Singapore in 1949 to supplement the work of information officers in the region. Initially, it was not very effective. Bowker wrote to Murray to complain about the special material which Rayner (the information officer there) had sent. He was disappointed that nothing had been done to provide the 'special material suitably prepared for Asiatic audiences, where necessary in local languages', which had been promised. He was concerned that more needed to be done to win over the Burmese socialists and quoted a conversation with U Kyaw Nyein, who had explained to him why many members of the party were still undecided as to whether they should follow

---

[351] Minutes by Watson recording his meeting with Healey, U Kyaw Nyein and U Maung Ohn, 3 November and follow-up on 19 November 1948, PR 983/71/913G, FO 1110/33.
[352] Note by Celia Kirwan on a meeting with Orwell, 29 March 1949, PR 1135/11/G, FO 1110/189.

Moscow or the British Labour Party. Many favoured Moscow mainly 'because it was revolutionary and therefore accorded with the early atmosphere of Burmese socialism'. Bowker added that its ideology was explained fully and clearly in textbooks which were easily available to Burmese – a further indication that IRD material was still not as readily available as he would have wanted.[353] Murray began to look for ways of increasing the effectiveness of the regional office in Singapore.[354] This led to greater activity: a larger number of articles were placed – including one by Healey on the communist peace offensive which was translated into Urdu and Tamil. Rangoon was given priority for second rights requests, Background Books (an IRD funded publisher) provided large numbers of cheap books for supply to Rangoon bookshops, and steps were taken to increase staffing.[355]

Labour Party support for the visit by U Ba Swe and U Aung Than.

Concerns about the need to increase the effectiveness of work in Burma to influence the Burmese Socialist Party also led the Foreign Office to request assistance from the Labour Party. This assistance went further than merely supporting the work of IRD. Thus in 1950, Healey arranged a visit to Britain by U Ba Swe, the Secretary-general, and U Aung Than, a senior leader of the Burmese Socialist Party. Healey accepted funding from the Foreign Office to look after their entertainment when they were in London.

The ambassador in Rangoon had reported in April 1950 that the TUC in Burma or TUC(B) was likely to pass a resolution affiliating to the WFTU. The TUC (B) was known to be a branch of the Burma Socialist Party, which controlled most of the seats in the Burmese Parliament. It was only the tacit support of this party which enabled the government of Prime Minister Thakin Nu to remain in power. Bowker

---

[353] Bowker to Murray, 14 October 1949, PR 3145/9/G, FO 1110/187.
[354] Minute by Murray, 1 November 1950, PR3224/G, FO 1110/187.
[355] Report on usage of IRD material in Burma, December 1950 (PR 60/5/51G), and minutes of a meeting to discuss work in Burma (PR 60/42G), FO 1110/415.

observed that it would be quite impossible for the TUC (B) to pass such a resolution without the high-level approval of the leaders of the Burmese Socialist Party.[356] An unsuccessful attempt had been made by the Foreign Office to invite U Ba Swe to Britain in 1949. The Foreign Office hoped that he could be invited again, and given a programme which could clearly demonstrate the strengths of British socialism and remove any lingering ideological sympathy which U Ba Swe might have for Moscow. The Foreign Office sought assistance from the Labour Party, which invited both him, and subsequently U Aung Than, as well.[357]

Since Healey and the Labour Party were asked to take on much of the responsibility for their programme, the Foreign Office took the unusual step of providing funds for their entertainment. Healey wrote a confidential letter to Glass in South East Asian Department asking if he could be provided with a cheque for £100 to cover their expenses. He undertook to submit a detailed account of their expenditure at the end of the visit, together with the unspent balance. He was given £75.[358] The Foreign Office wrote to the Treasury to inform it that since the two Burmese had paid their own air fares, the costs for the two of them would be less than the £350 which the Treasury had authorised the previous year when it was thought that U Ba Swe would be coming alone. Authorisation to pay the costs for both was requested. The Foreign Office did not, however, make clear who would be disbursing this money. The Treasury subsequently agreed that up to £200 could be spent on the visitors.[359] Healey subsequently submitted a bill for just over £120.[360]

---

[356] Rangoon telegram, 1 May 1950, FB 2181/2, FO 371/83226.
[357] Minute from Glass, South East Asian Department, 12 May 1950, FB 2182/9, FO 371/83226.
[358] Healey to Glass and minute from Glass, both dated 19 May 1950, FB 2181/9, FO 371/83226.
[359] Correspondence between the Foreign Office and the Treasury culminating in a letter of 27 June 1950 from E Church in the Treasury to HW Minshull in the Foreign Office, FB2181/19, FO 371/83226.
[360] Healey to Glass, 4 September 1949. The final bill was £121.9.2d, so Healey requested that the balance of £46.9.2d should be paid to him.
The letter was carefully drafted, and gave no indication of the purpose of the expenditure, or on whom the money had been spent. FB2181/40, FO 371/83226.

Healey went to considerable lengths to organise a programme for the Burmese. He enlisted the help of Woodrow Wyatt, who arranged dinners for the visitors with a series of senior Labour ministers, including Aneurin Bevan, Sir Stafford Cripps and Lytton Strachey. The TUC also organised a programme. Murray proposed that they should be given a copy of a new IRD paper on communist trade unions and how they worked to the disadvantage of the workers. It was agreed that Healey could pass a copy of this to U Ba Swe, but that he should attribute it to an unnamed research organisation and not to the British government. Before he could do so, the Burmese left for a visit to Poland and Czechoslovakia, to the disappointment of their hosts. However this visit did not go well: Poland was not the well-ordered and successful country they had been led to expect and they were poorly treated. They grew impatient at the long delay in obtaining a visa for Czechoslovakia and returned to London instead.[361] At the end of their visit, Gee minuted that he thought that there should be more scope for the transmission of information to them through Labour Party channels, and that this should be considered by South East Asian Department and IRD. Furthermore, it was agreed that a labour attaché should be posted to Rangoon.[362] The embassy in Rangoon later reported that Prime Minister Thakin Nu had expelled the leaders of the TUC (B) responsible for the decision to join the WFTU, and that the TUC (B) had been temporarily disaffiliated from the Burmese Socialist Party: the outcome of the visit could therefore be judged a success.[363]

The political situation in Burma did not stabilise and the communists gradually gained more support and established control in many provincial areas. Furthermore, in 1951 President Truman authorised the CIA to provide assistance to a Chinese nationalist warlord in northern Burma to enable him to attack the communist Chinese in Yunnan province, without informing the American ambassador in Rangoon. After failing to achieve very much, these

---

[361] Correspondence on FB2181/21, FO 371/83226.
[362] Minute by Gee, 18 July 1950, FB 2181/23. Agreement on a labour attaché for Rangoon is noted on FB 2181/31, FO 371/83226
[363] Rangoon telegram, 22 September 1950, FB 2181/44, FO 371/83226.

nationalist troops remained in the region, creating a further source of instability.³⁶⁴ A conference at British headquarters in Singapore, alarmed at the possibility of Chinese aggression in Burma which such actions might provoke, once again advocated making attempts to try to influence the Burmese Socialist Party. The conference recommended a visit by British Labour Party and trade union leaders with the aim of encouraging the Burmese to stand firm against communism. By now the Conservative party was in power, and the new parliamentary under secretary, Nutting, rejected the proposal on the grounds that Britain should not pander too much to the Burmese desire to learn from the British Labour Party – one of the first examples of the consequences of a change of government.³⁶⁵

Russian reactions to the work of IRD

In his first progress report on the work of IRD, Murray commented that he was satisfied that there had been no leakage of information about the work of the department.³⁶⁶ Nevertheless, from an early stage the Russian government would have been aware of the existence of IRD, and the nature of its work, as a result of reporting by a Soviet agent, Guy Burgess. Christopher Mayhew himself gave Burgess a job in the department on the recommendation of Hector McNeil, for whom Burgess had been working as a personal assistant.³⁶⁷ Since the Russians were aware of IRD, and must also have been concerned about the effectiveness of its work, why did they not take steps to try to limit or damage its activities? There is no significant evidence available to show that they did so. Defty draws attention to an article in

---

³⁶⁴ Aldrich, *The Hidden Hand*, p298.
³⁶⁵ Singapore telegram, 28 November 1951, minute by J D Murray, 24 December 1951, FB 1055/1, FO 371/92153.
³⁶⁶ Minute from Warner to Bevin covering a report from Murray 'Progress report on the work of IRD up to 31 July 1949', 14 October 1949, PR2919/112/G, FO 1110/277.
³⁶⁷ Christopher Mayhew, A *War of Words. A Cold War Witness* (I. B. Tauris, 1998), p24. Mayhew wondered whether the KGB might have instructed Burgess to join IRD, but subsequently concluded that McNeil had used the opportunity provided by the formation of IRD to get rid of him from his private office.

a Polish newspaper in April 1948, which suggested that the new propaganda policy might have been compromised. The article was repeated in the *Soviet Monitor* in Britain, and referred to recent instructions to British missions regarding an intensified anti-communist campaign 'including propaganda and the dissemination of false rumours'.[368] However, this does not appear to have been followed up, either in Britain or elsewhere.

The Russians might have been inhibited by the need to protect the position of their agent. However, this hardly seems likely because Burgess worked in IRD for only a few months before Mayhew dismissed him after Norman Reddaway, his private secretary, had drawn attention to the poor quality of his work.[369] Thereafter, the worldwide nature of IRD's work would have made it almost impossible to track down a leak of information so the Russians need not have been concerned about the consequences. Moreover, there were leaks from time to time which could have been exploited if the Russians had chosen to do so. For example, there was a problem in Finland in January 1951. McGhie, the information officer, reported to IRD that the two main Helsinki communist papers had exposed the fact that he had been sending background information to editors. The document which had fallen into their hands was 'The Soviet Peace Campaign', based on a long IRD brief. Both papers had printed the covering letter which McGhie had sent to the editors of the socialist papers. These papers had used the material, explaining that they were quoting it to show that similar material had been distributed in the past by the British, and that it was still being distributed. Interestingly, McGhie's response was to go on the offensive. After consulting the head of mission, he decided to duplicate a further 175 copies of the document and to circulate it much more widely than before. He pointed out in a covering letter to the recipients that the document was in no

---

[368] Andrew Defty, *Britain, America and Anti-Communist propaganda*, p76 Defty was informed about the article in the *Soviet Monitor* by Dr Sheila Kerr and quotes S. Kerr 'The Secret Hotline to Moscow: Donald Maclean and the Berlin Crisis of 1948' in A. Deighton (ed), *Britain and the First Cold War* (Macmillan, 1990), pp71-87.

[369] Mayhew, *A War of Words*, p24. Mayhew minuted that Burgess was 'dirty, drunken and idle'.

way secret and that it was intended as background guidance for publicists and others who were free to form an unbiased opinion of world events.[370] There is no evidence that this leak, which attracted plenty of attention in Finland, was followed up elsewhere.

It is also worth bearing in mind the scale of the Russian propaganda organisation which was already in place at this time. Writing in 1995, Norman Reddaway (who had become deputy director of IRD in 1955) commented on the extent to which propaganda was already an essential Russian foreign policy weapon even during the early post-war period. A huge apparatus had been constructed, supervised by three separate Politburo members with access to unlimited finance. They ran ran separate organisations through the international department of the Soviet Communist Party, Service A of the KGB and the information department of the Foreign Ministry.[371] It would have been a simple matter for the Russians to mount a campaign to expose the work of IRD. It is unclear why they did not: perhaps they were constrained by concerns about a counterattack by both Britain and the United States.

Given the circumstances of the time, it is to be expected that the Labour government would have sought to use its own party members to assist it in attempting to achieve a range of foreign policy objectives. The Labour Party was certainly well placed to make a valuable contribution through its links with well-disposed MPs both at home and abroad. Such MPs represented a broad spectrum of opinion within the party. There is evidence that even people such as Richard Crossman, one of the *Keep Left* group, were willing

---

[370] Letter from J I McGhie to IRD, 10 January 1951, PR 64/3, FO 1110/419. There are references on this file to papers which have not survived, so it is not possible to judge the reaction of the Foreign Office to this story. McGhie commented that, on balance, he thought that it had done more good than harm, although he would not want such things to happen too often. His successor, A H Noble, reported that after discussions in IRD before his departure, he had decided to suspend temporarily the distribution of all such IRD material to avoid a repetition of this incident. After an assessment on the spot, he decided to continue with its circulation. Noble to IRD, 20 August 1951, PR64/18, FO 1110/419.
[371] Copy of letter from Norman Reddaway, 22 August 1995, Mayhew archive, IRD, Box 4/1/1.

to cooperate by writing articles. (Indeed Crossman had written to McNeil in late 1947. He suggested adopting against the Soviet Union the sort of statistical methods which had been used to analyse German propaganda during the war to discover their underlying strategy. This had provoked extensive minuting about whether the newly formed IRD might implement his suggestion: there is no evidence that it did.[372]) It is therefore not particularly surprising to find proof in recently released papers that MPs such as Roy Jenkins were willing to allow articles to be published in their names, even though the material had been prepared with assistance from IRD. It is quite likely that further examples may be discovered in future, as there is still material retained in the IRD files, which might be released after further review.

The three countries examined in this chapter were chosen because they were among those countries given the highest priority by IRD. There were also considerable concerns about the growth of communist influence and fears that the communists might gain power in these countries. Their circumstances - and the effectiveness of their labour parties - were quite different from each other. The Labour Party was unable to build solid and effective relationships with any of the socialist parties in either France or Italy during this period. This did not prevent IRD from achieving some successes in disseminating its propaganda, particularly in Italy. It is ironic that its biggest success in France came from what Murray described as an own goal in the libel case. The Labour Party's relationship with the Burmese party was closer. Some worthwhile results were achieved, particularly following the visit of U Ba Swe. However, the political situation there was complicated and subject to a great variety of different influences. The British contribution, while effective when judged against the size of its input, was not on a sufficiently large scale to be able to prevent the communists gaining much support.

Throughout this period, there was never more than a handful of people in the International Department of the Labour Party. Its staff, particularly Healey, worked hard to

---

[372] Crossman to McNeil, 10 December 1947, N14492/14492/138, FO 371/66488B.

deal with a wide range of responsibilities, with a minimum of bureaucracy. It is remarkable that they achieved as much as they did. Finally, it is worth considering Murray's comment about the difficulty of assessing the value of propaganda: 'It is extremely difficult for us to judge what the effect of our work is in the various countries and what we might be doing there if we were really alive to countries' differing needs and the different markets for our wares. We are still working, indeed, too much in the dark'. It is rarely possible to assess the impact of propaganda, except by fairly crude means such as determining the number of times an article is reprinted and the circulation of the publication in which it is printed. Without access to all the relevant Russian archives, such an assessment could not be made. However, some documents have been obtained from the Russian Foreign Ministry which deal with concerns about anti-Soviet propaganda in Norway. These will be examined in the next chapter.

5 The impact of Information Research Department in Norway in 1948: an intimate relationship

The situation in early 1948

Once Cabinet had agreed to Bevin's proposals to establish Information Research Department, a circular was sent out to all heads of mission overseas. It outlined the new policy and invited them to suggest how it could be implemented in the country for which they were responsible.[373] Collier replied on 12 March, a fortnight after the Communist coup in Czechoslovakia which had already produced a powerful reaction in Norway.[374] The reaction was probably strengthened by Åke Ording's presence in Prague. He was there on UN business between 20 and 28 February while the coup took place. He wrote a very detailed report on events there and sent it to the Foreign Ministry, which forwarded a copy to DNA. The report included a poignant account of his meeting on 21 February with Jan Masaryk, who had visited Oslo only a few weeks before and who died shortly afterwards in mysterious circumstances. The Norwegians would therefore have been very well informed about what took place in Czechoslovakia, and the part played by the communist party and the Soviet

---

[373] Circular telegram No. 6, 23 January 1948, PR 1/1/913G, FO 1110/1.
[374] For many Norwegians, Czechoslovakia did not only have a special association because of its connection with Munich and the prelude to the Second World War. It also had special associations dating back to the beginning of the century when Bjørnstein Bjørnson, in powerful essays, had linked Norway's struggle for independence from Sweden with that of Czechoslovakia for independence from the Austro-Hungarian empire.

Union.[375] On 29 February, Einar Gerhardsen had made a speech at Kråkerøy when he launched an extremely strong attack on the NKP, describing them as Comintern communists and supporters of terror and dictatorship. This was therefore a most suitable moment for Collier to consider how to develop collaboration with Norway to work against the spread of communist influence. First, however, the Norwegian background deserves closer examination

Some senior members of DNA, such as Lie and Tranmæl, had long wanted a decisive confrontation with the NKP. In March 1947, they had tried to mount a press campaign through *Arbeiderbladet* criticising the NKP's stand over Svalbard. The NKP was the only party in favour of beginning negotiations with Russia. They had not then been well supported. Nonetheless, they had continued to work against the NKP. In June 1947, Collier submitted a report by the labour attaché, Inman, describing a vigorous campaign by DNA to discredit the leadership of NKP and to detach waverers among the NKP rank and file. This was pretty much what NKP, by a process of propaganda and infiltration, had also been trying to do to DNA since the liberation of Norway. Collier concluded that it would probably be necessary to wait until the local elections in November to assess the success of these tactics. However, he judged that the campaign had already helped check the progress of communist infiltration of the unions – for example by the earlier exposure in March 1947 of communist attempts to break up the seamens union by illegal strikes and other unauthorised activities. Although he commented on the skill of the leadership of DNA in waging this campaign, he acknowledged that progress remained slow.[376] Nonetheless, as Collier acknowledged, the government was still planning to encourage defections from the NKP. He reported that the government was not without hope of detaching some of the less fanatical Communists such as Kirsten Moe Hansteen. She was the widow of Viggo Hansteen,

---

[375] Report from Åke Ording on his visit to Prague from 20-28 February 1948, copied by the Foreign Ministry to DNA, Internasjonale forbindelser, D Dc 0005, Arbeiderbevegelsens arkiv.

[376] Collier to Bevin, 6 June 1947, describing relations between DNA and NKP and enclosing a minute by Inman, N6812/4496/30, FO 371/66059.

5 THE IMPACT OF INFORMATION RESEARCH DEPARTMENT IN NORWAY IN 1948

executed by the Germans in September 1941.[377] However, by the end of February 1948, the situation was different. The NKP had supported the Czech coup, which recalled memories of the way in which Quisling and the National Socialists had reacted to the German invasion in April 1940. The Russian government demanded a defence pact with Finland, and there were rumours that the communists may have been planning to sabotage iron ore shipments from Narvik.[378]

Stories had also appeared in the press of secret meetings between Norwegian communists and their Nordic colleagues in Oslo in February.[379] The embassy reported an unconfirmed story from the French embassy that one of these meetings discussed sabotage and subversion in Norwegian ships and harbours. It was also noted that Jensen, a Danish communist and first post-war Minister of Communications, had been at this meeting. This they considered significant.[380] Separately, Collier also reported that it had been confirmed that there had been separate meetings elsewhere in Oslo to discuss the affiliation of the northern communist parties to the Cominform, though there had been differences of opinion about the wisdom of this step. Furthermore, Norwegian communist leaders were making a special effort to recruit into the party ex-members of Quisling's Nasjonal Samling and other persons punished for collaboration with the Germans during the war. Collier thought that knowledge of this may also have contributed to Gerhardsen's strong attack on the communists at Kråkerøy.[381] Gerhardsen's speech called for a campaign against the NKP, whom he described as a threat to Norway's independence, freedom and democ-

---

[377] Collier to Hankey, 3 February 1948, FO 211/749 (British embassy, Copenhagen, Western Union file.)
[378] Øivind Stenersen, 'DNAs holdning til NKP 1945-50', in Bergh and Pharo (eds), *Vekst og Velstand. Norsk Politisk Historie 1945-64.* (Universitetsforlaget, 1989) p353
[379] *Aftenposten* 25 February 1948. Quoted in Udgaard, *Great Power Politics and Norwegian Foreign Policy* (Universitetsforlaget, 1973), p244.
[380] Oslo to Foreign Office, 9 March 1948, N2776/637/63, FO 371/71450.
[381] Collier to Bevin, 3 March 1948, N2840/637/63, FO 371/71450.

5 THE IMPACT OF INFORMATION RESEARCH DEPARTMENT IN NORWAY IN 1948

racy.[382] Although he asked that the campaign be fought by democratic methods, the ensuing reactions of the media were not very restrained. Collier also reported that informal purges were being carried out in organisations such as DNL (the Norwegian civil airline) where officials with communist leanings were being removed from their posts.[383] He added that the national executive of DNA had passed a resolution approving the Marshall plan and condemning the NKP as traitors to democracy.

In a subsequent report to Western European Information Department, Kenney observed that Gerhardsen had used the opportunity to take a decisive step in the campaign to isolate the communists in Norway.[384] Collier also commented on this speech in a despatch submitted on 3 March describing Norwegian opinions of communist policies and methods.[385] Shortly afterwards, in an internal embassy minute on 5 March, which does not appear to have been reported formally to the Foreign Office, Kenney reported to Collier. Kenney noted that he had heard indirectly from a DNA MP that Gerhardsen had drafted his speech largely with an eye on its effects abroad. The Norwegian ambassador in Washington, Wilhelm Morgenstierne, had been instructed to take the full text of the speech to Truman and explain the situation to him; he did so in an interview lasting over an hour and a half.[386] As tensions increased during this period, the Norwegian government obtained approval from the Storting for a further 100 million kroner for defence

---

[382] Trond Bergh and Knut Einar Eriksen demonstrate that the Norwegian security service (POT) had provided detailed reporting of the meeting of Scandinavian communist parties and the issues which they discussed, as well as on possible sabotage plans. See section on 'Kråkerøy-talen - nasjonal og internasjonal bakgrunn' in *Den hemmelige krigen – overvåking i Norge 1914 -1997* Volume One (Cappelen Akademisk Forlag, 1998), pp150-154. They demonstrate that POT had considered the Norwegian communists to be a security threat before the coup in Czechoslovakia, and that in formulating his speech, Gerhardsen would have been influenced by POT's assessment.
[383] Collier to Bevin, 9 March 1948, N3022/34/30, FO 371/71485.
[384] Kenney to FO (WEID), 6 April 1948, PR 232/1/913G, FO 1110/6.
[385] Collier referred to this despatch (N 9839/637/63) in his reply to circular telegram No 6, 12 March 1948, PR 97/1/913G, FO 1110/3. However, it has not been transferred to the archive.
[386] Kenney minute to Collier, 5 March 1948, FO 337/117.

expenditure. Leave of all naval and air-force personnel, and of fifty per cent of army personnel, was suspended until further notice. The intention was to prevent the virtual closure of service establishments which might have occurred during the Easter break.[387] This was the first in a series of preparatory measures taken by the Minister of Defence: for example, Hauge shortly afterwards sought advice from the Admiralty about measures to prohibit submarines without prior permission passing through territorial waters.[388] He then informed Collier that he was about to ask the Americans to provide certain military equipment which Britain could not provide.[389] High-level exchanges continued throughout the next few months between Hauge and Alexander, his opposite number in London, on assistance and advice to Norway.

Tensions remained high; but the Foreign Office maintained in a submission to Bevin in March that concerns about communist activities in Norway might have been exaggerated. The submission referred to reporting from top secret sources which suggested that there was no real subversive threat from the Communist Party within Norway. Nor was there any chance of their bringing off a coup without external aid – though isolated acts of sabotage were to be expected in the event of a major crisis. The submission went on to propose how Britain should react if the Soviet Union were indeed to propose the negotiation of a defence treaty with Norway.[390] The Norwegians received several hints that the Soviet Union might do just that, which contributed to the tension during this period. However, based on research in Russian Foreign Ministry archives, Korobochkin concludes that this was a false alarm. He maintains that the available Soviet sources give no indication that the idea of proposing a treaty was ever contemplated.[391]

---

[387] Oslo to Foreign Office, 18 March 1948, N3304/1794/30G, FO 371/71499.
[388] Oslo to Foreign Office, 10 April 1948, N4421/1794/30G, FO 371/71499.
[389] Oslo to Foreign Office, 13 April 1948, N4436/1794/G, FO 371/71499.
[390] Foreign Office submission to Bevin, 13 March 1948, N3337/2710/G30, FO 371/71504.
[391] M. Korobochkin, 'Soviet Policy towards Finland and Norway 1947-49', *Scandinavian Journal of History* (1995), p202.

5 THE IMPACT OF INFORMATION RESEARCH DEPARTMENT IN NORWAY IN 1948

Collier's proposals for the implementation of IRD work in Norway: emphasis on the need to establish still closer relations between the two Labour parties

Collier's reply to Bevin's circular about IRD was a comprehensive strategy paper. This provides a valuable insight into his assessment of the prevailing situation in Norway as far as the influence of communism and communist ideology was concerned. He also set out a series of recommendations for future action, which once again emphasised the need for establishing still closer relations between the two Labour parties. Collier may not have had any reason to suggest that Norway was uniquely vulnerable to communist influence. However, as the Foreign Office was to acknowledge in its reply, his analysis had an application which could go much wider than just Norway. The extent to which both labour parties were involved in assisting IRD's work in Norway certainly went beyond what was achieved in co-operation between labour parties elsewhere.

Collier referred to his recent despatch on changing Norwegian attitudes towards Communism.[392] He assessed that the situation had recently reached a turning point and that the majority of the population was now alert to the threat to the Norwegian way of life. He cautioned that it would be an over-simplification to use the anti-communist front as the basis for future propaganda work in Norway. He warned of the need to take account of the fact that

> as a people the Norwegians are tenacious of their established opinions, slow to accept new views, independently-minded and consciously wedded to the ideal of objectivity, with a sturdy reliance on the merits of their own judgements. Failing that, they may accept the views of a fellow-Norwegian, but for foreign views they have little use, unless they can assimilate them unconsciously and then regard them as Norwegian. It follows that the recent change of opinion concerning communism and

---

[392] Collier to Sargent, 26 July 1946, N9817/140/G, FO371/56786. This was examined in Chapter Four.

5 THE IMPACT OF INFORMATION RESEARCH DEPARTMENT IN NORWAY IN 1948

Russian policies must be given time to consolidate itself, that any overt or pushful attempt to influence Norwegian opinion will excite hostility, and that our own endeavour should be to make available the true facts of the situation without seeming to wish either to hurry, to excite, or to influence our public.

Anders Buraas would probably have agreed with him.

Collier also provided some recommendations about how this work should be carried out. He thought it necessary to expand the flow of factual and reliable news about the situation in communist-dominated areas and about the aims of the Cominform, and to let the facts speak for themselves. He maintained that such news should preferably come from trustworthy Norwegian sources, or from recognisably responsible sources abroad, such as might be found in speeches by the Foreign Secretary. He stressed that these should be short-term aims: the long-term strategy should be based on the axiom that the most potent argument against communism would be convincing evidence of the vitality and consolidation of western democracy. (A view, incidentally, which Bevin had long held.)

Collier then analysed the nature of the targets in Norway against which IRD should direct its work. He pointed out that with a few isolated exceptions, most of the government and administration were anti-communist and that the majority of the organised labour movement was by tradition hostile to communism. Referring to Gerhardsen's speech at Kråkerøy on 29 February, he pointed out that the Prime Minister had called for an ideological war against native communists. He concluded that those who were either undecided or pro-Russian were to be found among the following:
a. a dwindling band of left wing radicals and intellectuals
b. a section of the trade unions and other labour organisations, consisting mainly of middle-aged workers who had been educated along Marxist lines and were reluctant to abandon their beliefs and
c. the communists.

He concluded that there was nothing to be done with the hardcore communists, and that the waverers were already under pressure from DNA and the trade unions. However, he considered that there was plenty of scope for action against the first two groups, and set out some wide-ranging ideas on how this might be done.

Collier made seven proposals:

a. He considered it important to exert influence over Norwegian correspondents abroad, particularly those in London, so that their reporting took greater account of the views which the Foreign Office wished to put across,

b. He thought it essential to intensify the existing relationship between the British and Norwegian labour parties and to a lesser extent, between the British and Norwegian trade unions. The labour movements were on cordial terms, but there was still far too little traffic between them: a greater exchange of visits by lecturers, trade union delegations, study groups and so forth would yield valuable results,

c. He suggested expanding the use of the British press. He noted that the embassy was distributing 900 copies of British newspapers a week to the Norwegian press, which had accordingly come to depend largely on the UK press for opinion and news. He observed that newsprint shortages in the UK were restricting the amount of foreign news. He therefore suggested offering the inducement of a slight increase in newsprint allocations to those who were prepared to increase their foreign news coverage.[393]

d. Collier also proposed making use of the information services of different organisations, namely DNA, other Norwegian parties, the Norwegian trade union movement and the Norwegian press. He pointed out that the embassy was in touch with many of them already and through them could procure the publication and dissemination of anti-communist material.

---

[393] Newsprint was also in extremely short supply in Norway at that time. Kenney had reported in the 1947 Oslo Annual Review that the Norwegian press was only allowed 25,000 tons of newsprint in 1947, compared with a consumption of 127,000 tons by the Swedish press. N3433/3433/30, FO 491/2. It is worth noting here that the figure of 900 newspapers a week is remarkably high, given the constraints of the period, but it does not appear to have been questioned.

5 THE IMPACT OF INFORMATION RESEARCH DEPARTMENT IN NORWAY IN 1948

e. Returning to a theme raised by the embassy on previous occasions, he advocated producing a periodical in Norwegian designed to keep the Norwegian labour movement informed of developments in Britain and the Commonwealth.

f. He also wanted to make greater use of the Norwegian service of the BBC. (The BBC, at a senior level, was well aware of the existence and objectives of IRD and was co-operating with IRD.[394])

g. He proposed greater use of official statements in Parliament, which he thought should be combined with approaches to correspondents to draw their attention to the significance of such official statements.

Collier emphasised that the key to successful implementation of the new information policy in Norway would be the expansion of personal relationships between the British and Norwegian labour movements – a development which he continued to oversee successfully during the next two years. He stressed that no one was better placed to exert the sort of influence which was required than representatives of the British workers. He noted, though, that by Scandinavian standards the information side of the British labour movement, particularly in the international field, was distressingly inadequate. He provided some advice about how the material to be used might best be presented to a Norwegian audience, and stressed the need to avoid wartime 'black' propaganda. (This was a point which the Foreign Office would have borne in mind later in the year when the Chiefs of Staff showed themselves keen to re-establish a Political Warfare Executive. The Foreign Office was only prepared to plan for this on a contingency basis.[395])

Collier was too experienced a bureaucrat to miss the opportunity provided by this major new initiative, to make a bid to increase his establishment. He concluded by noting that it would be impossible to make any progress in implementing the new policy before a new second secretary

---

[394] Warner to Sir Ian Jacob, BBC Director General, 6 May 1948, PR/266/10/913, FO 1110/16.
[395] Warner to Sargent, 10 August 1948, PR 659/659/913G, FO 1110/104.

5 THE IMPACT OF INFORMATION RESEARCH DEPARTMENT IN NORWAY IN 1948

(Information) had been posted to Oslo.[396] (He received what he asked for remarkably quickly: a new second secretary left for Oslo just over two months later on 20 May.) A number of other European embassies also used the opportunity to request an increase in their staffing in order to meet these new requirements: Stockholm took a similar initiative.[397]

The Foreign Office response

Collier's despatch provoked some lengthy minuting in the Foreign Office. Western European Information Department was quick to dismiss the proposal for a journal to be published in Norwegian, pointing out that the embassy in Oslo had proposed a similar idea a year earlier: it had been rejected, largely due to cost (£1,250). Warner replied on 28 May. He informed Collier that his reply was one of the best received by the Foreign Office, and was most helpful. Addressing some of the specific points Collier raised, where action was required by the Foreign Office, he wrote:

a. that IRD would get in touch with the Norwegian correspondents in London. However, he was not sure how material might be passed to them because the Foreign Office was anxious to conceal its authorship of such anti-Communist material. (It did, of course, gradually become much more skilled at dealing with such modalities.)

b. that the question of increasing visits was being studied, not just as far as Norway was concerned. The problem was finance. The Labour Party could not increase what it was doing, and the use of government money for this purpose might be considered to be the use of public funds for party purposes. He added that there was a further problem: currency restrictions imposed by the Bank of England on union representatives going to conferences abroad. This was being taken up at ministerial level.

c. that following some recent comments by the President of the Board of Trade, it was clear that there was no hope of getting an increase in newsprint allocation.

---

[396] Collier to Bevin, 12 March 1948, PR97/1/913G, FO 1110/3.
[397] Henderson to Bevin, 17 March 1948, PR 98/1/913G, FO 1110/3.

5 THE IMPACT OF INFORMATION RESEARCH DEPARTMENT IN NORWAY IN 1948

d. that there was a plan to increase the output of labour news, and to improve it substantially. He thought that the recently established Socialist Parties information office (which later became known as the Socialist Information and Liaison Office – SILO) might be able to help.[398]

The Foreign Office did not at this stage formally draw up a graded list of the countries where it considered IRD should give priority to its work. However, there is evidence that Norway, because of its important strategic position and significant communist minority, was considered to be one of the more important countries. France and Italy were clearly the priority targets, particularly in view of concerns about how the Communists might do in the Italian general election in April 1948. Benelux and Scandinavia were near the top of a list put forward in a minute by Ralph Murray, the head of IRD, on 17 February. This list suggested target priorities for BBC broadcasting.[399] The circular, outlining the intended usage of *Freedom First* and inviting comments, was sent to a limited number of information officers in Western European posts, which included Oslo but neither Copenhagen nor Stockholm.[400] It is also worth noting that Oslo made very good use of material provided by IRD. By November 1948, there were only four other embassies (including Washington and Paris) which received a larger number of copies of publications sent out by IRD according to their standard distribution list.[401]

First successful results in Norway

The first major project undertaken by IRD was the production of a detailed series of reports on Communism and on conditions inside Soviet Russia and elsewhere in Eastern Europe. It was intended that the reports could be rewrit-

---

[398] Warner to Collier, 28 May, PR 97/1/G, FO 1110/3.
[399] Minute by Murray, 17 February 1948, PR22/10/913G, FO 1110/16.
[400] FO circular, 30 July 1948, PR 517/1/913G, FO 1110/11.
[401] Details of standard IRD distribution list containing details of posts and numbers of copies to be circulated to each, November 1948, PR 1102/57/913G, FO 1110/30.

5 THE IMPACT OF INFORMATION RESEARCH DEPARTMENT IN NORWAY IN 1948

ten by recipients in a way which suited local circumstances. The project soon produced worthwhile results in Oslo. A report from Kenney in May 1948 described the use which Haakon Lie had made of the first report in this series entitled 'The Real Conditions in Soviet Russia'. Kenney said that Lie had rewritten and added to it, drawing on his own personal experiences which came from the two visits he had paid to the Soviet Union before the Second World War. He noted that Lie had demonstrated a very skilful technique of laying damning facts about Communism before a working class audience in such a way as to give no impression of anti-Communist propaganda. Kenney was pleased with the IRD report, and commented that it was a prototype of the kind of material which could be used by the embassy. The article by Lie appeared in *Arbeiderbladet* on 29 April,[402] within three weeks of its completion in London.[403] The embassy continued to pass IRD material regularly to Lie, but did not thereafter comment in such detail on his use of their articles.

Those who collaborated closely with IRD were always on the lookout for people who would be willing to act as channels for disseminating IRD material. Denis Healey, who had been briefed on the work of IRD at an early stage, was also active in approaching European socialists whom he thought would be willing to provide support for IRD's activities. He wrote to his friend Adam Watson in IRD in November 1948, providing the names of three Eastern Europeans whom he thought might be able to help: Watson acted as an intermediary in passing on their names to the BBC.[404] Healey wrote again to Watson shortly afterwards, informing him that he had spoken confidentially to a number of European socialists during a recent Socialist Conference: Watson could now arrange

---

[402] Kenney to IPD, 26 May 1948, PR 396/57/913G, FO 1110/27.

[403] This was certainly not the only occasion when Lie showed that he was prepared to use unorthodox methods to achieve what he considered to be worthwhile objectives. He had a wide reputation for being a good friend of Israel: see for example Hilde Henriksen Waage, 'Norway: One of Israel's best friends' *Journal of Peace Research,* Vol 37 No 2 (March 2000), pp189-211, which describes his initiative in arranging for Norway to sell heavy water to Israel in 1958, a most controversial issue both at that time and afterwards.

[404] Healey to Watson, 2 November 1948, PR 993/1/913G, FO 1110/15.

to send them IRD material. The list of recipients which he provided included Haakon Lie, Kaj Bjørk (international secretary of the Swedish Social Democrat Party), Koos Vorrink (chairman of the Dutch Labour Party), Georges Brutelle (international secretary of the French SFIO), as well as several Italians. He undertook to provide in due course the name of a suitable Danish and Belgian recipient, and to obtain the their private addresses if Watson required them. He added that he would be prepared to circulate the material from Transport House if this was preferred. (This was an offer which, perhaps unsurprisingly, the Foreign Office did not take up. They would not have wished the Labour Party to be so visibly involved.) Healey concluded with the suggestion that the Foreign Office should inform information officers in the relevant embassies of the arrangements which had been made. Watson wrote to Kenney to inform him, and received a reply from Mason, Kenney's successor, who pointed out politely that Haakon Lie had already been receiving IRD material for more than six months.[405]

Over the next few months, IRD produced a series of detailed reports on conditions in the Soviet Union and elsewhere in Eastern Europe. In a letter of 23 June 1948, Kenney commented to Murray that he particularly liked a paper on 'Labour and the Trade Unions'; he thought it met the need in Norway for a completely dispassionate and objective analysis of communist policy and the Soviet setup. He intended to pass it to the international secretary of LO at the earliest opportunity. He asked for six copies of the papers which IRD had by then produced (which included reports on subjects such as 'The facts of Soviet expansion', 'Some facts about communism and freedom of the press', 'Poland as an example of how communism gains and consolidates control in a state' and 'Notes on the communalisation of justice in Eastern Europe'). He also asked for twelve copies of each paper produced by IRD in future.

---

[405] Healey to Watson, 8 December 1948, and subsequent correspondence, PR 1211/1/913G, FO 1110/15. In view of the significant numbers of recipients of IRD material in most countries in Western Europe, it is scarcely surprising that Watson had overlooked Kenney's earlier report about Lie's use of IRD material to write an article in *Arbeiderbladet*.

5 THE IMPACT OF INFORMATION RESEARCH DEPARTMENT IN NORWAY IN 1948

Kenney left Oslo in December 1948. His successor, F. C. Mason, wrote to Murray shortly afterwards, replying to a request which the latter had made for information about usage of IRD material, and for suggestions about how it could be better employed. He said that since he lacked the intimate knowledge which Kenney had possessed, his preliminary reply would be sketchy. However, he noted that Kenney regularly distributed IRD reports to a carefully selected group of recipients which included: Haakon Lie, John Sanness (foreign editor of *Arbeiderbladet*), Bjørn Bunkholdt (foreign editor of *Aftenposten*), Trygve Width (foreign editor of *Morgenbladet*), Walter Wilson (director of Høyres Pressekontor, the conservative press agency) and Arnulf Øverland, a former left-wing idealist who was one of the leading poets and writers in Norway.[406]

Some of the subsequent comments in this letter suggested that Mason was initially not as enthusiastic about active IRD propaganda work as Kenney had been. He thought that the best way to put across anti-Communism was to stress British achievements and qualities, merely slipping in here and there a comparison with some fact or failing from the Soviet Union which spoke for itself.

Offer by Murray of materials for DNA use as propaganda and in elections

IRD occasionally picked up some encouraging indications of the extent to which senior members of DNA valued their product. A particular (and very successful) example occurred during the United Nations General Assembly in Paris in October 1948. F. Warner wrote in November 1948 to Mayhew to report a conversation which he had had with Aase Lionæs, the head of the women's branch of DNA and a delegate at the UNGA. When Warner asked her what she thought of the British tactic of occasionally attacking the Russians in debate, Lionæs replied that it had been a tremendous relief to her and her colleagues. In the past they had often had to sit under a rain of Russian insults without replying: she thought it unmanly and unnatural. She had been especially impressed by the

---

[406] Mason to Murray, 17 December 1948, PR 1317/57/913, FO 1110/30.

speech made by Mayhew on Russian forced labour camps (a speech based on a brief which, as Mayhew very well knew, had been prepared by IRD). The speech was different from all previous statements as Mayhew had been able to quote real Soviet sources and had not just reported comments by anti-Soviet refugees. Lionæs was so impressed by this speech that she had sent copies back to DNA's headquarters in Oslo for use in preparing material for the next election.[407]

Murray saw this letter and copied it to Kenney in Oslo. He thought that Kenney might find it useful, in case it gave him an opportunity to use more IRD material in some way. He carefully warned Kenney not to show knowledge of the interest shown by Lionæs in his discussions with DNA.

Murray then offered some further assistance from IRD. He knew that there would be an election in Norway the following year, and suggested that if DNA was in need of material in a big way for election propaganda, IRD could produce various studies if DNA could specify what it wanted. The papers which IRD had issued hitherto had been designed for common denominator distribution to information officers: the idea was that the papers might be useful to publicists who could perhaps base articles on them. However, IRD was getting a certain amount of research done. Since they were strengthening the department considerably, they could if required produce quite a lot of new material. For example, they had what he described as 'a terrific document on trade unions in the Soviet Union. It would be quite useless for publicity as it stood because it was so vast - but it did contain a great deal of research not done by anyone else'. He wondered whether an assiduous DNA official might be able to use such a paper as a quarry. He also offered a study of human rights in the Soviet Union, which could similarly be used as a source of information

By this time, Kenney had left Oslo, and Mason replied. He temporised, saying that he had just arrived, and that he would not wish to ask for special material until he had got to know his way around a bit better.[408] IRD were not deflected

---

[407] F. Warner to Mayhew, 15 November 1948, PR 1069/760/913, FO 1110/112.
[408] Mason to Murray, 7 December 1948, PR1229/760/913, FO 1110/112.

5 THE IMPACT OF INFORMATION RESEARCH DEPARTMENT IN NORWAY IN 1948

by this cautious response and clearly wanted to ensure that their material was put to good use as quickly as possible. Watson therefore wrote to Mason soon afterwards telling him that the human rights brief would be rehashed. However, the trade union brief was different. The latest document contained a mass of new evidence and detail which had never been published outside Russia. He acknowledged that it was unsuitable for publicity as it stood, but said that the collective view in IRD was that DNA might like to use it as a source of information. He therefore instructed Mason to pass it to Haakon Lie.[409] In a conversation in July 2005, Haakon Lie said that he had made good use, for anti-communist propaganda purposes, of material passed to him by the British although he had also benefited from material provided by other sources, including the Americans who had also provided him with some briefing. However, not surprisingly he was unable to remember the use to which any specific documents may have been put.[410] There was, throughout this period, close co-operation between the British and the Americans over anti-communist propaganda. Foreign Office guidance issued in May 1948 advised that the two countries should aim to 'shoot at the same target from different angles'.[411] This also provided authority to exchange information with local US counterparts so as to avoid overlapping. There is no documentary evidence of the extent of local collaboration in Oslo, although contacts certainly took place. In December 1948, Mason replied to a letter encouraging local cooperation, saying that he had not yet met his American colleague as he was away on leave, but that Kenney had been on excellent terms with him.[412]

This was not the only time that IRD provided assistance to DNA in their preparations for an election in Norway. They did so again in 1953, by which time Michael Cullis had replaced Mason and was responsible for IRD work in Norway. An article based on 'Facts about the

---

[409] Watson to Mason, 21 December 1948, PR 1229/760/913, FO 1110/112.
[410] Conversation with Haakon Lie, 5 July 2005.
[411] Foreign Office circular telegram, 12 May 1948, PR229/1/913G, FO 1110/6.
[412] Mason to IRD, 16 December 1948, PR1188/865/913G, FO 1110/229.

Soviet Taxpayer', produced by IRD, was published by DNA as their main pamphleteering effort directed against the Communists in the elections in that year.[413]

Speaking in 2007, Adam Watson said that he had not had direct responsibility for IRD's work in Norway. This was overseen by Murray. However, he had sufficient oversight to observe that the relationship between the two Labour parties was particularly intimate. It was extremely effective in enabling IRD to achieve its objectives in Norway. Watson considered that this relationship represented the essence of the way in which IRD liked to work.[414]

Freedom First

Thought was also given to trying to reach a wider trade union readership. Mayhew approached Herbert Tracey of the Defence of Democracy Trust, a TUC-funded organisation, and suggested to him that he should consider producing an international edition of *Freedom First*, a newsletter which was already being produced by the Trust. In a minute to Warner in June 1948, Mayhew pointed out that the Trust was handicapped by a shortage of funds. He wondered whether the Foreign Office could not appropriately purchase copies of the home edition of *Freedom First* for distribution to information officers and labour attachés in a limited number of carefully selected missions overseas. He also asked what sort of financial assistance could be given to an overseas edition.

Warner was initially cautious. He did not see how any trade union body in the UK could produce a newsletter sufficiently interesting to have a wide circulation in foreign countries. 'For surely the trade unionists, for example in Norway, are unlikely to be very interested in such a newsletter unless it contains a good deal about domestic

---

[413] Minutes of Western European Regional Meeting discussing IRD work, 10 December 1953, PR103/14/G, FO 1110/615. Cullis was at that time directly employed by IRD. It had been necessary to close the Information Section of the embassy in Oslo for reasons of economy at the end of March 1952. However, it was decided that IRD operations should be continued and that Cullis, who had been responsible for information work, should be offered employment as a member of IRD.
[414] Conversation with Adam Watson, 3 April 2007.

5 THE IMPACT OF INFORMATION RESEARCH DEPARTMENT IN NORWAY IN 1948

matters in Norway of interest to Norwegian trade unionists.' However, he changed his mind and agreed once Mayhew had explained to him the extent of the planned close collaboration with IRD and the detail of IRD input. Mayhew wanted the newsletter to be translated into French, Italian, German and Norwegian – 300 copies each, except for 500 copies in German. He requested that information officers be asked to provide mailing lists, and preferred that the newsletter be mailed directly to recipients, and not sent out through information officers.[415]

A circular telegram was sent in July 1948 to information officers in Western European posts (though not at this stage including Denmark and Stockholm), as well as to certain posts in Latin America. This outlined the project. It asked for the names of proposed recipients, and it specified these names should extend down the trade union hierarchy as far as possible. It envisaged local branch officials as suitable readers, as well as members of central trade union organs. It expected that the lists put forward in smaller countries would consist of perhaps fifty or more names, and requested that the labour attaché, if one existed, also be consulted.[416]

Kenney replied on 14 August, suggesting the names of 130 recipients. He noted that he had collaborated closely with Inman in preparing the list. He pointed out that while the list might seem large for a country as small as Norway, it should be borne in mind that the labour movement there was extremely highly developed and widespread and was numerically greater than the organised movements of many larger countries. The list of names which he provided included: Konrad Nordahl, chairman of LO, Gunnar Braathen, deputy chairman of LO, Alfred Skar, Press Department of LO, Trygve Bratteli, Deputy Chairman of DNA, Haakon Lie, secretary of DNA, Anders Mørk, Arbeidernes Opplysningsforbund, Harald Haraldson and Martin Tranmæl from *Arbeiderbladet* and over

---

[415] Mayhew minute to Walker, 3 June 1948, and subsequent minuting, PR517/1/913G, FO 1110/11.
[416] Circular telegram on Freedom First, 30 July 1948, PR 517/1/913G, FO 1110/11.

120 more from trade unions, local youth organisations and local DNA branches both in Oslo and around the country.[417]

In the end, however, an international edition of *Freedom First* never got off the ground. There were disagreements about which languages should be used and concerns about its quality and lack of authenticated information. Moreover, as Kenney also argued after he had seen a trial version, there were problems with its rather unsophisticated approach to propaganda, which was too crudely anti-communist. Kenney also considered that it used the wrong language and was repetitious.[418] Attempts continued to be made - mainly by Mayhew - to overcome these problems, but the plan finally had to be abandoned following the Lynskey Tribunal, a hearing which took place later in the year. (This was an investigation into allegations that bribes had been paid to government ministers and officials: *Freedom First* received some publicity when it emerged that the central figure in the investigation by the Tribunal had paid for a subscription to the newsletter with a cheque which bounced.) IRD sent a circular to information officers on 31 January 1949, describing this background and explaining that the idea of *Freedom First* would have to be abandoned because of this unfortunate publicity.[419] Mayhew continued unsuccessfully to try to find another way of restarting the project. In March 1949, Murray asked for a paper to be prepared for Mayhew which would set out the case why the TUC was considered incapable of running an international newsletter. He wondered whether it might be worth considering approaching the Labour Party to do the job instead.[420]

The effectiveness of IRD in Norway: Russian reactions

It is notoriously difficult to estimate the effectiveness of propaganda and the extent to which it is responsible for informing

---

[417] Kenney to IRD, 14 August 1948, PR 681/G, FO 1110/98.
[418] Kenney to IRD, 13 September 1948, PR 772/G, FO 1110/98.
[419] IRD circular letter to Information Officers, 31 January 1949, PR 50/22/G, FO 1110/213.
[420] Minute by Murray, 18 March 1949, PR 110/G, FO 1110/213.

5 THE IMPACT OF INFORMATION RESEARCH DEPARTMENT IN NORWAY IN 1948

and changing the views of those against whom it is aimed. The best assessment that can usually be made is to monitor the number and range of publications in which an article is replayed and to use that as a measure. IRD soon started to request usage reports from posts to which it was supplying material. Thus in December 1948, Murray wrote to Mason to ask him about the extent to which IRD material was used in Norway. However Mason, newly arrived, was only able to give him a fairly sketchy reply and to provide the names of the most prominent recipients.[421] By the middle of the following year, Murray was able to go into rather more detail in his report on the work of IRD up to July 1949. He noted the very successful response to the publication of the Codex on forced labour in the Soviet Union, which had been prepared for use at the Economic and Social Council of the UN which met in Geneva. As will be shown in Chapter Eight, IRD gradually developed better systems of monitoring and assessing usage of their material, to try to ensure that their product was tailored to produce more effective outcomes.

It is also worth attempting to assess quite how the Russians reacted to IRD's work, so as to form a view of the extent to which it had an impact on them, as well as on the Norwegians against whom it was principally directed. This has been done by a study of documents exchanged between the Russian embassy in Oslo and the Russian Foreign Ministry in Moscow, obtained from the archives of the Russian Foreign Ministry. While these documents give some fascinating insights, it should be borne in mind that they do not represent a complete picture of Soviet policy-making during this period: access to the documents of other Soviet departments, in particular those of the Politburo, are not yet available – a point made by Korobochkin.[422]

The Russians had been concerned about the extent of British influence in Norway for some time and made a number of attempts, which do not appear to have been particularly successful, to counter it. In July 1946, the Fifth European Department of the Soviet Foreign Ministry (which

---

[421] Murray to Mason, 2 December 1948, PR1105/57/913, Mason to Murray, 17 December 1948, PR 1317/57/913, FO 1110/30.
[422] M. Korobochkin, 'Soviet Policy Towards Finland and Norway', p186.

was at that time, according to Korobochkin, still very optimistic about the prospects for the Soviets to increase their influence in Norway[423]) sent a memorandum to Molotov. It stated that Russia could not permit Norway, with its common borders and which was so important to the safeguarding of security in northern Europe, to be incorporated into the sphere of influence of the Anglo-Saxon powers, particularly Britain. The memorandum observed that when Anglo-Soviet relations became tense in 1946, the British had sought to prepare solid support in Norway, out of concern for international complications. It cited a range of actions as evidence of the British policy, including the activities of the military, the removal of the pro-Soviet General Ruge, the appointment of the 'British agent' Hauge as Defence Minister and the close connections between the two royal families. It also noted Laski's visit to Oslo in September 1945 at the invitation of DNA, and commented that Laski had made a significant contribution to the worsening of relations between the Labour Party and the Soviet Union. The memorandum made a series of recommendations aimed at overcoming this situation, and strengthening political, economic and cultural ties with Norway. The political proposals included tasking Ambassador Kuznetsov to explore the possibility of achieving a friendship treaty between the Soviet Union and Norway and obtaining agreement to open a Russian consulate in Kirkenes to strengthen control over the west coast of Norway. It also proposed improving the quality and quantity of staff in the Russian embassy in Oslo and increasing the size of the TASS office in Oslo. An editorial footnote to this document, which appears in *Norge og Sovietunionen 1917-1955 En utenrikspolitisk dokumentasjon*, notes that Molotov commented that 'this must be discussed'.[424] However, the proposals were not considered any further. Korobochkin

---

[423] Ibid, p199.
[424] Memorandum from Aleksandr N. Abramov, Ivan M. Maevski and Mikhail S. Vetrov, Fifth European section of the Foreign Ministry to Molotov, 2 July 1946 in Sven Holtsmark (ed.), *Norge og Sovietunionen 1917-1955 En utenrikspolitisk dokumentasjon* (Cappelens Forlag, 1995), p379.

considers that the reason was that Molotov became too busy preparing for the Paris Peace Conference.[425]

The Soviet Foreign Ministry returned to the charge early in 1947, when Novikov, a member of the Foreign Ministry's collegium, sent a further memorandum to Molotov. He referred to the earlier memorandum and Molotov's comment that it should be discussed. He observed that it had not actually been discussed at all in relation to a series of important international meetings which had taken place. However, it remained as important as it had been before for Russia to strengthen its position in Norway. Novikov cited a number of ways in which the British and the Americans had improved their position, noting that the British in particular were doing so through an increase in the influence they were exerting over all the armed forces. Furthermore, the British were strengthening their propaganda in Norway, and the country was being overrun by British tourists, military, students, industrialists and businessmen. (He provided no evidence to support these observations.) He also noted that at the Paris peace conference, Norway had voted with Britain and the United States on all the most important questions. Indeed, since the liberation of Norway, Russian-Norwegian relations had not been worse. He put forward a series of recommendations aimed at improving this situation. These were more detailed and wide ranging than those made by the Fifth European section a few months earlier. He suggested completing negotiations with Norway over Svalbard, aiming at achieving a joint declaration on joint defence of the Svalbard archipelago and the abrogation of the 1920 Paris Treaty on Svalbard. He also suggested granting permission to *Arbeiderbladet* and *Friheten* to send permanent correspondents to Moscow and broadening information and propaganda work. On the economic side he suggested, among other proposals, Soviet participation in the Norwegian aluminium industry and the creation of a joint venture company. His suggestions on the cultural side were equally wide-ranging. A footnote observes that Novikov's proposals were submitted to the Central Committee, but it was not clear what had happened as a result. It appears that the

---

[425] Korobochkin 'Soviet Policy towards Finland and Norway', p199.

subject was further discussed, but that no steps were taken to realise all of his proposals.[426]

It is interesting that these proposals were initiated within the Russian Foreign Ministry, rather than within the Russian embassy in Oslo. However, the embassy was not inactive. There is evidence that the Russians had complained specifically about anti-Soviet propaganda from as early as mid-1947. Haakon Lie told an American diplomat in July 1947 that a Russian, whose name he could not remember,[427] had recently called on him. He complained about an article Lie had written in *Arbeiderbladet* about the International Socialist Congress in Zurich. He then referred to other articles also published in *Arbeiderbladet* which he considered unfriendly to the Soviet Union, particularly a series earlier in the year on the Communist party in America.[428] The author noted that Lie thought this conversation significant because it was the first time that the Russians had bothered to protest at any deviation from a pro-Russian line. By January 1948, the Russian embassy had become so concerned about the extent of what it perceived as anti-Soviet propaganda that it made a very strong protest to the Norwegian Foreign Ministry.

In some subsequent correspondence during that year, the Russian embassy did not distinguish between British and American propaganda, and lumped them together. For example, Afanasiev wrote to Zorin in Moscow in June 1948 enclosing a report from Cherkasov on what Cherkashov described as the Anglo-American campaign, aimed at threatening Norway with the prospect of Soviet expansion. He noted that this campaign, supported by Norwegian reactionaries, had had a series of consequences. These included an increase of 100 million kroner in the defence budget, the

---

[426] Memorandum from K.V. Novikov, member of the collegium of the Foreign Ministry, to Molotov, 5 January 1947, in Holtsmark (ed.) *Norge og Sovietunionen*, p392.

[427] This was probably Cherkasov, who had a meeting with Lie on 20 June 1947. Foreign Policy Archive of the Russian Federation, Moscow, (hereafter AVPRF), f.0116, op.38, p.140. d.8 11. 88-92. Cherkasov's minutes from meeting with Haakon Lie, 20 June 1947.

[428] Memorandum from the American ambassador in Oslo to State Department, No 1228, 17 July 1947, containing an account of a conversation between Lie, Walter Galenson and the unnamed author in mid July 1947. Document provided by Sven Holtsmark.

exclusion of communists from the important defence and foreign affairs committees in the Storting, and more frequent speeches by prominent politicians, including Prime Minister Gerhardsen, about the possible creation of a Scandinavian military bloc. He concluded that these developments were in part the result of Anglo-American propaganda.[429] However, the report made no mention of specific articles or reports which it considered to be the results of British or American propaganda, such as the one written by Lie on the 'Real Conditions in the Soviet Union'. IRD had assessed this article to be one of the first successful results of their work when it was replayed in *Arbeiderbladet* a few weeks earlier. The correspondence assumed that such a campaign existed, without adducing specific evidence. The report made no recommendations as to what might be done to try to counter the impact of the campaign which the embassy had identified. Further evidence of Russian reactions to what it considered to be the Anglo-American anti-Soviet propaganda campaign will be examined in Chapter Eight.

Secret briefings for Hauge

IRD was not the only department which was providing briefings on communism and Soviet activities. On 22 September 1948, Hankey wrote a top secret and personal letter to Collier in which he referred to arrangements which had been made to supply periodical reports on communism which would be produced by the Joint Intelligence Committee (JIC).[430] The first of these reports was taking longer to produce than had been anticipated, and in order not to keep the Norwegians waiting, Hankey had commissioned some interim material. At his request MI6 had provided him with some recent reports on various aspects of communism which were suitable as they stood for transmission to the Norwegians. He asked Collier to pass them to Hauge, the Norwegian Minister of Defence, in accordance with the procedure which had been

---

[429] Afanasev to Zorin, 2 June 1948, AVPRF, f.0116, op.36, p.140, d.2. 12.
[430] These papers were retained for 45 years because of their sensitivity, given the references to MI6 and the provision of JIC papers to the Norwegians.

arranged between him and Alexander, his British opposite number. Collier replied on 5 October that one of these not very impressive reports was incomplete and he had not yet given them to Hauge.[431] They were never passed because Hankey sent the first completed JIC report to Collier to give to Hauge on 26 October.[432]

It is scarcely surprising that the high tension and seriousness of the situation during this period created misunderstandings between the two countries. Some of these took place at a very senior level, creating the potential for awkward consequences which were only avoided because of the common sense of Hauge and Collier. Thus, the passing of briefing papers to Hauge was again delayed shortly afterwards for a more sinister reason: in November, the British military attaché, Treseder, had expressed doubts as to the reliability of General Ole Berg, the Norwegian Chief of Staff.[433] Treseder and his naval and air attachés thought that Berg had unnecessarily close relations with the Russians and reported that he had a very weak character and that the Russians found it easy to extract information from him.[434] It was decided that JIC briefings to Hauge should be suspended. This matter escalated into an unpleasant incident. Hauge, approached by Treseder, was quick to come to the defence of Berg when the subject was raised and he expressed his strong support for him. Hauge's assurances were accepted, but Berg himself unfortunately also came to hear of the allegations about him. When reporting to London and attempting to draw a line under this issue, Collier suggested inviting Berg to the UK, perhaps to visit the Staff College, as a means of placating him and demonstrating that the British continued to retain confidence in him. He defended his attachés up to a point when he wrote to Hankey that they would not have been doing their duty if they had not reported their suspicions. However, Collier also noted

---

[431] Collier to Hankey, 5 October 1948, N11287/27120/G30, FO 371/71504.
[432] Ibid.
[433] These papers were also withheld for 45 years because of the sensitivity of the comments about Ole Berg.
[434] Crowe, chargé d'affaires, to Hankey, 11 November 1948, N12765/1794/G30, FO 371/71499. Treseder to War Office, 7 December 1948, N13127/1794/G30, FO 371/71499.

that if they had had longer experience of serving in Oslo and working with Norwegians, their suspicions might not have been aroused.[435]

This was not the only occasion - during this time of great tension - when members of the British military expressed doubts about the reliability of Norwegians. They – and the Americans – also shared concerns about Vilhelm Evang, the head of the Norwegian Intelligence Service (NIS). Matthew Aid quotes a report from a senior American official who noted that NIS was headed by one of the most powerful communists in the army. He adds that whatever distrust may have existed about Evang did not prevent American intelligence officials from accepting any high-grade intelligence that NIS was willing to share.[436] On another occasion, improbably enough, some doubts were raised about Hauge himself - although fortunately on that occasion the report was not circulated much beyond the War Office. As in the case of Berg, the allegations turned out to have been based on the injudicious circulation of unsubstantiated gossip and rumours which were not verified before being passed on – an explanation which probably accounts for many of the rumours about other Norwegians which were circulating at a time of such sensitivity. Briefings for Hauge were resumed with the handing over of JIC papers on the defence of Scandinavia. Collier, however, requested that one of these documents should be withheld from the Norwegians: it was a paper which discussed ways of meeting a Russian attack on Scandinavia, which emphasised the weakness of Norway's position without Swedish assistance. He was assured that no documents such as these would be given to the Norwegian defence authorities except through him and with his approval.[437]

---

[435] Collier to Hankey 15 December 1948, N13468/1794/G30, FO 371/71499. These papers were also withheld for 45 years because of the sensitivity of the comments about Ole Berg.

[436] Msg, S4837, HQ EUCOM Frankfurt to WDGID, 13 May 1947, RG-18, Entry 5 AAF Decimal File 1942-1947 Box 42, File: MC7200-7399 April-June 1947, NA, CP. Quoted by Matthew M. Aid, 'US Sigint Relations with Scandinavia, 1945-1960' *Journal of Strategic Studies* (August 2006), pp583-584.

[437] Collier to Foreign Office, 21 December 1948, Foreign Office to Oslo, 23 December 1948, N13576/1794/G30, FO 371/71499.

5 THE IMPACT OF INFORMATION RESEARCH DEPARTMENT IN NORWAY IN 1948

By the time that IRD was established in early 1948, the embassy already had close and wide-ranging contacts with members of the Norwegian labour movement at different levels. This research shows that the embassy was able to exploit these links quickly and effectively to disseminate information as IRD wished. The fact that a large number of papers have been withheld, and are not available in the archives, makes it impossible to establish a clear picture of all the activities in which they were involved. There is nonetheless sufficient evidence to show that the parties had discussed the nature of their collaboration at the highest level, that senior members such as Lie and Healey were actively involved in assisting with the dissemination of material which had been produced by IRD, and that they were also benefiting from the briefing which IRD was providing. Watson's comments provide valuable confirmation of the way in which IRD was able to take advantage of the particularly intimate links between the two parties. Although the embassy was also providing material to journalists and members of other parties, the files show that the collaboration was much less effective - partly because their links were not so close, but largely because DNA was better placed to disseminate IRD's propaganda effectively.

The material which has been described in this chapter further supports the conclusion put forward in Chapter Three that the key elements were to be found in a triangular relationship between the two Labour parties and the British embassy in Oslo. The strategic direction which was provided by Collier, exemplified particularly in his earlier despatch of 20 March 1946, and that of 12 March 1948, was of great importance. In the prevailing circumstances - and in particular after the coup in Czechoslovakia - it is certain that the two parties would have found common cause anyway, but the development of their links was facilitated by the support which they received both from the embassy in Oslo and the Foreign Office in London. Just as it suited both parties to work closely together to counter the threat of growing communist influence, so it suited the Foreign Office to accept Collier's advice and to encourage this process as far as possible.

6 Spain

This chapter will make a comparative study of the extent to which the two labour parties were able to cooperate in attempts to achieve the removal of Franco. Throughout the period, the labour movements in both Norway and Britain worked hard to persuade their own governments to adopt policies directed towards his removal. However, while they were able to influence the thinking and attitudes of senior government ministers, they did not have a decisive effect in changing policy. Both governments, in Britain in particular, were concerned to try to preserve their trade with Spain which provided minerals considered important for post-war reconstruction. British policy seemed to be largely passive, depending on the Spanish people to take action to remove Franco and neither interfering nor allowing the use of significant international pressure to unseat him. Norway was more proactive, but did not wish to take action in isolation. Representatives of the Norwegian labour movement made several visits to London to try to gain insights into the thinking of their British counterparts and Labour politicians, both to explore possibilities for more concerted action against Franco and to seek assistance in resolving a specific Norwegian problem with Spain in early 1947. This co-operation did not produce significant results.

Despite the impression given by the Foreign Office throughout this period – both publicly and privately - of a passive policy towards Franco, there are documents in the Norwegian Labour Party archive, and also in the Norwegian national archive, which together with some indicative material in the British national archive, provide evidence which demonstrates that in 1946 Britain was indeed working to remove Franco and was much more proactive in this process than has hitherto been believed.

6 Spain

When the popular front government was elected in Spain in 1936, it faced an armed revolt by the nationalists, led by Franco. Fascist Italy and Nazi Germany provided extensive financial and military aid to him, while Britain and France observed the policy of non-intervention which all powers had ostensibly accepted but which they alone maintained. Only the Soviet Union gave assistance to the Spanish republicans. While volunteers went to fight for both sides, there were many from labour movements across Europe who went to fight for the republicans. Preston comments that in a Europe which was still unaware of the crimes of Stalin, the communist-organised brigades seemed to be fighting for much that was worth saving in terms of democratic rights and trade union freedoms. The volunteers believed that by fighting fascism in Spain, they were also fighting it in their own countries.[438] The labour movement in Britain was split. Most of the leadership was never willing to mount an active campaign to supply arms to Spain, or to do more than support humanitarian aid. Like other trade union leaders, Bevin sympathised with the Spanish republicans, but continued to defend the policy of non-intervention. Weiler points out that he also feared that strong support for the republicans might divide the labour movement, since a number of Catholic workers opposed the aims of the republicans. For the left wing of the movement, Spain was the great political cause of the decade. [439] It certainly played a significant part in influencing the decision of many young left-wing students and intellectuals to join the Communist party in the late 1930s, as Denis Healey described in an interview in 1991.[440]

The level of interest in Spain was certainly no less in Norway during this period. The war was widely reported, and the scale of the suffering caused much interest and concern.[441] Senior representatives from both labour parties were sent

---

[438] Paul Preston, *A concise history of the Spanish Civil War* (Fontana Press, 1996), p5.
[439] Peter Weiler, *Ernest Bevin* (Manchester University Press, 1993), p93.
[440] Healey interview with Andrew Whitehead, 13 September 1991, CP/HIST/01/01, Labour Party Archive, Manchester. Healey also wrote about this in his autobiography, *The Time of my Life*, pp33-34.
[441] It has also been widely written about. Paul Preston estimated that by 1996, more than 15,000 books had been published about the civil war.

6 SPAIN

to Spain to see what might be done to help the republicans. Together with Rolf Gerhardsen and Willi Midelfart, Haakon Lie visited in the autumn of 1936, and spent Christmas in Madrid. Shortly after their return, on a very cold night in Oslo, they addressed an open-air meeting of over 8,000 people, who wanted to hear about the situation there – the size of the audience reflecting the widespread concern about Spain. Indeed, Lie wrote later that no war was ever followed with greater interest in Norway than the Spanish Civil War. More than 300 Norwegians were among the many thousands of volunteers fighting on the republican side. Norwegian donations per head were greater than those of any other nation. The Norwegian Seamens' Union boycotted ships which had sailed into Franco's harbours. Members were instructed to disembark if their ships starting loading cargo destined for Franco. (This was judged to be illegal, and the union subsequently had to pay some compensation.) When Franco's troops boarded some Norwegian ships on their way to Spain, Foreign Minister Halvdan Koht proposed that a Norwegian minesweeper be sent to the Mediterranean to protect the ships and their crew. He was only with difficulty dissuaded from resigning when this proposal was not implemented.[442] Similarly, Attlee visited the republican forces in Spain in December 1937. In recognition of this fact, and the support provided by him and by the Labour Party, the British battalion of the International Brigade, formed on a volunteer basis to assist the Spanish republicans, included a Clement Attlee company.[443] Attlee maintained his pro-republican views during the Second World War as well. In late 1944, as deputy prime minister, he wrote a minute to the War Cabinet stating that Britain should stiffen its attitude towards the Franco regime and use whatever methods were available to assist in bringing about its downfall.[444]

In common with most countries, the Norwegian government recognised the Franco regime in 1939. It was careful

---

[442] Haakon Lie, *Loftsrydding* (Tiden Norsk Forlag, 1980), pp323-325.
[443] Trevor Burridge, *Clement Attlee A political biography* (Jonathan Cape, 1985), p127.
[444] Attlee to War Cabinet, 4 November 1944, PREM 8/106, quoted by Paul Preston in his introduction to *Britain, Franco and the Cold War* by Qasim Ahmad (Garland, 1992), p xvi.

to point out that this was not a recognition of Franco, but an expression of the fact that the republicans had lost the civil war. Norway established a legation in Madrid. When the minister there died in 1942, he was not replaced. Norway was represented by a chargé d'affaires, Sven Ebbell, who remained until the decision of the UN General Assembly in November 1950 to allow the return of ambassadors to Spain. During the war, Franco tried to break off relations with the Norwegian government in exile, and to establish them with the Quisling regime. This was successfully prevented by a policy of careful prevarication. No Spanish representative was therefore sent to Oslo.[445]

In view of the widespread detestation of the Franco regime and its close links to both Germany and Italy, it was not surprising that after the collapse of the Axis powers and the end of the war, labour movements in both Norway and Britain expected their respective Labour governments to take action quickly to remove Franco and liberate Spain from its dictatorship. However, this did not happen. Bevin soon indicated that the Labour government would follow many aspects of the foreign policy of its predecessor, including that towards Spain. He made this commitment more explicit in his first speech in the House of Commons on 20 August 1945, when he said that the western powers would not take action against Franco, that the question of the regime in Spain was one for the people of Spain to decide and that 'I am satisfied that intervention by foreign powers in the internal affairs of Spain would have the opposite effect to that desired and would probably strengthen General Franco's position'.[446]

A number of factors contributed to this change of view. First, the protection of trade. Both Britain and Norway were reliant on Spain to some degree for raw materials which were of importance to their reconstruction programmes. Spain needed little from either country, and was able to exploit this factor to considerable advantage, particularly with Norway.

---

[445] 'Fakta for talere og tillitsmenn: Spania-spørsmålet.' A DNA publication for use by party members, April 1946. Internasjonalt utvalg, D Da10, Arbeiderbevegelsens arkiv.

[446] Quoted by Alan Bullock, *Ernest Bevin: Foreign Secretary 1945-51* (Heinemann, 1983), pp71-72.

Secondly, throughout this period, Britain was concerned that open intervention in Spain risked causing another civil war. Thirdly, Britain thought that such an intervention risked causing instability which could be exploited to the full by the communists. By early 1946, the British Chiefs of Staff and the Foreign Office were inclined to the American view that the Russians wanted to see a civil war provoked in Spain. This was one of the main reasons why they were reluctant to allow the Spanish question to be put before the UN Security Council: it would have given the Soviet Union an opportunity to influence events.[447] On 10 May 1946, Gerram in Northern Department summed up the situation as follows:

> The Soviet government have been taking an increasing interest in Spain during the last eight months and have intensified anti-Franco propaganda. It is clear that they see in the situation in Spain a heaven-sent opportunity for making trouble for western democracies, and the possibility of bringing about a revolution in Spain, resulting in the establishment of an extreme left-wing government which would give them a sphere of influence of considerable strategic importance in south-western Europe. Maisky talking to Roberts (the British chargé d'affaires in Moscow) and Gromyko at the UN Security Council have said quite frankly that they would like to see a revolution in Spain.[448]

As was discussed in Chapter Four, arguments such as these contributed to the first attempt to establish a programme to disseminate counter-Soviet propaganda. Finally, there were also senior officials, such as Warner, who argued that it was very important not to create a precedent by interfering in the internal affairs of another country.[449] The Soviets might later do the same thing with other countries whose internal conditions they did not like.

---

[447] Paul Preston, *Franco* (Fontana, 1995), p553.
[448] Minute by P. Gerram, 10 May 1946, N6344/605/38G, FO 371/56832.
[449] Colban to Norwegian Foreign Ministry (UD), describing a meeting with C F A Warner on 26 April 1946, Boks 559 25.4/102, Riksarkiv.

Throughout this period, few governments found it easy to agree on a common policy towards Spain. Their policies were not consistent, nor were they effectively co-ordinated, as the intensive manoeuvrings during successive meetings of the UN General Assembly showed. Governments, and sometimes politicians, occasionally took their own initiatives. Preston notes that France, given intense public hostility to Franco, was potentially the most anti-Francoist of the three western powers. However, in 1945 both Bidault, the Foreign Minister, and de Gaulle, the President of the Council of Ministers, were hostile to action against him. De Gaulle even sent Franco a secret message to inform him that he would resist left-wing pressure and would maintain diplomatic relations with him.[450] However, this was not sustained and on 1 March 1946, just a few days before the issue of the Tripartite Declaration by France, Britain and the United States,[451] France announced that it was unilaterally closing its border with Spain. Similarly, the United States decided in late 1945 not to replace its ambassador in Madrid, Armour, when he left Spain on retirement, though at the time his departure was officially described as due to private reasons. This significantly diminished the impact of the UN resolution in December 1946 to withdraw ambassadors from Madrid. Such a thread of inconsistency ran through many of the main events of the next few years: in November 1950, Britain and France abstained from voting on the resolution to rescind this resolution, whereas the United States voted for it.

Labour movement agitation over Spain.

Both in the immediate aftermath of the war, and throughout this period, labour movements in Britain and Norway undertook a series of actions to pressure their respective governments to take effective action over Spain. Union conferences and congresses passed resolutions, and individual unions and

---

[450] Paul Preston, *Franco*, p 543, quoting Randolph Bernard Jones, *The Spanish Question and the Cold War 1944-53* (Unpublished PhD thesis, University of London, 1987), pp 49-51 and Florentino Portero, *Franco aislado: la cuestion espanola* (Madrid, 1989), pp 133-38.
[451] The Tripartite Declaration condemned the Franco regime, but described the Franco problem as an internal Spanish matter.

branches regularly wrote considerable numbers of letters to their MPs, as well as to ministers and prime ministers. They frequently asked them to monitor or intervene in judicial cases in Spain, where there were sometimes suspicions of miscarriages of justice and many executions. Their actions often led to representations being made to the Spanish foreign minister.[452] Delegations of party and trade union leaders frequently sought meetings with ministers to lobby them. This occasionally produced results. It led to a situation in Britain where to appease the Labour Party, Bevin publicly maintained a strong anti-Franco position, though he consistently refused to agree to policies which risked damaging British economic or political interests in Spain. The Spain Committee was set up in Norway in 1946 to co-ordinate similar work, although the committee did not always find it easy to agree on how far they could go in working against Franco without damaging Norwegian interests. Haakon Lie was a member of this committee and opposed the idea that Norway should take isolated diplomatic and economic measures against Spain.[453] William Warbey was prominent among the activists in the Labour Party in this respect, asking frequent parliamentary questions about Spain and joining delegations. It was shortly after he had met McNeil to lobby him on Spain, as a member of the External Affairs Committee of the Parliamentary Labour Party, that the Foreign Office commented that it would not be wise for him to go to Oslo, because he might argue for breaking off relations with Spain, and the Norwegian government would not be pleased.[454]

---

[452] One of those frequently involved was Colonel Leslie Sheridan, who in 1946 was the public relations adviser in Britain to the Spanish republican government in exile. He was subsequently recruited into IRD by Ralph Murray in early 1948 and played a prominent role there for over fifteen years. Healey worked with him on Spain, and continued to do so once he had joined IRD.
[453] Stein Bjørlo, 'Et bål av vilje. Haakon Lie – et portrett', in *Arbeiderhistorie 2005* (Årbok for Arbeiderbevegelsens arkiv og bibliotek, 2005), p184.
[454] Note from McNeil, 15 March 1946, describing the visit of the delegation from the Parliamentary Labour Party External Affairs Group, Z2674/36/41, FO 371/60353. Subsequent minute from Ewart, Northern Department, 6 May 1946, on possible problems which might arise if Warbey were to go to Norway, N 4417/219/30, FO 371/56284.

6 SPAIN

While these lobbying activities may not have actually changed policy towards Spain, it is clear that they had some influence on shaping attitudes during the early postwar period. For example, Bevin sent a personal message to the ambassador in Spain, Sir Victor Mallet, on 3 February 1946. He wrote that the Spanish situation was giving him great cause for anxiety. He had not wanted to intervene too much in the internal affairs of Spain in the hope that the Spanish people would be able to resolve their future themselves. However, world opinion was becoming very strong, and he was afraid that the situation could not be held for very much longer. He instructed Mallet to impress on the Spanish government the imperative need for a solution at the earliest possible moment.[455] Mallet saw Foreign Minister Artajo the following day and reported that he had been quite shocked, as well as embarrassed at the prospect of having to confront Franco over his retention of power. Artajo had also emphasised the impropriety of an ambassador thus directly attacking a head of state.[456]

Over the next few months, during a series of visits to London, and at meetings and international conferences both in Britain and elsewhere in Western Europe, the Norwegians sought to explore the potential for more widespread and effective action against Spain.

Haakon Lie's visit to London in early March 1946

There followed two visits to London in quick succession by senior members of the Norwegian labour movement. The first substantive contact took place when Haakon Lie went to Britain in early March. His visit occurred shortly after France had unilaterally decided to close its border with Spain, and began on the day that Britain, the United States and France had issued the Trilateral Declaration. (Soon afterwards, Collier reported that on 6 March, *Arbeiderbladet* had published an editorial which criticised the Tripartite Declaration as likely to be ineffective and which maintained that the Spanish question should be brought before the UN

---

[455] Bevin to Mallet, 3 February 1946, SP/46/2, FO 800/504.
[456] Mallet to Bevin, 4 February 1946, SP46/3, FO 800/504.

- which should not shrink from military action if necessary.[457]) Lange informed Colban of Lie's visit, instructing him to provide assistance and if necessary to forward any report directly to him.[458] Collier reported that the purpose of Lie's visit was to discuss urgently with Morgan Phillips and other British labour leaders the request from the NKP to local DNA branches for joint discussions and mass demonstrations concerning Spain.[459] He added that the Norwegian government was anxious not to be forced into taking action before the major allies did so. If the communists had orders from Moscow to agitate for the rupture of diplomatic relations and an economic boycott, then the position of the government and DNA would become very difficult, unless they could give the public a clear and satisfactory picture of British policy. Western Department suggested that once the Labour Party had determined its line over Spain, it might be worth Bevin giving a briefing to Phillips. Bevin instructed that Mayhew should do so, and a meeting for this purpose took place on 16 March. In the report which he wrote on his visit, Lie described its aim slightly differently. He considered that his most important objective was to find out whether Britain and the United States had any plans which would lead to an immediate and decisive break with Franco. He confirmed that they did not.[460]

It is worth noting the range of people whom Lie saw during this visit. They included Phillips, Healey, Creech Jones (minister for the Colonies and already well known in Norwegian DNA circles), William Warbey (and other young Labour MPs), Trygve Lie (who by that time was UN Secretary-General but happened to be in London), Sam Berger (labour attaché in the American embassy in London, a close friend of Healey and well placed to exert influence on British foreign policy[461]) and Julius Braunthal (editor of

---

[457] Collier to Bevin, 7 March 1946, Z2454/1977/41, FO 371/60444.
[458] Lange to Colban, 1 March 1946, Boks 10504, 25.4/106, Riksarkiv.
[459] Collier to FO, 28 February 1946, Z1977/1977/41, FO 371/60444.
[460] Report from Haakon Lie on his visit to London, 4-8 March 1946, Lie arkiv, D Dc0004 Arbeiderbevegelsens arkiv.
[461] Healey describes his relationship with Berger, and his view of the importance of the links between Berger and the British labour movement, in his autobiography, *The Time of my Life* (Michael Joseph, 1989), p 113.

Socialist Forum and already very much involved in international socialist circles in London). After talking to these people, Lie judged that it was not necessary to seek a meeting with Bevin.

Lie's report carefully assessed all the relevant issues which he had discussed with his interlocutors. He considered the possibility of swiftly breaking off relations with Franco, and judged that Britain had no plan for this. He was not impressed by the Tripartite Declaration, and considered that it did not go significantly further than the Potsdam Declaration. (This supported Spain's exclusion from the UN on the grounds of the origins and Axis links of the Franco regime. Contrary to Stalin's wishes, however, it did not mention possible intervention against Franco.[462]) He noted that both the TUC and the international sub-committee of the Labour Party had recommended breaking relations with Franco, adding that the National Executive Committee of the Labour Party had not yet reached a decision about this issue. He concluded that the leadership of the Labour Party did not have significant influence over the government. (This was a judgement which - as far as this issue is concerned - was shown to have been justified.) He also wrote that neither the TUC nor the international sub-committee of the Labour Party had proposed a break in trading relations with Spain – noting the importance of iron ore imports to the steel industry in Britain at that time. He added that the possibility of some sort of disruption of trade with Spain was not an issue which had been publicly discussed in Britain. On the possible involvement of the UN, he repeated Trygve Lie's comment that at present the UN had no machinery for dealing with complicated questions such as Spain. Finally he described the difficulties in Britain, noting that opinion there was more divided than it was in Norway. He concluded that if Norway were to break off relations with Spain, Britain would strongly disapprove. He thought anyway that independent action by Norway would be a waste of time, and that the only way forward in the circumstances should be action

---

[462] Paul Preston, *Franco*, p540.

through the United Nations. There was no justification for going further than that.[463]

In *Skjebneår 1945-1950,* Lie described his meeting with Trygve Lie. He asked the latter whether as UN Secretary-General he could bring up the question of Spain in the UN Security Council, on the grounds that the Franco regime represented a threat to world peace. In addition to repeating that the UN had no machinery for dealing with such a complicated matter, Trygve Lie stated that it was clear that neither the United States nor Britain wished to see the matter raised in this way.[464] During his time as Secretary-General, Lie used to write regular private letters to the Norwegian prime minister, Einar Gerhardsen. He used this as an unofficial channel to brief him, to discuss problems and occasionally to ask for assistance. He wrote one such letter in late March 1946, shortly after his meeting with Haakon Lie, to express his surprise that none of the interested parties such as France or Mexico had tried to bring up the issue of Spain in the Security Council. He also expressed in quite strong terms his disappointment that the British Labour Party, with its government now in power, was no longer working to meet the needs of the Spanish people for freedom and independence. He was concerned that this setback would affect the influence of the British labour movement elsewhere in Europe, when it should have been taking the lead in all international progressive policies.[465]

Visit to London and Paris by John Sanness from LO, late March 1946

The conclusions drawn by Lie from his visit were not universally accepted in Oslo. There were many in the government, DNA and LO who had hoped for more positive results from his trip. Shortly afterwards therefore, LO decided that they also wished to send a representative to both London

---

[463] Lie's report on his visit to London, Lie arkiv, D Dc0004, Arbeiderbevegelsens arkiv
[464] Haakon Lie, *Skjebneår 1945-1950* (Tiden Norsk Forlag, 1985), p120.
[465] Trygve Lie letter to Einar Gerhardsen, 27 March 1946, Jostein Nyhamar arkiv, D12, Arbeiderbevegelsens arkiv.

and Paris, to investigate the possibilities of an international blockade of Spain. They chose John Sanness, who was the international secretary of LO and who had developed close links to many exiled Spanish republicans during the civil war. He travelled later in March. His visit was supported by the Foreign Ministry, which agreed to meet his costs. A report on his visit was circulated by DNA to party members.[466] However, a more detailed report, with wide-ranging comments and recommendations, is in the Foreign Ministry archive.[467] In London, Sanness met Bell (international secretary of the TUC), Healey, Warbey (whom he had known during the war years), Hector McNeil in the Foreign Office and Oldenbroek (International Transport Workers' Federation).

He noted that British dockers had hitherto not undertaken any sort of action, whether official or unofficial, against Spain. He considered it unlikely that the TUC would be willing to go any further that it had already. But more importantly, he concluded that spontaneous union demonstrations had not had, and by themselves alone would not have, any significant influence on the situation in Spain. Effective action would need to be taken by governments in concert with each other. He commented that the French border closure reflected the weak French position in international politics and doubted that it would have any significant effect on the Spanish economy.[468] He advised against any unilateral Norwegian action, which might cause some real misunderstandings about Norwegian policy. He stressed that if any independent step were to be contemplated, it would be wise to warn the British government first, with a view to obtaining their understanding of and support for Norwegian intentions. Reinforcing his argument against

---

[466] 'Fakta for talere og tillitsmenn', April 1946, Internasjonalt utvalg, D Da10, Arbeiderbevegelsens arkiv.
[467] Report from Sanness to Lange, 13 April 1946, Boks 10504, 25.4/102, Riksarkiv.
[468] Nor was its enforcement completely effective. In September 1946, the Norwegian embassy in Paris reported that the border between France and Spain was sometimes opened to allow the passage of both people and goods, after the agreement of local authorities on both sides of the border. This was done without the knowledge of the Quai d'Orsay. Letter to Oslo, 28 September 1946, Bind VIII, Boks 10505, 25.4/102 Riksarkiv.

any unilateral Norwegian action, he commented that such a step would have no effect on the attitude of the American or British governments – a point which Lange sidelined when reading the report, noting his agreement with it.

However, Sanness judged that the situation was not set in stone, and there were still prospects for changes in British policy.[469] He ended by advising that there should be action on several fronts: LO should put pressure on the TUC, DNA should do the same with the Labour Party and the Norwegian government should continue to demand action from the British government. Finally, LO should also put pressure on its own government. The situation could still change quickly to Norwegian advantage. His conclusions therefore were much the same as Lie's. Lange also presented an account of Sanness' visit, and his assessment of the possibilities for further action against Spain, at a meeting of the international committee of DNA on 24 April. No decisions were taken on that occasion.[470]

Throughout this period, the Norwegian embassy in London kept in touch with a wide range of British ministers, officials and politicians. As a result, they were generally able to identify those who were likely to be more favourably disposed towards the Norwegian position on Spain than they were to their own British position. Not surprisingly, Philip Noel Baker was a key interlocutor, particularly while he was a junior minister in the Foreign Office. Colban met him in early March 1946, when Noel Baker commented that there were strong grounds against taking up the issue of Spain at the UN, but Colban was not completely convinced by the arguments. In his report to Lange, Colban commented that, while he was able to accept the viewpoint of others,

---

[469] As an example of this, Sanness mentioned that when he had seen Hector McNeil, the latter had made it quite clear that Britain was not contemplating any sort of international blockade against Spain. However, he had mentioned the possibility of a halfway move through the recognition of the republican government in Paris. Sanness was sure that this was not a casual remark by McNeil: Warbey thought that it showed that McNeil and Bevin must have discussed this option in some depth. Consequently, among Labour Party MPs there were real hopes that this possibility might be taken further. Sanness report to Lange, ibid.
[470] Minutes of meeting of the international committee of DNA, 24 April 1946, Internasjonalt utvalg, D Da 10, Arbeiderbevegelsens arkiv.

Noel Baker was personally and emotionally ready to support a more active role than Bevin and the Foreign Office.[471] Nonetheless, despite identifying Noel Baker and others who were more favourably disposed to the Norwegian position on Spain, the Norwegian embassy did not then appear to try to lobby them very much.

Discussion of Spain at the conference of European socialist parties in Clacton, May 1946

Åke Ording, a member of the Central Committee of DNA, attended the first major post-war conference of socialist parties which was called by the Labour Party and held in Clacton from 17-20 May 1946. Representatives from nineteen different parties, mainly from Europe but also from the Americas and Australasia, took part. The Labour Party fielded a heavyweight delegation of four ministers (including Hugh Dalton, Chancellor of the Exchequer and Aneurin Bevan, Secretary of State for Health), as well as Harold Laski, Morgan Phillips and Healey and other members of the NEC. As will be further discussed in Chapter Seven on the Socialist International, the Norwegians would have been well satisfied with the results. When Haakon Lie had written to Phillips on 20 March to inform him that Ording would attend this conference, he had also notified him that Ording would wish to bring up the question of strengthening socialist co-operation by proposing the establishment of an office with a full-time secretary in London. He asked for this to be placed on the agenda.[472] This was done and at the conference Ording's proposals were accepted. During the general discussions, it was also Ording who brought up the question of Spain. He demanded in strong terms that effective and concerted action should be taken to deal with the issue. Other parties supported his proposal. The French representative agreed to arrange a conference of socialist parties in Paris later in the summer to discuss Spain. At this stage, though, no country made any specific proposals on what

---

[471] Colban to Lange, 7 March 1946, Boks 559, 25.4/102, Riksarkiv.
[472] Lie to Phillips, 20 March 1946, Internasjonalt utvalg, D Da 10, Arbeiderbevegelsens arkiv.

should be done. Ording noted that all countries, including Britain, agreed that such a conference would be useful, and the resolution to hold it was carried unanimously.[473]

Åke Ording remained in England after this conference to do some further research on Spain. He spoke to a wide range of British, Spanish and other European socialist contacts, in particular Ilse Barea, an Austrian woman married to a Spanish refugee. Barea had lived for many years in Spain and retained good contacts with the underground movement there. She was living in London and working for the Fabian Society.

Ording sent his report, which contained a range of balanced and considered views, to Lange on 4 June. He said that it was worth remembering that for Norway, Spain was the only surviving element of the fascist regime. However, for Britain, it was one of many problems which needed to be dealt with before a peaceful and stable world could be achieved. He mentioned that there had still not been free elections in many of the European countries which had been liberated, referred to continuing violence in Central Europe and the Balkans, and noted the tension in Palestine, the Arab world and Iran. On the other hand, he highlighted the influence exercised by the Spanish through companies such as Rio Tinto Zinc, which had the largest copper mine outside Russia and whose headquarters was in London. He also described the very active political opposition, especially in the British parliamentary Labour group, where many MPs felt that Spain provided a good opportunity for the British Labour government to show that it had a new democratic and socialist policy which was considerably different from the old imperial policies of the Conservatives. He noted that Francis Noel Baker (son of Philip Noel Baker, and recently elected an MP) had just been to Toulouse to attend the Spanish socialist conference and had spoken out for action against Franco.[474]

---

[473] Report from Åke Ording on the International Conference of Socialist parties at Clacton.on-Sea, 17-20 May 1946, Internasjonalt utvalg, D Da 10, Arbeiderbevegelsens arkiv.

[474] In his report, Noel Baker wrote that the Spanish socialists were much depressed by the expansion of British economic activity in Spain, noting that there were recent reports of big new contracts negotiated by ICI. A copy of his report is in the Spain file for 1946 in the Labour Party archive in Manchester.

Ording was sure that there was a will in the government to get rid of Franco.

He made a series of recommendations to Lange. The most important was that Norway should maintain direct contact with the Giral republican government, in exile in Paris, by inviting a representative to base himself in Oslo. He thought that Norway should also maintain direct contact with Giral's government in Paris. He did not believe that it would be necessary to establish diplomatic relations in order to achieve this.[475] In common with all significant reports on Spain throughout this period, the Foreign Ministry marked this paper to the prime minister.[476]

The establishment of links between Norway and the Giral government had already been discussed several days earlier in Oslo, when Lange met Lizaso, one of Giral's representatives, on 1 June. Lizaso handed over a letter from Giral, in which he requested that Norway again consider giving his government formal recognition. Lizaso said that he supported this request, and commented that he knew that the British government would look benignly on such recognition by the Norwegians. He added that the Czechoslovak government had taken a decision in principle to recognise Giral, but would not make any announcement until a western European government had done so. Lange replied mildly that the Norwegian government's information was that the British government would not look kindly upon unilateral recognition of Giral by Norway. (The most recent British expression of this had been on 31 May when the Danish Minister in London met Hoyer Millar in Western Department. Hoyer-Millar said that Lizaso was going to visit Denmark and other Scandinavian countries with a view to persuading them to recognise Giral. Although he thought well of Giral personally, Hoyer Millar said that he did not think that he would be able to take over if Franco fell, and there was therefore no case for recognising his

---

[475] This remained the case, although the Norwegian government later gradually allowed the republican representative, Tell Novellas, certain diplomatic privileges, mainly to facilitate his importation of duty-free goods.

[476] Åke Ording to Lange, 4 June 1946, Boks 10505, 25.4/102, Riksarkiv.

government.[477]) Lange agreed to maintain contacts with representatives of Giral both in Oslo and in Paris, and said that he would nominate a diplomat from the Norwegian embassy there as the point of contact.[478]

Unproductive meeting between Attlee and Lange in Luxembourg, 3 August 1946

The Norwegians continued to try to find ways of presenting their case to the British. Lange sought a personal meeting with Attlee in Luxembourg, during the Paris peace conference, saying that he wanted to get to know him personally and that he believed there were great possibilities for co-operation between the Labour governments in their two countries. After discussing reconstruction in Norway, he reassured Attlee that – despite the concerns to the contrary which he knew had been expressed by Collier in Oslo – Norway would not revert to an isolationist position in international politics. Then he brought up Spain. The result was not what he would have hoped for. Lange asked whether Britain would change its policy during the forthcoming UN General Assembly and agree to the implementation of some joint action against Spain. Attlee replied that his impression was that international action against Franco had so far strengthened rather than weakened him. Lange responded that Franco's position might have been strengthened because the unilateral French action in closing the border with Spain had demonstrated the lack of unity in the democratic world on the Spanish question. Attlee replied that on the basis of the information which the British government had, he could not share Lange's view on this issue. One of the main problems for the British government over Spain was that there was no viable alternative to Franco: he did not think that Giral commanded enough support within Spain to be an acceptable successor. His government largely consisted of emigrants who had lived outside Spain for more than seven

---

[477] Minute by F.R.Hoyer Millar, Western Department, 31 May 1946, Z5463/36/41, FO 371/60361.
[478] Note by Lange recording his meeting with Lizaso, 1 June 1946, Boks 559, 25.4/102, Riksarkiv.

years, who were out of touch with conditions there and who could not agree among themselves. When Lange replied that he had the impression that the Giral government had managed to unite the main émigré groups and to gain support from all republican forces inside Spain, Attlee retorted again that on the basis of the information which his government had, he was very doubtful about that.

Commenting on this conversation, Lange noted that Attlee was so dismissive in his statements on this subject, he thought it would be pointless to discuss it further. The conversation therefore returned to a discussion of Norwegian reconstruction.[479]

Meeting of the international conference of socialist parties to discuss Spain in Paris, August 1946

It was decided that Lange and his foreign policy adviser Arne Ording would attend the French Socialist Party conference and, separately, that Ording, Terje Wold and John Sanness would then also represent DNA at the conference on Spain which was to follow it.[480] This conference took place from 27-28 August. Following an introduction by Leon Blum, there was a heated intervention by Llopiz (a member of the Giral government) on the presence of Negrin, the Minister of Finance in the National Front government during the civil war. This reflected the difficulties of the Spanish émigré groups in achieving a degree of unity among themselves, an issue which was to continue to complicate the subject throughout the next few years. Llopiz then spoke in strong terms to demand that all the participating countries break diplomatic ties with the Franco government, institute an economic blockade of Spain and recognise Giral's republican government in exile. Healey stated that this was not consistent with British policy, and he could not therefore be a party to a

---

[479] Note by Lange on his meeting with Attlee in Luxembourg, 3 August 1946, Boks 10505, 25.4/102, Riksarkiv. No one else was present at this meeting, and no record of it has been found in prime ministerial papers in the British National Archives.
[480] Letter to the Central Committee of DNA, 24 August 1946, based on a discussion with Halvard Lange and Martin Tranmæl, Internasjonalt utvalg, D Da 10, Arbeiderbevegelsens arkiv.

resolution which would put pressure on his own government. He said that it should be a relatively easy matter to get rid of Franco, but it was necessary to ensure that he was replaced by a real democracy, elected on a general franchise. He said that the British government had been the targets of many unreasonable attacks recently as it had not been possible to give the full details of what was going on. He compared the criticism with that which had met Blum's non-intervention policy in 1936. Blum then felt obliged to defend his policy, and there followed a series of attacks on Healey and Britain by many of the participants, including Negrin. Ording presented the Norwegian view that Franco should be removed by international action, preferably through the UN, and that the conference should produce a unanimous resolution, because anything else would be to Franco's advantage.

It is probable that a combination of the desire to defend the British position and the need to find agreement then led Healey to be more forthcoming on the following morning. He told the conference that he wanted to inform them in the strictest confidence that the British government was indeed working systematically to remove Franco. For some months Bevin had been trying to unite all the opposition elements, including the monarchists, although he had had to give up on the monarchists and it was possible that the work which was ongoing in Spain would have to take on a new form. Britain was the only country which was working actively to get rid of Franco, and the British government were anxious about any other actions which might damage their plans. Healey said that, naturally, he could not go into detail, but he himself thought that the plan had a chance of succeeding. He added that both Negrin and Llopiz knew that such work was going on, which was the reason for the relative moderation of the views which they had been expressing.

In the report which he wrote, Ording noted that the proposals which were then put forward were influenced by the need for the care which had to be shown in light of Healey's comments. Although others still wanted to achieve a resolution that the UN should vote for a diplomatic break and an economic blockade, Healey would not support such a move. It was eventually agreed that individual countries would decide for themselves whether to recommend that the UN implement an economic blockade. Healey also stated that the British Labour Party would not commit itself to support Giral's government, and with agreement from him and Llopiz the final resolution simply proposed that the parties should work 'to rebuild the constitutional and legal republican government'.[481]

In his diary, Ording commented that during the general debate later on 27 August, Negrin was surprisingly moderate. He also noted that Healey was absent during the afternoon, probably to confer with McNeil.[482] There is no direct account of this conference in any British archive, whether official or party. The British embassy, which would not have been represented at such a party meeting and which would presumably therefore have depended on Healey (the only British delegate) or another participant for the details, reported that there had been a strong demand for recognition of the Giral government and for economic sanctions. They wrote that the UK delegate Healey, *supported only by Norway*,[483] had succeeded in steering the conference away from these proposals and finally secured the adoption of a more moderate resolution. The desk officer for Spain, Sloan, commented that this report was somewhat perfunctory. His senior, Horsfall Carter, agreed and thought it would be useful to have a more detailed commentary but none was forthcoming.[484]

In view of the lack of supporting evidence, it would have been natural for the Norwegians to wonder whether Healey might have been exaggerating the extent of British activity to undermine Franco so as to deflect the attacks on British policy by many of the twenty other parties which attended the Paris conference. This conclusion would probably have been supported by Colban's account of a meeting with Sir

---

[481] Report by Arne Ording, 2 September 1946, on the International Socialist Conference on Spain held in Paris, 27-28 August 1946, Internasjonalt utvalg, D Da 10, Arbeiderbevegelsens arkiv. This report was copied to the Norwegian Foreign Ministry and is also held on one of their files, Boks 10505, 25.4/102, Riksarkiv.

[482] Arne Ording, diary entry for 27 August 1946, *Arne Ording Dagbøker 1945-1949*. (Universitetsforlaget, Oslo), p152.

[483] Author's italics. Arne Ording does not refer to his actions in supporting Britain either in his report or in his diary.

[484] Duff Cooper to Bevin, 8 September 1946, and subsequent Foreign Office minuting, Z8017/9/41, FO 371/60337.

Orme Sargent on 6 September. At the meeting, Sargent had agreed unreservedly with Colban's statement that he understood that the British government had no plans for the time being for any further steps to bring down the Franco government. Sargent repeated to Colban that he wanted to get rid of Franco. However, he thought that the only ways to do this would either be after an attack by republicans reinforced with arms supplied from abroad, or by waiting passively until internal political developments took the direction which both countries wanted – and which would only be delayed by continued demonstrations against Franco.[485]

Trifon Gomez briefs Lange and Ording on British moves to remove Franco

The Norwegians obtained an explanation of what lay behind Healey's comments when Lange and Ording met Trifon Gomez in Paris shortly afterwards, on 14 September. In his report on this meeting, Ording noted that Gomez was the representative of the Spanish UGT (roughly the equivalent of the TUC) in the Giral government. He had known Bevin well from their joint work on TGWU activities and he was very close to the leading Spanish socialist, Prieto. Gomez said that he had had a long talk with Bevin recently in Paris. In his opinion it was correct that Bevin had been working for quite some time to get rid of Franco. Bevin's aim was to do this without a new civil war: his plan was therefore based on achieving the change in the government of Spain by working through the Spanish generals. For that reason, Bevin had wanted to avoid any steps which would cause any national humiliation in Spain. He believed that the French closure of the border in March had strengthened Franco just when there was a prospect that his plan would succeed.

Gomez acknowledged that Bevin had the best of intentions but he was clearly in doubt about whether Bevin's plan would work. He thought that some time ago an external action against Spain might have produced the result which Bevin had described. But a very important change had taken

---

[485] Report from Colban to UD on his meeting with Sir Orme Sargent, 6 September 1946, Boks 10505, 25.4/102, Riksarkiv.

place recently. At the outset, the opposition generals had been working to get Franco to withdraw voluntarily. Now they were clear that this would not work, and that Franco must be removed. As a result, these generals were in some danger. In contrast to their earlier position, the generals and the other opposition forces with which the British were now working (whom Gomez did not further describe to his Norwegian interlocutors) desired an international action against Franco. Ording noted that Gomez repeated this several times, and also provided examples of the ways in which these circles had now sought contacts with illegal labour movements and socialist émigrés.[486] He did not, however, provide any further details of the other opposition forces with whom the British were working, which agency or agencies were entrusted with this work, or what their plans were. Nor did Ording elaborate on the means of contact which were being used.

Ording's report of this meeting thus provides interesting and hitherto undiscovered evidence of some of the methods used by the British government to try to remove Franco. In his diary, he also observed that it had been an interesting lunch and that Gomez had been very willing to talk. He noted the agreement in the accounts put forward by Bevin and Gomez – which might perhaps suggest that Bevin (or Collier) may separately have given a privileged account to the Norwegians which has not been recorded in any papers found so far in Norwegian archives. He also described the difference between the views expressed by Bevin and Gomez on the one hand, and those given by Sargent to Colban on the other, noting that Sargent had said that it was not possible to remove Franco. Ording, no doubt correctly, concluded that this might possibly have been due to cautiousness on Sargent's part.[487]

---

[486] Berg, minister in Paris, to UD, 17 September 1946, enclosing the report written by Ording of the meeting with Lange and Gomez on 14 September. The report was copied to the king, prime minister and ambassadors in Washington, London and Moscow on 26 September and was given a very restricted circulation within the Foreign Ministry, Boks 10505, 25.4/102, Riksarkiv.

[487] Arne Ording, diary entry 14 September 1946, *Arne Ordings Dagbøker*, p164.

No further documentary material has been found elsewhere in the Norwegian archives which throws any light on how the Norwegian government reacted to the revelations provided by Trifon Gomez of an undisclosed British policy on a topic which was of such significant interest and importance in Norway. Perhaps, given the circumstances in which he obtained this information, Lange felt constrained in making use of it with Collier or Bevin. However, it is also possible that a description of the consequences is contained in further archival material which has not yet been discovered.

The information provided by Gomez to Lange and Ording shows that, even if he did not go into detail, Healey took quite a risk during the Paris conference in disclosing information to such a wide audience about what Britain was doing to remove Franco. It is not clear what he hoped to achieve by doing so, apart from moderating the criticism from his socialist colleagues of Britain's policy on Spain . Nonetheless, his confidence appears to have been respected. There was, however, an inadvertent and potentially awkward disclosure from the British side three months later. The Associated Press (AP) news agency ran a story in December reporting that British diplomats had been meeting right to centre left political leaders in Madrid to explore the possibility of forming an interim coalition government to replace Franco. This story was based on a somewhat garbled version of an article written by Morgan Phillips in a Labour Party newsletter. In the newsletter, he replied to an attack on Bevin by the Spelthorne divisional Labour Party, and wrote that Britain was the only power in the world which was working continuously inside and outside Spain for a means of removing Franco. It was this comment which had prompted AP's interest. Phillips had added that the Labour Party would not support gestures which did not bring positive results: there was no use imposing sanctions when an agreement with Argentina would provide Franco with all he needed. Western Department commented on 20 December that this statement (roughly similar to the terms which Healey had used three months earlier in Paris) had not been cleared with the Foreign Office. McNeil then admitted with some embarrassment that the statement had been cleared with him, but that he had concentrated on the Soviet references. He had overlooked what had been written about Spain. The context of his comments, and his apology, suggest that British actions to remove Franco were therefore still ongoing at the end of December 1946.

Sir Orme Sargent considered sending a letter to Phillips asking him to be more careful about his references to Spain in future, then thought an oral message might be better - but eventually did not take it up with Phillips at all. He did not give a reason for this.[488] The Spanish Foreign Ministry, predictably, protested.[489] Mallet recommended to the Foreign Office that he be authorised both to reply to the Foreign Ministry and to issue a public denial, because he was concerned that the British position might be misunderstood. However, the Foreign Office concluded that he should not say anything publicly but simply tell the Foreign Ministry that the stories had been based on a complete misunderstanding of the position and that there was no truth in the allegations that members of the embassy had exceeded their proper role.[490] This was a further indication that the Foreign Office hoped that this story would die quietly, and did not wish to risk reviving it by issuing any sort of a rebuttal.

The fragmentary nature of the evidence does not permit a judgement to be made about the extent of British actions against Franco, still less to attempt to determine how effective they may have been. However, the fact that evidence comes from three separate and independent archival sources, one party and two governmental, gives confidence in the credibility of the conclusions which can be drawn. This disparate material provides insights, albeit tantalisingly limited ones, into what British policy actually was at that time. It reveals signs of active British engagement in planning to remove Franco, and of the extent to which this contrasted with the frequently and publicly repeated statements of the passive policy of leaving it up to the Spanish people themselves to determine their future. It shows that British policy went

---

[488] Western Department minuting between 18 and 24 December 1946, Z10586/36/41, FO 371/60371.
[489] Note verbale from the Spanish Foreign Ministry, Z10664/36/41, FO 371/60371.
[490] Exchanges between Sir Victor Mallet, Western Department (Hoyer Millar) and Sir O. Harvey, December 1946, Z10665/36/41, FO 371/60371.

appreciably further than has been hitherto disclosed. The comments of Phillips also show that it was not only Healey among senior Labour Party officials who were briefed on the sensitive details of British policy towards Spain – a further indication of the remarkable extent to which the party was taken into the confidence of the government at that time on issues of considerable sensitivity. (The fact that both Healey and later Phillips were guilty of indiscretion must call into question the extent to which that confidence was justified.) It is also worthy of note that following Healey's remarks, quite a wide range of foreign socialists as well as others in opposition to Franco were aware at least in outline of what was going on. In view of the controversy which was caused, especially among the left wing of the labour movement, it is remarkable that Healey's confidences were protected by so many different parties, not all of which necessarily had quite the same interests.

UN General Assembly resolution to request the withdrawal of ambassadors and ministers from Spain.

Labour movements in both countries continued to be active in rousing support for action against Franco. In the autumn, the TUC Congress in Brighton passed a resolution supporting the breaking of diplomatic and economic links with Spain. Commenting the following day, the *Times* noted that Congress had voted for this resolution by a large majority, showing the clear difference between the British labour movement and the policy which the secretary of state considered correct.[491] It was clear from a personal telegram which Bevin sent to the prime minister from New York on 4 November that this resolution had influenced his thinking: he made clear that in view of the growing pressure it was difficult for him to continue to countenance the existing position and therefore to continue to oppose the movement for a change.[492]

---

[491] Extract from *The Times*, 26 October 1946, clipping contained in Boks 559, 25.4/102, Riksarkiv.
[492] Personal telegram from Bevin to Attlee, 4 November 1946, SP46/13, FO 800/504.

6 SPAIN

It was during this period that the UN General Assembly began and the Secretary-General, Trygve Lie, caused some controversy when he chose to raise the Spain issue during his opening address. Ebbell reported that this speech, and the proposal by the Norwegian delegation that Spain should be handled as a special issue by the UN, caused a strong and bitter reaction in Madrid. The Norwegian delegation, led by Halvard Lange, continued to be very active in pushing for strong measures to be taken against Franco. In a personal letter to Prebensen (secretary-general of the Foreign Ministry and soon to succeed Colban as Norwegian ambassador in London), Lange wrote on 29 October that the situation had become quite complicated. The delegation needed to work to clarify things, so as to ensure that Norway was not the only country which suffered economically as a result of its attitude towards the governing regime in Spain.[493] Although it was Poland which took the lead in steering this proposal through the UN processes, Norway played a very active supporting role. The outcome of their work was a decision by the UN General Assembly in December to adopt a resolution on Spain which recommended that members should withdraw their respective ambassadors and ministers from Madrid, and which also excluded Spain from all UN specialised agencies. This was a compromise solution, just acceptable to Britain and the United States, and less than Norway wanted. The British ambassador, Sir Victor Mallet, accordingly left Spain in late December.

The perceived Spanish threat to prevent Norwegian shipping from sailing to Spanish ports

The resolution of the General Assembly produced a powerful reaction in Spain. Ebbell reported large demonstrations in Madrid and concerns by himself and the Belgian and Danish chargés d'affaires (the only other countries represented there which had led the action against Spain at the UN) that their trade was suffering at the expense of other countries such as the Netherlands. There were problems over the Spanish

---

[493] Personal letter from Lange in New York to Prebensen in Oslo, 29 October 1946, Boks 10505, 25.4/102, Riksarkiv.

refusal to bunker a Norwegian ship, the *Garnes,* in a Spanish harbour. These took considerable efforts to resolve.[494] Then on 3 January, Ebbell was called to the Foreign Ministry and told by Navascues, the head of the economic and political section, that throughout 1946 Norwegian ships visiting Spain had been provided with bunkering and whatever other facilities they had requested. However, Spanish ships visiting Norwegian ports had continually met with a variety of difficulties. The Spanish government had decided that in future they would provide assistance only to such countries as were favourably disposed to Spain. Ebbell tried to clarify what Navascues meant, and reported that at first he replied that the Spanish would 'impede' Norwegian ships sailing to Spanish ports. He later changed this to 'prevent' Norwegian ships from visiting Spanish ports. The written note verbale which he undertook to provide, and which was delivered the following day, did not include such direct and threatening language. Referring to the perceived difference in treatment accorded to Norwegian and Spanish shipping, the note said

> In this circumstance, my government asks whether it is possible to continue to accept in the long run a situation which shows such a clear and unjust disparity and to reassess the not only correct, but also friendly, attitude which it has up to now taken towards Norwegian ships in Spanish territorial waters.[495]

This report produced no immediate response from Oslo. However, a month later Ebbell reported a conversation with Suner, a counsellor in the Spanish Foreign Ministry whom he found more liberal and less unfriendly to Norway than Navascues. They discussed trade, and on being told that Norway was working to normalise trade relations with Spain, Suner said that was of course quite acceptable. However, he noted that Norway was more interested in normalising trade with Spain than Spain was interested in normalising trade with Norway. A normalisation of trade

---

[494] Reports by Ebbell to UD on 10, 16 and 18 December 1946, Boks 559, 25.4/102, Riksarkiv.
[495] Ebbell to UD, 4 January 1947, Boks 559, 25.4/102, Riksarkiv.

should be accompanied by a normalisation of diplomatic relations. Quite a few countries wanted to normalise their trading relations with Spain, but just asking to do so was not enough. Suner requested Ebbell tell the Norwegian government that after the British ambassador Mallett had been withdrawn, the British embassy had put forward a proposal for an increase in trade which would more than double the level which existed between the two countries. This was a positive proposal which would be of significance to Spain. He expected that it would be accepted by the British Parliament and it would then provide Spain with the opportunity to gain access to the entire Sterling Area. In his report, Ebbell commented that there was a strong desire on the Spanish side to come to an understanding with Norway. However, this would need to be linked to some diplomatic or political concession from the Norwegian side.[496]

When, shortly afterwards, the subject was discussed in a secret meeting of the Storting, Lange disclosed that before the Spanish civil war, between 2,000 and 2,400 Norwegian ships had visited Spanish ports every year. In 1946, the figure was down to 339, with very considerable economic consequences.[497] At the same time, Lange also revealed that the level of bilateral trade between Norway and Spain was only at about the same level – thirty million kroner in each direction – as it had been before the civil war. Lange asked Finn Moe, the Norwegian delegate to the UN, to discuss with Trygve Lie whether Norwegian trade discussions with Spain could be considered a breach of the UN resolution. He concluded that the carefully qualified reply which he received was sufficient for him to proceed. A meeting was held in the Foreign Ministry on 14 February, attended by Lange and Prime Minister Gerhardsen, to discuss the next steps. Lange said that he wanted to achieve a normalisation of trade with Spain, but it would be necessary to proceed carefully in view of the emotional reaction which such a decision would cause among the Norwegian people. There was some discussion with the shipowners about how the case could be presented.

---

[496] Ebbell to UD, 4 February 1947, Boks 559, 25.4/102, Riksarkiv.
[497] Lange's speech to a secret meeting of the Storting, 30 January 1947, Boks 10506, 25.4/102, Riksarkiv.

Gerhardsen said that it was important to consider appearances. The Norwegian government should not allow the dockers to determine their foreign policy, but some of the dockers' earlier actions had shown what could be at risk if their union became involved.[498]

Following this meeting, the Foreign Ministry informed Ebbell that the matter had been discussed by the government, and that the Storting had been briefed at a secret meeting. Ebbell was accordingly authorised to inform the Spanish government that the Norwegian government was considering a step towards the normalisation of relations with Spain. However, he was given no details yet of how this might be achieved.[499]

Threatened action by the International Transport Workers' Federation: visit by Nordahl and Haugen to London and Paris

However, a problem then arose. On 17 February the management committee of the International Transport Workers' Federation (ITWF) discussed a report that the Franco government was considering a ban on Norwegian ships entering Spanish ports. The committee issued a public statement declaring solidarity with Norwegian sailors and stating that the threatened action, if undertaken by the Franco government, would not fail to meet with effective counteraction by the members of the unions affiliated with the ITWF. On 19 February, Lange rang Prebensen, now ambassador in London, and drew his attention to the communiqué. He wanted to know the background. Prebensen immediately arranged to see McNeil, who offered to arrange for the British chargé d'affaires in Madrid to tell the Foreign Ministry that Spain would be very 'ill-advised' to take action to ban Norwegian shipping. Prebensen said that he would seek instructions. He spoke to Lange on 20 February. Lange said that he was minded to accept the British offer of assistance. This problem with

---

[498] Note of meeting held in UD on 14 February 1946, attended by Gerhardsen, Lange, Evensen and a number of senior Norwegian shipowners, Boks 10505, 25.4/102, Riksarkiv.
[499] UD to Ebbell, 6 February 1947, Boks 559, 25.4/102, Riksarkiv.

6 SPAIN

Spain had caused a very difficult internal political situation and he was no longer sure that it would be possible to carry through the original plan to come to a *modus vivendi* with Spain.[500] Collier reported these events to London in a despatch on 22 February expressing similar views.[501] McNeil wrote to Prebensen on 20 February to confirm that he had spoken to his officials, and that if Prebensen wished to proceed, he should get in touch with Western Department. He added a personal assessment which raised doubts whether the ITWF would be able to deliver effective action and how long it might take.[502]

The implied threat of Spanish action was taken very seriously in Norway. Between 5 February and 14 March 1947, representatives of DNA in the Storting held fourteen separate meetings to discuss the issue.[503] Furthermore Nordahl, chairman of LO, and Haugen, leader of the Norwegian Seamens' Union, immediately arranged to visit London and Paris between 23 and 28 February to try to resolve the matter. They met a variety of leaders from the unions concerned in both capitals. They sought a meeting with Bevin, but this could not be arranged until after they were due to have left for Paris, so it did not take place. While they were in London, the *Arbeiderbladet* correspondent Anders Buraas reported that he had spoken to the press attaché at the Spanish embassy, who had stated specifically that the Spanish had not made any threats to discriminate against Norwegian shipping. (The Norwegian embassy subsequently contacted the Spanish press attaché to confirm this.[504]) Buraas also spoke to Healey, who had said that the British government would be against any industrial action by British workers directed against Franco. Nordahl assumed that by this he was referring to a general economic blockade whose purpose was to bring

---

[500] Reports from Prebensen to UD, 17 and 20 February 1947, and note by Lange, Boks 559, 25.4/102, Riksarkiv.
[501] Collier to Bevin, 22 February 1947, Z 2096/1940/41, FO 371/67902A.
[502] McNeil to Prebensen, 20 February 1947, Boks 559, 25.4/102, Riksarkiv.
[503] Haakon Lie, *Skjebneår*, p122.
[504] Prebensen to UD, 25 February 1947, Boks 559, 25.4/102, Riksarkiv.

down the Franco government.⁵⁰⁵ Howard, the British chargé d'affaires in Madrid, subsequently reported that he had discussed the issue with Ebbell. Ebbell said that although there had been no actual threat that Spanish ports would be closed to Norwegian shipping, there had been an implication that unless the Norwegian government brought their policy into line with other members of the UN, the Spanish government might take action against them. Ebbell did not think that the Spanish had actually intended to do this, and if things had been left alone, agreement might have been reached. However, the matter leaked, making it much more difficult for the Norwegian government to take any action.⁵⁰⁶

It subsequently emerged that the Norwegians had themselves been inadvertently responsible for publicising this issue. In a letter written on 6 March, Haugen revealed that the seamens'union had learned of the possible threat to Norwegian shipping on 27 January. The union had written to Bratteli, the labour attaché in London, asking him to take this up with Oldenbroek, the general secretary of the ITWF, and to enquire whether the ITWF might be willing to become involved. Oldenbroek had replied that such a request should be put in writing. This was done on 14 February, but when the management committee of the ITWF considered the matter a few days later and decided to support the Norwegian unions, it determined to make their decision public without referring back to the Norwegians who had asked for their assistance.⁵⁰⁷ This action effectively prevented consideration for some considerable time of any further Norwegian progress in regularising Norway's trading relations with Spain.

The British responses – particularly the one from ministerial level in the Foreign Office, less so from the Labour Party - were helpful in ensuring that the issue was not further protracted, although it would probably not have suited Spanish interests either to allow the matter to drag on.

---

⁵⁰⁵ Report written by Nordahl and Haugen on their trip to London and Paris, 23-28 February 1947, Internasjonale forbindelser, D Da 15, Arbeiderbevegelsens arkiv. This report was copied to UD and is also contained in Boks 559, 25.4/102, Riksarkiv.
⁵⁰⁶ Howard to FO, 5 March 1947, Z 2485/1940/41, FO 371/67902A.
⁵⁰⁷ Letter from the Norwegian Seamens' Union to UD, 6 March 1947, Boks 559, 25.4/102, Riksarkiv.

6 SPAIN

However, the reaction at desk level in the Foreign Office was less sympathetic than that provided by the minister of state. Internal Western Department minuting concluded that whatever the Spanish government may have said or done, it had certainly given the impression that it would close Spanish ports to Norwegian ships. Sloan hoped that Howard, the chargé d'affaires, would get a reassuring response when he took he matter up with the Foreign Ministry. Otherwise, he thought, the Norwegian government might have difficulty in restraining their own unions from independent retaliation, or from mobilising others in support, including British unions. Hogg added that it was no bad thing for the Norwegians to get a jolt about their Spanish policy, which had been both self-righteous and mischievous. He noted however that the Norwegians did not need to trouble themselves any further on this issue, as the Spanish had climbed down first.[508] By then, Lange had sent a personal telegram to Ebbell in Madrid explaining that the difficult negotiations of the last few days had shown that, for internal political reasons, it would not be possible to go further with the normalisation of relations with Spain. It would therefore be necessary to try to win time and to do everything possible to try to prevent Spain implementing any sort of discrimination against Norway.[509]

Difficulties over trade

This was shortly after the Norwegians had learned that Britain had signed a trade agreement with Spain.[510] Throughout this period, both the Norwegian and British embassies provided reporting on the trading activities of the other country, and of course on their main competitors as well. Colban had first done this in April 1946, and Prebensen subsequently provided regular updates. Throughout the next three years, Norwegian progress towards the beginning of trade negotiations continued to be slow. Spain continued to

---

[508] Western Department minuting, mainly between Sloan and Hogg, 3-4 March 1947, Z 2096/1940/41, FO 371/67902A.
[509] Personal telegram from Lange to Ebbell, 21 February 1946, Boks 10506, 25.4/102, Riksarkiv.
[510] Ebbell to UD, 17 April 1946, Boks 10506, 25.4/102, Riksarkiv.

use this as a lever to influence to their advantage Norwegian policy towards Spain, and to achieve Norwegian agreement to an accredited Spanish diplomat visiting Oslo without conceding anything significant in return. For example, as late as May 1949, Collier reported that Lange had informed the Storting that the trade negotiations which were due to have begun in Madrid during that month had been postponed indefinitely. The Spanish Foreign Ministry had told Ebbell that the Spanish government regarded the Norwegian vote in the political committee of the UN General Assembly, against the resolution for a restoration of normal diplomatic relations with Spain, as hardly compatible with a desire for a commercial agreement. The Norwegian government had replied that they were not prepared to alter their attitude but were still willing to negotiate a trade agreement. On 18 May however, the Spanish government announced that negotiations must be postponed until further notice.[511]

Given the importance which trade considerations played in shaping the policies of many governments towards Spain during this period, it is not surprising that some academics have subsequently attempted to reassess the validity of the arguments put forward, especially by the British government, for avoiding the use of sanctions as a weapon against Franco. Qasim Ahmad assesses this in some detail in his book *Britain, Franco and the Cold War*.[512] In his prologue to this book, Paul Preston comments that 'Qasim Ahmad's intriguing analysis of British economic policy towards Spain shows that alternative sources of supply were available for products imported from Spain. Accordingly, the choice to continue trade with Spain reflected both a higher strategic necessity and also the parlous state of the British economy.'[513] However, it is worth noting that the information and assessments which were considered by Cabinet at that time were not so detailed and wide-ranging as these subsequent academic analyses. For example, a paper put to Cabinet in

---

[511] Collier to Bevin, 30 May 1949, N4103/11330/41, FO 371/79735.
[512] Qasim Ahmad, *Britain, Franco and the Cold War* (Garland,1992). See in particular Chapter 6: 'The Economic Considerations; A Flawed Rationale, 1945-50' pp 135 – 162.
[513] Ibid, Prologue, pp xvii-xviii.

January 1947 which examined the impact of economic sanctions on Spain, noted that

> The supply of foodstuffs essential to the diet of the British people would be seriously diminished. The production of foodstuffs would be seriously reduced. British heavy industry would be further hampered, if not curtailed. Requirements of coal would rise and output of steel would probably fall. ... It would also create fresh financial difficulties for the British government and seriously prejudice the interests of British creditors, who after some years are in the process of securing repayment from Spain. Furthermore, the interests of British companies established in Spain, such as the important Rio Tinto mines, and of British shipping companies trading with Spain, might be seriously affected.[514]

It would have been on the basis of papers such as this that government policy was shaped. Norwegian government policy was determined by similar considerations. Jakob Sverdrup noted that both Trygve Lie and later Halvard Lange had emphasised the importance to Norwegian reconstruction of Spanish imports – in particular zinc ore to produce zinc at Odda, potash and superphosphates for agriculture, as well as salt for the fisheries industry. Sverdrup pointed out that the export of Norwegian goods and shipping to Spain provided valuable income which the country used to buy exports from other countries, which were also needed for reconstruction. Spain, on the other hand, had little interest in Norwegian exports. It was clear therefore from an early stage that a trade war, following the imposition of economic sanctions, would damage Norway much more than it would damage Spain.[515]

March 1947- October 1951: a change of direction

Shortly after the visit of Nordahl and Haugen in March 1947, Lange wrote to Gerhardsen from London. He had discussed

---

[514] Cabinet paper, 3 January 1947, Z270/3/41G, FO 371/67867.
[515] Jakob Sverdrup, *Inn i storpolitikken* (Universitetsforlaget, 1996), p246.

their visit with Prebensen. Prebensen's conclusion was that Norway's friends had given her a helping hand because of good will. They had given him the clear impression that the transport and seamens' unions were serious about a sympathy action if Norwegian ships were excluded from Spanish ports. However, not one leader considered that such an action should lead to worldwide union activity to attempt to get rid of Franco. He noted that, in London, the question of Spain was a dead issue. The statement of the ITWF on solidarity with Norwegian seamen had not been published in any British paper, nor had any of the British media covered Lange's speech to the Storting the previous week. It was necessary to ensure that Norway achieve a normalisation of relations with Spain. Media coverage would be important. Norwegians should understand from *Arbeiderbladet* and elsewhere that this was now entirely an internal Norwegian problem, not an international one.[516]

This visit by Nordahl and Haugen was effectively the high-water mark of attempts between the British and Norwegian labour movements to co-ordinate their activities directed against Spain. No further visits or meetings took place specifically to discuss the subject, though it continued to be of great interest and concern to both parties. Spain was almost always on the agenda of meetings of COMISCO and other socialist conferences, and resolutions were regularly passed calling for a break in diplomatic relations and the imposition of economic sanctions. Occasionally, COMISCO became more directly involved. For example, Julius Braunthal, the secretary of the International Socialist Conference, wrote to Haakon Lie in October 1950 to express concern that Norway was about to change its policy at the UN over maintaining the withdrawal of ambassadors from Madrid. He raised possible ways of continuing to prevent this, and sought Lie's advice about the wisdom of approaching Moe, who was leading the Norwegian delegation. Lie replied that he thought that the government had already made up its mind, and would abstain on the vote, because Norway could not afford to take a stand different from that

---

[516] Lange to Gerhardsen, 1 March 1947, Boks 10506, 25.4/102, Riksarkiv.

of all other Western European countries.[517] When the vote was taken at the General Assembly on 4 November 1950, the United States supported the resolution to rescind the operative parts of the 1946 resolution. Britain and France abstained. Both Britain and Norway subsequently sent an ambassador to Madrid.

During this period, the Norwegians conducted a complex series of negotiations with Spain. They wanted to move towards a position where they could begin the negotiation of a trade agreement to replace the compensation trade which they still carried out. Spain wanted a diplomatic representative in Oslo, and ultimately to achieve the restoration of relations at ambassadorial level. Since bilateral trade mattered much more to Norway, and to Norwegian shipowners in particular, this was a situation where the Spanish held a decided advantage.

Spanish diplomats raised the subject of representation in Oslo at regular intervals in Madrid, in London - and even in Copenhagen when Lange was approached by the resident Spanish Minister Count Agramonte during a visit to Denmark to attend the funeral of King Christian in April 1947.[518] The Spanish Foreign Ministry insisted that it would be necessary to have a chargé d'affaires in Oslo before trade negotiations could begin. The Norwegians were concerned about public reactions if a Spanish diplomat were to be based in Oslo: eventually a compromise was worked out whereby Count Torata, who was nominated as chargé, would be based in Copenhagen and visit Oslo as necessary. This was announced on 3 June 1947 and Torata made his first visit to Norway at the end of that month. This diplomatic success for Spain provided little obvious benefit to Norway. Subsequent Norwegian attempts to begin trade negotiations were tortuous and long drawn out. It took a long time before they were successful.

---

[517] Braunthal (Administrative Secretary of the International Socialist Conference) to Lie, 11 October 1950. Lie reply to Braunthal, 13 October 1950, Internasjonalt utvalg, D Da 36, Arbeiderbevegelsens arkiv.

[518] Ebbell to UD, 5 March 1946 and 12 May 1946, Prebensen to UD, 12 March 1946 and 22 May 1946, note by Lange on his meeting with Count Agramonte on 30 April 1946, Boks 559 and Boks 10506, 25.4/102, Riksarkiv.

6 SPAIN

Jakob Sverdrup comments that there was relatively little interest in international affairs in Norway in the immediate post-war period. The main concern of both government and people was reconstruction and the raising of living standards. However, the issue of Spain was an exception. It aroused great bitterness that the fascist regime should continue there when those in Germany and Italy had been removed: Norwegians were more engaged on this question than in almost all other countries in Europe. Sverdrup considers that the explanation for this might be that it was a moral question which had clear parallels with the resistance campaign against Germany within Norway itself.[519]

However, despite the high expectations which were aroused among labour movements across Europe in the aftermath of the Second World War, it proved to be extraordinarily difficult to achieve any effective degree of international consensus on what should be done about Spain, and about removing Franco. Labour movements passed resolutions at their congresses, and their branches and smaller groups sent considerable numbers of letters and messages to their governments to make their views clear. Party and union groups lobbied ministers and governments frequently. It is clear that they influenced the thinking and attitudes of ministers, but they did not have a significant effect in changing policy.

The views of the Labour parties and labour movements in Norway and Britain were broadly similar throughout this period. The publicly expressed policies of their governments were not, however, and the leaders of both made clear that they did not wish their labour movements to determine how they should deal with the problem of Spain. The view of historians has been that for a variety of reasons, many of them self-interested, Britain preferred to adopt a passive policy, hoping that the people of Spain would somehow be able to find a way of removing Franco for themselves, and only moving reluctantly and as little as possible to accommodate considerable pressure at the United Nations to take the minimum steps possible against Franco. The evidence provided by the report of Healey's speech at the Paris conference of European Socialist parties in August 1946, and

---

[519] Sverdrup, *Inn i storpolitikken*, p199.

of the meeting between Lange, Ording and Trifon Gomez in September, shows that British policy during this period was more active and interventionist than had been thought. The British government did take measures to attempt to remove Franco. The limited nature of the evidence available makes it hard to judge how comprehensive these efforts may have been, and (despite Healey's optimistic comment) harder still to come to a conclusion about their likely prospects of success. Such a judgement must await the release of more material to the archives. From the outset, the aim of Norwegian policy had been to find a way of removing Franco, and to do so by promoting the breaking of both diplomatic and economic links to Spain. The problem for Norway was that a trade war with Spain would damage Norwegian interests much more than Spanish interests. It was therefore only possible for Norway to pursue its policies by means of international action through the UN. Norway played a prominent role at the UN in promoting measures to this end. This produced a compromise resolution leading only to the withdrawal of ambassadors, but even that step produced a series of Spanish reprisals or reactions against Norwegian interests. Jakob Sverdrup comments that Norway's policy towards Spain failed because it was constructed on a purely emotional basis, which did not take account of international realities. In its bilateral relationship with Spain, Norway pursued a policy which made itself vulnerable. Sverdrup notes that this had happened once before at the beginning of the 1920s, when Spain and Portugal had forced Norway to moderate its alcohol ban by threatening to stop imports of dried cod.[520]

The British and Norwegian Labour parties may have shared similar and strongly held views, but in neither country were they able at any stage to exert a telling influence over the policy of their government. The British Labour Party may have been able to open doors for their Norwegian visitors to meet a range of ministers, politicians and activists when they came to London in 1946 and 1947, but they were unable to do more than that for them or for that matter to do more on their own account either. The truth was that there was no identity of national interest, and no reason for the

---

[520] Sverdrup, *Inn i storpolitikken,* p255.

two countries to work more closely together, as they were increasingly to understand that they needed to do in other areas, particularly against the threat of growing communist influence. As the two parties realised this, they chose to concentrate their co-operation elsewhere. In an interview in 2005, Haakon Lie said that Britain had done a little to help, but that it was fairly soon clear that there was not enough common ground for effective co-operation between the labour parties on Spain.[521]

---

[521] Interview with Haakon Lie, 18 July 2005.

7 The Socialist International

Although many socialists were interested in the idea of re-establishing the International after the war, it soon became apparent that this would be premature, and that it would be better to establish a liaison committee instead. During the early post-war years, much of the work of this committee, and of international socialist conferences, was focused on establishing an independent organisation and on admitting to membership only those socialist parties which were truly independent and which were not susceptible to communist pressure or influence. The British Labour Party did much of the organisational work, and until the International was re-established, the administrative headquarters was based in London. The Scandinavians in general, and Norwegians in particular, co-operated closely with the British Labour Party over the work of the international socialist conference. Expert conferences, which began in 1948 and which covered a wide variety of subjects, provided a valuable forum. IRD made use of the organisation to disseminate anti-communist propaganda. The most notable example was Morgan Phillips' speech at the 1950 Copenhagen conference, drafted by Denis Healey, who drew mainly on material provided by IRD.

However, the work involved was considerable, and some of the participants questioned afterwards whether it really justified the efforts which they had put into it. Apart from its work to contain the spread of communist influence, perhaps its greatest immediate value may have been the opportunities which it offered for regular contacts between socialists to exchange ideas and experiences as they struggled to rebuild their societies and economies during a period of growing tension between Eastern and Western Europe.

7 THE SOCIALIST INTERNATIONAL

Dissolution of the Labour and Socialist International: early post-war consideration of the re-establishment of an International

After the First World War, the Second International was reconstituted as the Labour and Socialist International (LSI) in 1923. By the time of its fourth congress in 1931, the LSI represented a total membership of over six million, composed of parties from nearly every country in Europe. Its office was in Brussels, and its secretary was Friederich Adler. When the Germans overran Belgium, Adler escaped, but the offices were taken over and all records, documents and the library were lost. Very little material was recovered after the war. After the fall of France, the LSI ceased to function. During the war, European socialists in exile in London set up a committee which met occasionally to discuss matters of common concern, and especially the idea of a new International after the war.[522] A more detailed discussion took place in the margins of the Labour Party annual conference in London in 1944, when Labour Party leaders held the first informal conference of socialists from liberated Europe.[523] There was, initially, much interest in the prospect of re-establishing the International as soon as possible, and the international subcommittee of the Labour Party later considered a memorandum to that effect which was submitted by Healey. It was anticipated that the British would provide the lead for this.

However, it gradually became clear that such a course of action would create significant difficulties. The issue was discussed during the conference of the Dutch Social Democratic party in Amsterdam in early February 1946, where delegates from many European socialist parties were present. Healey subsequently wrote to Dalton, the chairman of the international sub-committee, outlining the problems which had been identified. He explained that countries under

---

[522] Letter from Edith Loeb, Secretary of the Socialist and Labour Information Office to Greaves at the LSE, 14 June 1948, File 491, General correspondence, Socialist International archive, Amsterdam.
[523] Foreword written by Morgan Phillips, secretary of the Labour Party and chairman of the Socialist International, introducing a pamphlet of the Socialist International, February 1953. Socialist International papers, Labour Party archive, Manchester.

Russian pressure or with large communist parties (especially Czechoslovakia, Poland and Italy) would find it embarrassing to participate in an International under British leadership. Furthermore, the Scandinavian countries retained their old mistrust of an International which was limited to the passing of ambiguous but inflammatory resolutions. Neither did they want to complicate their own relations with Russia. He concluded that it would be less embarrassing and of more immediate value to set up a liaison committee of socialist parties, which could discuss practical problems where common action was possible and desirable. There was general support for such a step among those who took part in the conference. Healey also pointed out that a liaison committee would not have to function in the glare of publicity, and would not be committed to expressing a unanimous opinion on every international problem which arose. [524] Dalton replied that he 'would not be broken-hearted if we did simply fall back on a Liaison Committee'.[525] Writing some years later, Healey provided a further, perhaps more compelling, reason which was that 'the British and Scandinavian parties, fortified by recent election victories, were not prepared to consider any external interference into their own affairs'.[526]

The Scandinavian parties had discussed their positions in advance of the conference.[527] Phil Heller, the chairman of the international affairs committee of Socialist Party USA had written to DNA in early 1946 calling for a speedy reconstitution of the International.[528] Haakon Lie, who had attended the conference in Amsterdam, replied in mid-February. He explained it had been agreed that it would be

---

[524] Healey to Dalton, Chancellor of the Exchequer and chairman of the international sub-committee of the Labour Party, 12 February 1946, Healey papers, Labour Party archive, Manchester.
[525] Dalton to Healey, 18 February 1946, Healey papers, Labour Party archive, Manchester.
[526] Denis Healey, 'The International Socialist Conference 1946-1950', *International Affairs* 26 July 1950, p366.
[527] Unsigned letter from DNA to Sven Andersson, secretary of the Swedish Social Democratic Party, 15 January 1946. (The letter is actually dated 1945, but it is clear that this was a typographical error.) Internasjonalt utvalg, D Da 10, Arbeiderbevegelsens arkiv.
[528] Circular letter from Socialist Party USA to all socialist parties, January 1946, Internasjonal utvalg, D Da 10, Arbeiderbevegelsens arkiv.

better to start by setting up a liaison office rather than by establishing an International, which would be unlikely to do more than the liaison office committee would do if it were properly led. He added that the British Labour Party had been asked to organise an international conference at the end of May to discuss the matter.[529] At the same time, Lie wrote to Healey to inform him that when he had reported to the executive committee of DNA on the conversation which they had had in Amsterdam about future international cooperation, the committee had fully agreed with the policy which Healey had outlined, and would be represented at the conference which the Labour Party would be organising.[530]

The first conference of international socialist parties at Clacton, May 1946

On 21 February 1946, Morgan Phillips wrote to eighteen socialist countries, mainly in Europe but also in the Dominions, calling them to an informal conference in Clacton from 17-20 May. The main objective of the conference would be to re-establish contacts broken by war, to exchange information and to work out, if possible, common policies on problems of common and mutual interest.[531] The proposed agenda was discussed at a meeting of the international committee of DNA on 15 March. It was agreed that a socialist liaison office should be set up in London, and that the British Labour Party should be responsible for administration and staffing, as well as for the initial costs which would be incurred. Lie replied to Phillips on 20 March, telling him that Åke Ording (member of DNA's executive committee and secretary of their group in the Storting) would represent DNA and asking him to arrange

---

[529] Letter from Haakon Lie to Phil Heller, Socialist Party U.S.A., 13 February 1946, Internasjonalt utvalg, D Da 10, Arbeiderbevegelsens arkiv.
[530] Lie to Healey, 13 February 1946, Internasjonalt utvalg, D Da 10, Arbeiderbevegelsens arkiv.
[531] Circular letter from Morgan Phillips, 27 February 1946, File 234, International Socialist Conferences, Socialist International archive, Amsterdam. Copies of this and subsequent correspondence on this subject were also viewed in the relevant files in the Arbeiderbevegelsens arkiv in Oslo and the Labour Party archive in Manchester, which contain full sets of the newsletters and briefs which were circulated.

for DNA's resolutions to be put onto the agenda.[532] He would have had a chance to discuss this in person with both Phillips and Healey earlier in March when he had visited London to discuss Spain with his British colleagues, though there are no separate records to show whether this happened.

Notwithstanding the differences between them, the Clacton conference was a triumphant reunion of socialist parties whose links had been interrupted or fractured by the war. Åke Ording introduced the debate on future co-operation, and put forward proposals to establish a liaison office. They were unanimously agreed, and it was decided that the office should be known as the Socialist Information and Labour Office (SILO) and would be established in Transport House, the headquarters of the Labour Party. The British Labour Party would also be responsible for the administration of the office, appointment of staff and, initially, all the other expenses which would be incurred as well. The other main topics which were discussed were relations with the Soviet Union and the communists, democracy in the countries of Eastern Europe, Germany and German social democracy and Spain. These issues were going to occupy much of the attention and energies of socialists throughout the next few years.[533] Reflecting these discussions Laski, then chairman of the party, noted afterwards that this conference had not been an attempt to revive the Second International, and that it would be premature to try to do so until a resolute attempt had been made to reach some sort of understanding with their Russian colleagues.[534] There were probably more obstacles to co-operation after the war than there had been before it. Furthermore, Western European socialist parties were not homogeneous: there were significant differences

---

[532] Minutes of a meeting of the international committee of DNA on 15 March, and letter from Lie to Phillips on 20 March 1946, Internasjonalt utvalg, D Da 10, Arbeiderbevegelsens arkiv. It was, incidentally, this meeting which also recommended that the first Norwegian labour attachés should be sent to London and Paris.
[533] Report by Åke Ording on the International Conference of Socialist Parties at Clacton, 3 July 1946, Internasjonalt utvalg, D Da 10, Arbeiderbevegelsens arkiv.
[534] Undated note by Laski on the Socialist Conference at Clacton, International Sub-Committee papers, Labour Party archive, Manchester.

between the parties in Britain and Scandinavia on the one hand, and those in France and Italy, which were more rigid, on the other.[535]

Laski made these observations just a few days after Churchill had made his well-publicised speech in Fulton on 5 March, setting out a very different view of the situation in the Soviet Union and Eastern Europe. Quite a number of socialist parties considered establishing closer links with the communists during this period. DNA itself had had a series of discussions with the Norwegian Communist Party (NKP) in 1945 about the possibility of establishing a joint list for the election to be held that autumn. A joint programme had been agreed upon, in which the communists acknowledged the principle of peaceful transition to socialism. This came to nothing when, following a press campaign throughout Scandinavia, the proposals were rejected by NKP. The parties campaigned separately. However, a further attempt was made in March 1947 through what was known as the Vestfold proposals, when the local parties agreed on fusion largely on the basis of the joint programme which had been worked out in 1945, but their proposals were again not accepted by the executive committee of NKP.[536]

Bournemouth: significant differences of views between Eastern and Western European Socialist parties

The next conference was held six months later in Bournemouth, from 8-10 November 1946. Haakon Lie represented DNA. He subsequently reported that in order to reduce the administrative burden on the British Labour Party, it had been agreed that a consultative committee should be set up and meet regularly in London in between the international conferences. (Lie would occasionally attend these committee meetings himself, but for the next year,

---

[535] Healey, *The Time of My Life*, p364.
[536] Nordahl to Vincent Tewson, 19 July 1947, International sub-committee papers, Labour Party archive, Manchester. There are further details contained in a note made by Healey of a conversation with Bratteli on 23 July 1947, Healey papers, Labour Party archive.

until the creation of the Committee of the International Socialist Conference, COMISCO, the responsibility was usually delegated to Olav Bratteli, the labour attaché at the Norwegian embassy in London.[537] Problems caused by differences of view between the Eastern and Western European parties were already becoming apparent, even over minor procedural or administrative matters. The Pole, Kuriewicz, noted that the establishment of a consultative committee in London would mean a deepening of the political split, while the Czech, Vilim, maintained that the establishment of the committee in London would weaken the position of his party in Czechoslovakia. Healey avoided a more serious problem by minimising the significance of the committee and by explaining that its job would only be to carry out information work, and to organise conferences, thereby enabling a unanimous resolution on its establishment.[538]

However, it was clear that the Labour Party and the Foreign Office were disappointed that it had not been possible to achieve more progress. Hankey noted to Warner that Bournemouth had been a complete flop because the Poles and Czechs had prevented anything concrete from being agreed. He reported that Harrison, from the American embassy, had found it amusing that Western European socialists should have any real illusions about the affiliations or practical freedom of socialists from countries behind the Iron Curtain. Harrison had also heard that the Eastern European socialists might be organising their own conference in Prague later in the year, in a possible attempt to make a rival International under Communist control. (This would eventually become the Cominform.) Hankey hoped that Healey might be able to provide some information about this.[539] He and Warner subsequently attended Healey's meeting with Mayhew at which the subject was further discussed. There was, at this stage,

---

[537] This was decided at a meeting of the international committee of DNA on 3 January 1947, Internasjonalt utvalg, D Da 15, Arbeiderbevegelsens arkiv.
[538] Report by Haakon Lie on the International Socialist Conference at Bournemouth, 8-10 November 1946, Internasjonalt utvalg, D Da 10, Arbeiderbevegelsens arkiv.
[539] Personal minute from Hankey to Warner, 14 November 1946, N14860/14860/63, FO 371/56244.

some understanding of the constraints which circumscribed the freedom of manoeuvre of the Poles and Czechs and which prevented them from provoking the communists by more open advocacy of an International. Healey subsequently attended the conference of the Hungarian Social Democratic party in January 1947: he was optimistically encouraged to advise them to show a greater degree of independence in their dealings with the communists. He reported that it now seemed likely that the Prague conference would be postponed indefinitely.[540]

Much time would be spent at future conferences debating the question of whether certain European socialist parties qualified for admission to these International Socialist Conferences, either as participants or as observers. The question would generally hinge on whether the party concerned was a genuinely independent socialist party, or whether it was to a greater or lesser extent subservient to the local communist party. Speaking fifty years later, Healey noted

> ... when the war ended, I was International Secretary to the Labour Party.... The Soviet government took the view that it could not win control of any capitalist country without first destroying democratic socialism in the labour movement and so one of its major objectives, on which it spent a lot of time and money, was trying to get the socialist parties to lie with the communists and be swallowed by them. And I spent six years travelling all over Europe, particularly Eastern Europe, trying – in Eastern Europe unsuccessfully – to slow that down. That was also the period when the Russians genuinely believed in the theory of the two camps.[541]

The most contentious issue at this conference was whether the German Social Democratic Party (SPD) should be admitted. Morgan Phillips urged that it should be, and was supported by the Scandinavians among others. However, the

---

[540] Healey to Mayhew, 30 December 1946, R310/11/21, FO 371/67169.
[541] Statement by Healey at a colloquium organised by the Foreign and Commonwealth Office, recorded in 'Spies, Secrets and Diplomacy', *Occasional Paper No 15* (FCO Historians, January 1999).

Eastern Europeans, led by the Poles, maintained that the Germans were too nationalistic and that to admit them would be offensive to the Soviet Union.[542] A compromise was agreed, whereby the German SPD would be invited to the next conference and permitted to answer questions as a preliminary to further discussion.

The changing situation: Zurich, June 1947

By the time of the next conference, held in Zurich in June 1947, the situation was changing significantly, not least for the socialist parties in Eastern Europe. The speech by George Marshall, which led to establishment of the European Recovery Programme, received a positive response from most of the Eastern European socialist parties – until they were informed by Moscow that participation would be considered an anti-Soviet action, or were bribed with a promise of increased Russian assistance, or were threatened that their prisoners of war would not be released if they voted for the programme.[543] Furthermore, the Secretary-General of the Hungarian Smallholders' Party (who had won fifty-seven per cent of the votes in the 1945 election) had been arrested, charged with espionage and had disappeared. Twenty-one MPs from that party had been arrested and imprisoned. In Bulgaria the leader of the Farmers' Party, Petkov, had been arrested. Over 200 socialists had been arrested in Poland and charged with espionage.[544] Lie wrote to Bratteli in March, setting out the views of DNA on the subjects which were expected to be the main agenda items at the Zurich conference. Bratteli, who had recently arrived in London, had already found Healey to be very helpful and the source of some useful introductions. He gave this letter to Healey, who replied to Lie that the position of the British Labour Party was just about the same on all points.[545]

---

[542] *The Times*, 11 November 1946.
[543] Haakon Lie, *Skjebneår*, p 203.
[544] Lie, *Skjebneår*, p209.
[545] Healey to Lie, 2 May 1947, Lie arkiv, internasjonale forbindelser, Dc0004, Arbeiderbevegelsens arkiv.

It was not therefore surprising that the attitude of the Eastern European socialists at Zurich would be at best circumscribed, if not actually more hostile. Haakon Lie subsequently discovered that the delegates from Poland and Czechoslovakia had met in Berne beforehand and worked out a common strategy on how to deal with the proposal to admit the German SPD.[546] There was similarly much correspondence beforehand between the Western European socialist parties as they tried to work out a satisfactory way of ensuring that the German SPD would be admitted. Healey wrote confidentially to Schumacher in May to assure him that he anticipated that the result would be satisfactory.[547] It was not. The Poles and Czechs submitted a large number of questions, clearly drafted for later publication at home, and to cause the maximum disruption. It was finally agreed that the subject should be discussed again at the next international conference, which would be held in Antwerp at the end of November – Haakon Lie proposed this, for the Norwegians were among the keenest to see the SPD admitted as soon as possible.

There was little progress on other issues, either, but it was agreed that a two-thirds majority would suffice in future for the admission of new members – though the Hungarians and the Czechs had wanted the decision to be unanimous. It was not possible to agree on the admission of other parties: representatives or liaison groups were charged with trying to mediate between the different factions of the Spanish and Italian socialist parties. There was also further discussion of a proposal to consider the reconstruction of the International, 'bearing in mind the experience of the past, and the present needs of international socialist action'.[548] The French and the Belgians were most enthusiastic about this idea, and were prominent among those pushing for the proposal: following opposition from the Hungarians and Rumanians, the conference decision (proposed by Phillips) to set up a committee to consider it was an effective way of delaying any further

---

[546] Lie, *Skjebneår*, p209.
[547] Healey to Schumacher, May 1947, File 235, Socialist International archive, Amsterdam.
[548] Healey to Mayhew, 28 June 1947, enclosing the minutes of the Conference, File 235, Socialist International archive.

consideration. The Norwegians remained as unenthusiastic as the British about a new International. In the autumn, Lie wrote to Bratteli, shortly before a meeting of the consultative committee in London, to make clear that DNA remained of the opinion that it was too early to consider any such step.[549]

Following the Zurich conference, the gap between east and west widened. The discussions of the Marshall plan, which took place in Paris between Bevin, Bidault (the French foreign minister) and Molotov, broke down in early July. Following a meeting of the Soviet and Eastern European communist parties in Silesia in Poland in October 1947 (also attended by French and Italian delegates), a decision was taken to establish the Communist Parties' Information Bureau, known as the Cominform, which was based in Belgrade.[550] This effectively marked the end of any prospect of worthwhile co-operation between the parties of Eastern and Western Europe, though it took a few months more before this was openly acknowledged. During the year, Healey travelled widely in Eastern Europe, attending socialist party conferences in Hungary in January, in Czechoslovakia in November and in Poland in December. All of these conferences were characterised by strong influence exerted by the communists. The Czech Social Democrats rejected heavy pressure to agree to fusion with the communists and rejected the motion of their leader, Fierlinger, who was regarded as a Soviet stooge. Their resistance did not, however, last long: the government was replaced following a communist coup in February 1948. The Polish socialists also soon agreed to fusion with the communist party in a new workers' party. Healey did not find this surprising because he noted that the post-war Polish socialist party represented only those who had worked in the war with the communists, rather than the government in exile.[551]

---

[549] Lie to Bratteli, 8 October 1947, Lie arkiv, Internasjonale forbindelser, Dc0005, Arbeiderbevegelsens arkiv.
[550] Lie, *Skjebneår,* pp 217-218. Lie notes that the directives were given out through a document called 'For lasting peace and popular democracy', which he considered to have been the most boring paper to have been printed outside the Soviet Union.
[551] Healey, *The Time of My Life,* pp85-88.

Little progress at Antwerp

Against this background, and strikes in France during the autumn, it was not surprising that the Antwerp conference at the end of November – the last attended by the Eastern European parties as full members - produced few concrete results. Although Laski made a speech intended to prevent any further economic and political division of Europe, it had little effect. The Italian delegate, Basso, supported by the Poles and the Hungarians, advocated an alliance with the communists and rejection of the Marshall plan.[552] The Czechs were resolute enough to oppose this, but it was to be their last demonstration of independence. However, there were some signs of progress: the conference was able to agree (through use of the two-thirds majority) that the German SPD should be admitted to the International Socialist Conference. Furthermore, it was agreed the Committee of International Socialist Conferences (COMISCO) should be established to replace the consultative committee. COMISCO could exercise wider powers between the six-monthly meetings of the full conference. Nonetheless, despite these achievements, there was a feeling that the international socialist movement had made little progress during the year. Writing in *Arbeiderbladet* in December 1947, Haakon Lie reflected these views. He noted that the socialist parties in Eastern Europe had chosen to make themselves spokesmen for Russian views in order to buy for themselves some freedom of manoeuvre at home, and that the creation of the Cominform must strengthen this tendency.[553]

The second meeting of COMISCO, held in London in March 1948, agreed to expel the former social democratic parties of Rumania, Bulgaria and Hungary, none of whom had sent representatives to take part. COMISCO noted that the Czechs had clearly shown their desire for independence at their conference in Brno the previous November, but that they had been betrayed. The present leadership of the Czech

---

[552] Haakon Lie noted that there was about to be an election in Italy, and that the Italian socialists had an electoral agreement with the communists: he concluded that this was the reason why Basso took this position. *Skjebneår*, p228.
[553] Article by Lie in *Arbeiderbladet*, 1 December 1947, Boks 25.2/59, International Socialist Conferences, 1947-1949, Riksarkiv.

party could not therefore be accepted as representative of socialism. They were also expelled. The Polish and Italian parties were given an ultimatum and told to prove their commitment to socialism.[554] In the event, the Poles withdrew their membership after this resolution: it took rather longer to resolve the issue of Italian membership.

Conference of European Socialist parties to discuss the Marshall Plan.

The background to the conference of European socialist parties to discuss the Marshall plan was discussed in Chapter Three. The proposal was made to Healey by Haakon Lie, after some Eastern European socialist parties had attacked the plan during the Antwerp conference. They agreed that at the first meeting of COMISCO, in London in January 1948, Lie would propose a conference of European socialist parties to discuss (and support) the Marshall plan.[555] The other Scandinavian parties did not wish to associate themselves with this proposal, though it was enthusiastically endorsed by the French and Belgians. They had wanted COMISCO to take responsibility for organising the conference. It was, however, eventually agreed that such a step was not within the competence of that body and that the British Labour Party should assume responsibility for arranging and hosting the conference.[556] Lie's report shows that eleven voted against the idea of COMISCO organising the conference, and only five for it. Such a move would presumably have been considered undesirable by those who were concerned about the inclusion of Eastern European parties. It would also have been considered undesirable by the Eastern European parties themselves (who were not expelled until the next meeting of COMISCO in March). Morgan Phillips reminded the delegates that it had been agreed at Antwerp that regional

---

[554] COMISCO circular, March 1948, File 265, COMISCO meetings, Socialist International archive.
[555] Conversation with Haakon Lie, 18 July 2005.
[556] *Daily Telegraph*, 12 January 1948, File 265, COMISCO meetings, Socialist International archive.

conferences could be held, and this approach provided the solution which permitted only certain parties to be invited.[557]

Vienna: agreement to arrange expert conferences

It was also Haakon Lie and the Norwegians who took the initiative to propose Vienna as the venue for the first conference of 1948, held from 4-7 June.[558] It was marked by further debate about the membership of the Italian socialists. A decision was taken to suspend (but not expel) the Partito Socialista Italiano (PSI), led by Nenni and Basso. A commission (which included both Healey and Lie) was set up, with the intention that it should make an appeal to the PSI before their conference in Genoa on 27 June. It was given a mandate to take the initiative to help to reunify the forces of Italian socialism after the conference.[559] However, its work was not successful. At their congress in Florence in December 1948, the PSI leadership was again taken over by Nenni and his pro-communist associates, and the next International Socialist Conference, held in Holland at Baarn from 14-16 May 1949, finally decided to expel the PSI. The Unita Socialista, which had split away from the Nenni party, was admitted instead as the Italian member of the conference, although work continued to try to achieve the unification of Italian socialists.[560]

By the time of the conference at Baarn, as Healey noted, on many major international issues the socialist parties differed almost as widely among themselves as with other parties – their disagreements over European unity at Baarn were a striking example.[561] This explains why some of the most useful work now began outside the regular conferences and the intervening meetings of COMISCO. A significant

---

[557] Report by Lie on the first meeting of COMISCO in London, 10 January 1948, Lie arkiv, Internasjonale forbindelser, Dc 0005, Arbeiderbevegelsens arkiv.
[558] Lie, *Skjebneår,* p419.
[559] Report by Lie on the Vienna conference, 9 June 1948, Lie arkiv, Internasjonale forbindelser, Dc0005, Arbeiderbevegelsens arkiv.
[560] International Socialist Conference newsletter, May 1949, File 265, Socialist International archive.
[561] Healey, *The Time of My Life,* p368.

step taken in Vienna was the decision to organise expert conferences on special subjects. The first two were the administration of nationalised industries, and the international control of basic industries in Europe. The British Labour Party undertook to organise the first conference on nationalised industries. It took place at Buscot Park, the home of the Labour peer Lord Faringdon, from 6-10 December 1948. Arne Drogseth, state secretary in the Ministry of Industry, was the Norwegian delegate. Despite the complexities of the subject, and the differences of approach between the countries concerned, it was held to have been useful. It was therefore decided to hold another conference, to look at the international control of basic industries. This was held at Bennekom, Holland in March 1949. Although it was not always possible for the parties to find someone sufficiently qualified to attend (the Norwegians for example were unable to find a suitable delegate to send to Bennekom[562]) these conferences continued. By 1950, it was the practice to run two conferences a year, meeting for five days and studying current problems. Other conferences which took place in 1949 and 1950 studied subjects as varied as the Saar commission, the refugee commission, the drafting committee on the principles of international democratic socialism, as well as propaganda and organisation.[563]

During this period, at the suggestion of the Swedish Social Democratic Party, SILO undertook an investigation of communist policy and activities in the countries represented in the International Socialist Conference. SILO sent out a circular letter asking for a range of information about communist parties, their main positions of strength, relations with socialist parties and their activities - especially those which might affect economic reconstruction and political democracy. It was hoped to collate and publish the information

---

[562] Lie to Healey, 10 March 1949, Lie arkiv, Internasjonale forbindelser, Dc 0005, Arbeiderbevegelsens arkiv.
[563] Circular letter from Julius Braunthal, 5 September 1950, File 491, General correspondence, 1947-1950, Socialist International archive.

which was obtained.[564] Lie provided a very detailed reply.[565] Although there is no record in the archives that SILO passed this material to IRD, it is likely that they did so. It would certainly have usefully complemented the regular reports on communist activities which at that time were being provided by embassies abroad.

Involvement of IRD

Given the objectives of COMISCO and the close links between the British Labour Party and their Western European counterparts during this period, it would have been surprising if IRD had not made some significant attempt to use the organisation in its work against the spread of communist influence. No evidence has been found in the archives to show whether or when a specific policy decision was made to exploit the opportunities which the movement offered. However, Foreign Office files, as well as those of the Socialist International, reveal some interesting examples both of the way in which IRD material was used and also of the way in which the Labour Party sought to make use of the Socialist International for its own purposes.

A significant example occurred during the International Socialist Conference in Copenhagen from 1-3 June 1950. The conference was opened by Hans Hedtoft, the Danish Prime Minister, who set the tone by referring to the evils of communism and the part to be played by united social democracy in the struggle against it. He was followed by Erich Ollenhauer from Germany, who presented a long report on forced labour in Eastern Europe. He quoted statistics suggesting that there were between ten million and fifteen million slave workers in Eastern Europe, including about one million taken to Russia after annexation of the Baltic states. His arguments were supported by some telling statistics. He noted for example that 1.23 million people had been removed from Poland to

---

[564] Letter from Edward Thompson, editor of *Socialist World* (at that time a quarterly magazine published by SILO) to Haakon Lie, 27 August 1948, Lie arkiv, Internasjonale forbindelser, Dc0005, Arbeiderbevegelsens arkiv.
[565] Lie to Thompson, 1 November 1949, Lie arkiv, Internasjonale forbindelser, Dc0005, Arbeiderbevegelsens arkiv.

Russia, and that about 445,000 of them had disappeared. On the following day, Morgan Phillips delivered a powerful speech on the position of socialism in the struggle for world peace, beginning with a forceful exposition of the falsities of Soviet peace propaganda. He pointed out that work in the UN Security Council had been paralysed by Soviet obstruction, and noted the extent to which western democratic countries had reduced their defence forces to a fraction of their pre-war figures, while those of Russia still totalled more than half of their strength in 1945. In his report the ambassador, Randall, concluded that the main interest of the conference lay in the way in which it had re-opened the whole question of the doctrinal basis of socialism, and also in the very effective counter-propaganda which it provided to the Soviet-inspired peace campaign. He considered that in the latter respect Phillips, who had just come out of a London hospital for this purpose, had made an outstanding contribution.[566]

Commenting on this despatch, IRD noted that while they may have helped to stimulate Ollenhauer's report on forced labour, they could not take the full credit. The SPD had its own sources of information on forced labour in the Soviet zone of Germany. Ollenhauer's figure of 400,000 slave workers in the uranium areas of Saxony was larger than IRD's own estimate, but might well be the correct figure. It was excessively hard to obtain firm facts. Adam Watson added with satisfaction that the bulk of that part of Phillips' speech dealing with Soviet imperialism was in fact drafted by Healey from material supplied by IRD. A great many of the sentences were textually those of IRD. He thought that, between them, Healey and Phillips had put the speech together very well.[567] This represents an interesting example of the extent to which

---

[566] Randall to Younger, 8 June 1950, reporting on the first International Socialist conference to be held in Scandinavia since the war, N1023/1, FO 371/86147.

[567] Minuting by Wilkinson and Watson (IRD), 23 and 29 June 1950, N1023/1, FO 371/86147. These papers were to be retained until 2026, but after review they were released in 2004. Without mentioning IRD, Healey refers to the part he played in drafting Phillips' speech in his autobiography, commenting that in those days it was possible for him to write a speech claiming that the Labour Party owed more to Methodism than to Marxism. *The Time of My Life,* p 93.

IRD, with the willing co-operation of the Labour Party, was able to make telling use of a major international conference to produce a significant propaganda impact.

There are occasional references in IRD files to their use of COMISCO. For example, in early 1950, IRD wanted to use COMISCO to ensure that the subject of forced labour in communist countries – where IRD considered its work to have been very successful since the publication of the Codex – was kept in the public eye. Watson minuted to Murray that he was considering further steps to keep the subject alive.

> The most promising field is the International Confederation of Free Trade Unions (ICFTU), which has the subject on its agenda and which hopes to debate it in the near future. By arrangement with Mr Healey, the various foreign members of the organisation will receive through COMISCO some substantial documentation on the subject prepared by us, which will ensure that the debate is on a high and informed level.

Murray commented that IRD was in some danger of lacking a forum from which to conduct publicity about forced labour in the Soviet Union and other communist countries. He considered that this threw into relief the importance of anything which could be done by COMISCO, the ICFTU or other independent bodies to which IRD could supply information confidentially.[568] IRD were subsequently able to strengthen their contacts in the ICFTU after Healey wrote to Peck at the end of 1950 to recommend Edward Thompson, head of the publications department of the ICFTU, as a worthwhile contact. He informed Peck that Thompson had been in the Intelligence Corps during the war, that he had formerly been one of the secretaries of COMISCO and that he was thoroughly reliable. When Peck passed Thompson's name to the information office in Brussels, he noted that Thompson

---

[568] Watson minute to Murray, 8 March 1950, Murray minute to Watson, 27 March 1950, PR 14/41/G, FO 1110/288.

had actually been receiving IRD material in the form of the Digest since 1948.[569]

In a further example, without any apparent prior introduction and without providing any details about the organisation which he represented, in May 1951 Stephen Watts wrote from an anonymous address in central London to Julius Braunthal, the administrative secretary of the International Socialist Conference. In his letter, Watts offered to provide Braunthal with a batch of Background Books which he thought might be of interest to COMISCO. In an opaque preamble, he explained that the booklets were on sale in the ordinary way at home and abroad; they had also been taken up by some of the organisations interested in disseminating informative literature on current affairs written from the western democratic point of view. He wondered whether there might be an outlet through COMISCO. He offered further booklets in the series on the Cooperative movement, the future of South East Asia and a symposium 'Why Communism must fail' by Bertrand Russell, Leonard Schapiro and others. Braunthal replied, thanking him and looking forward to the books which he was going to publish. He thought that the only way in which he might be able to help disseminate this informative literature would be by publishing extracts of those books of special interest through the COMISCO information service.[570] Background Books was a series which was initially published by the Batchworth Press from early 1951, under IRD auspices.[571] Watts, who edited the series, had worked for the Security Service during the war. The first volume in the series which he produced was entitled *What is Communism?* The Foreign Office bought 5,000 copies for distribution to British posts, and the Colonial Office a further 10,000. The series, which was also published by Phoenix House and Bodley Head, comprised almost 100

---

[569] Healey to Peck, 8 December 1950, and Peck to Lockhart in Brussels, 19 January 1951, PR 18/3/51/G, FO 1110/380. Sheridan minuted enthusiastically on Healey's letter that the more that IRD could get into the ICFTU magazine, the better.
[570] Watts to Braunthal, 25 May 1951, reply from Braunthal, 28 May 1951, File 492, General Correspondence, Socialist International archive.
[571] There are a number of references to Background Books in the IRD files, of which FO 1110/573 is an interesting example.

titles.[572] Another of the first booklets which Watts produced was *Trade Unions: True or False* by Vic Feather.[573]

A further interesting example of the way in which the Labour Party sometimes used the International as a means of influence is demonstrated by a letter which Phillips (who by then was the chairman of the Socialist International) wrote to Braunthal in January 1952. Writing from Transport House without any explanation of the background to his purpose, he enclosed a draft of a letter which he wished to be sent to Oldenbroek, the general secretary of the ICFTU, in Brussels. The draft first asked for guidance on what steps might be taken to secure more effective co-operation between the ICFTU and the newly created International. It referred to the expert conferences which the International had been running, noted that one would shortly be taking place in Dorking on the problem of production, rearmament and a higher standard of living, and offered Oldenbroek an invitation either for himself or for his representatives if he wished to take this further.

More significantly, the draft described the extent of the problem faced by the International in countering aggressive totalitarian communism, particularly in Asia and other underdeveloped countries. It explained that the International had already established contact with a number of parties in Asia, and that the Japanese were affiliated and the Indians were observers. It also noted that a conference was shortly to be held in Rangoon of a number of Eastern democratic socialist parties to consider their future development. Knowing that the ICFTU had a wide variety of contacts in many of these territories, the draft suggested that a frank exchange of opinion on the problems to be faced would be of great value to the organisation. It concluded that the author (i.e. Braunthal) would be happy to have Oldenbroek's private advice on the possibility of effecting private co-operation between the two organisations. Braunthal wrote to Oldenbroek in these

---

[572] Andrew Defty, *Britain, American and Anti-Communist Propaganda 1945-1953* (Routledge, 2004), p165.
[573] Paul Lashmar and James Oliver, *Britain's Secret Propaganda War 1948 – 1977* (Sutton Publishing, 1998), p100.

terms without amending the draft in any way.[574] There is no trace of a reply in the Socialist International archives, nor any record of this correspondence in IRD files, but an initiative of this sort could be expected to have come from IRD.

In general, the papers which have been found in the archives reflect discussion of the dissemination of IRD material, and some discussion of the internal affairs of the conference and its governing committee. There is nothing to show that IRD as such made any covert efforts to influence the conference or its leadership. Once the Eastern Europeans had been expelled, there would have been no reason to do so. COMISCO and IRD would have had very similar objectives.

Reconstitution of the Socialist International

Although the French and Belgians had continued to encourage consideration of reconstitution of the International, there was little significant progress until the end of 1950. The main opposition continued to come from the British and Scandinavian parties. An article in *Arbeiderbladet* in March 1951 noted that these parties did not want to create the illusion that an International had the ability to solve international problems. The writer noted how difficult it was to work out common lines for domestic and foreign policies in the relatively homogeneous and limited Scandinavian area.[575] However, at their conference in December 1950, the Belgian Socialist Party passed a unanimous resolution that work should now be undertaken to re-establish an International, and expressed their impatience that this had not been done sooner. Larock, the secretary of the party, followed this up with an open letter to Phillips which made a similar request. The situation by then had stabilised sufficiently that the British and Scandinavians did not feel justified in continuing to maintain their opposition. Following some detailed preparatory work, in March 1951 COMISCO

---

[574] Phillips to Braunthal, enclosing the draft, 9 January 1952. Braunthal sent a letter to Oldenbroek two days later, without amending the draft, File 492, General Correspondence, Socialist International archive.
[575] Article in *Arbeiderbladet*, 1 March 1951, Boks 25.2/59, International Socialist Conferences, Riksarkiv.

adopted the necessary resolutions. The International was re-established at the next International Socialist Conference in Frankfurt in July 1951. The headquarters of the German SPD were in Frankfurt, and many socialists thought that it was appropriate that a town in Germany should provide the cradle for the new International.[576]

Speaking in 2005, Haakon Lie said that although the views of the Norwegian and British Labour parties were often identical (particularly on the question of delaying the re-establishment of the International), he did not think that the work which they did together at these meetings was of particular significance in their overall relationship during this period. He added that others probably shared this view. However, there could be no doubt of the importance of the work to ensure that the movement remained as free as possible of communist influence. Lie added that he had also found it very useful to meet Healey, Phillips and other British socialists so regularly in the course of committee meetings and conferences.[577] This was certainly of significant benefit. Healey went a little further. He concluded that this work had helped to accelerate and consolidate trends which would otherwise have developed more slowly and painfully in the individual parties, though their work had achieved this in the main by acting as a forum for the exchange of experiences.[578] He added that socialism was the only existing movement capable of competing with communism as a political force, and that by emphasising the international traditions of socialism, the conference had helped some of the weaker parties to maintain or increase their support.[579] Given the importance of the work which they were doing, it is not surprising that IRD decided to make use of COMISCO and the conferences as outlets for their material.

However, the administration and co-ordination work involved was considerable, and some of the participants questioned afterwards whether it really justified the efforts which they had put into it. Apart from its work to contain the

---

[576] Lie, *Skjebneår*, p 422.
[577] Conversation with Haakon Lie, 18 July 2005.
[578] Healey, *The Time of my Life*, p372.
[579] Ibid. p373.

spread of communist influence in the movement, perhaps its greatest immediate value may have been the opportunities which it offered for regular contacts between socialists to exchange ideas and experiences as they struggled to rebuild their societies and economies during a period of growing tension between Eastern and Western Europe.

8 The relationship at work and its sudden end: 1949 to October 1951

New Labour Party initiatives to strengthen socialist links

By 1949, the relationship was well-established and functioning effectively. But as party resources became stretched, work was still needed to maintain it at that level. At the end of January 1949 Mennell, assistant secretary of the International Department of the Labour Party, wrote to Haakon Lie to inform him that Harry Earnshaw, the General Secretary of the National Union of Beamers, Twisters and Drawers, would attend the DNA congress in mid-February.[580] This was shortly after Healey had written a circular letter to Haakon Lie to announce the appointment of a new assistant in the International Department, Eric Randall, whose main function would be to extend and develop direct contact between the local organisations of the Labour Party and socialist parties abroad. Healey commented that the British Labour Party felt that international socialist solidarity could not become fully effective as long as contact between the socialist parties was confined to their elected leaders and officers. The British party thought that local party organisations, women's sections and youth and student organisations should be encouraged to develop relations with corresponding groups in other countries.[581] The Danes replied shortly afterwards that they were interested in the

---

[580] Mennell to Haakon Lie, 29 January 1949, Internasjonalt utvalg, D Da 26, Arbeiderbevegelsens arkiv.
[581] Healey to Lie, 11 January 1949, Lie arkiv, Internasjonale forbindelser, Dc0006, Arbeiderbevegelsens arkiv.

idea, but considered that a lack of English at a local level might prove a hindrance.[582] Even with the reinforcement provided by Mennell and Randall, the international department of the Labour Party was still very small, and – judging from the correspondence which has survived – most of the burden throughout this period was still carried by Healey. It appears that the Danish reservations may have been justified, because there is little evidence to show that Randall was successful in building up closer organisational links.

The appointment of Randall was not the first initiative Healey had attempted, to develop links with other countries. A minute written by Mayhew to Warner in May 1948 had described a meeting which he had held with Morgan Phillips and Healey to discuss the possibilities of increasing the influence of the Labour Party in countering communism in other countries. One of the subjects which they considered was the proposal to adopt a town in Italy or France on a party basis. They also discussed the question of strengthening the Labour Party in both staff and money. Mayhew urged that more financial assistance should be given to enable Labour MPs to travel abroad, but was told that the general consensus was that this would be too expensive a commitment for the party. It was pointed out that available funds could more profitably be spent by expanding the staff of the international department, a conclusion which eventually led to the recruitment of Mennell and Randall.[583] Mayhew also asked about the possible organisation of visits of foreign socialists to Britain to be trained in party and trade union organisation, with a view to combating communism. Phillips replied that they had recently had a French socialist over for three months for just such a purpose, but he considered that the results had not been worthwhile.[584]

---

[582] Letter from the Danish Labour Party to Lie, 9 March 1949, Lie arkiv, Internasjonale forbindelser, Dc0006, Arbeiderbevegelsens arkiv.
[583] Minute from Mayhew to Warner, 6 May 1948, PR 442/1/913/G, FO 1110/10.
[584] Ibid. This meeting is also described in a note by Mayhew recording this meeting in the Mayhew papers, Establishment of IRD, Box 4/1/1, Liddell Hart archive.

8 THE RELATIONSHIP AT WORK AND ITS SUDDEN END: 1949 TO OCTOBER 1951

The DNA conference: historic debate on the Atlantic pact

Shortly afterwards, at the beginning of March, Collier sent a report by Inman on the recently concluded DNA conference, attended by Earnshaw. He noted that the conference came at a key time during the process of evolution of Norwegian policy towards an Atlantic pact. It included a major debate on foreign policy, when Gerhardsen said that he supported Lange's view that defence co-operation with the western powers was the right course for Norway. Many key members of DNA – including, significantly, Halvdan Koht - spoke in favour of such a resolution.[585] Lange noted subsequently that when Koht rose to speak, his foreign policy adviser Arne Ording left the room, because he could not bear to hear Koht defend his neutrality policy again. Lange added that Ording was wrong: Koht supported the resolution, and his speech was one of those which made the greatest impact on the conference.[586] Collier commented that the presence of a British delegate was of assistance in persuading the conference to accept the point of view of the Norwegian government and DNA leadership on the question of the Atlantic pact – although the DNA report of the conference makes clear that Earnshaw, while stressing the importance of the subject as it dealt with nothing less than peace and freedom, took care to emphasise that he was not going to offer any advice.[587]

---

[585] In a conversation with Paul Engstad on 23 December 2004, Haakon Lie described the atmosphere during this debate, when there was a small but significant minority opposed to Norway signing the Atlantic pact. On the basis of Koht's known views on joining such alliances, Lie was apprehensive of the adverse influence which his speech might have, and was most relieved when Koht supported the motion. The leader of those opposing signature was Olav Oksvik. After the resolution had been won by 329 votes to 35, Oksvik spoke again the following day and said that he wished to withdraw his minority resolution, so that the decision could be reached unanimously. When he returned to his seat he said to Lie: 'I think that we are making a mistake, but if we are going to make a mistake, then we should all do it together.' Conversation with Paul Engstad, 18 January 2005.
[586] Halvard Lange, *Norges Vei til NATO* (Pax Forlag A/S Oslo, 1966), p55.
[587] DNA, Landsmøteprotokoll 1949, Arbeiderbevegelsens arkiv.

8 THE RELATIONSHIP AT WORK AND ITS SUDDEN END: 1949 TO OCTOBER 1951

The DNA conference: Collier's concerns over Labour Party doubts about British participation

Collier added that he had been informed that Earnshaw's presence was greatly appreciated and that the conference was interested in the facts of British social and economic achievements provided in his speech. He also observed that numerous personalities in the Norwegian labour movement would have been glad to make his acquaintance and to discuss with him matters of common interest, had his stay in Oslo been less brief. Then, sounding a note of warning, Collier continued

> As I have previously reported and Inman has emphasised during his trips to London, the Norwegian labour movement is at present most anxious to develop its connections with its British counterpart. This was clear both from the warm wording of the invitation from DNA to the Labour Party and from the terms of the Norwegian Prime Minister's speech of welcome to Earnshaw, which were stronger than those in which he welcomed any other foreign delegate. In these circumstances it was surprising to learn from Mr Earnshaw that there had been considerable doubt at Labour Party headquarters as to whether it was worthwhile to send any representative to the conference.[588] I venture to suggest the desirability of representing in that quarter that gathering contacts of this sort provide a unique opportunity for developing contacts between the British and Norwegian movements. This conference, for example, was attended by nearly all the national leaders of the Norwegian labour movement and by many of the more important local figures and among

---

[588] This was not the only occasion during this period when the Labour Party was reluctant to attend a foreign conference: it had declined an invitation to attend the fiftieth anniversary celebrations of the Finnish Social Democratic Party in November 1949. It took a personal letter from Leskinen to Healey before this decision was reviewed, and Michael Foot was despatched as the Labour representative. Mikko Majander, 'Britain's Dual Approach: Labour and Finnish Social Democracy 1944-1951', in Aunesluoma (ed.), *From War to Cold War. Anglo-Finnish Relations in the 20th Century*. (SKS/Finnish Literature Society, 2005), p132.

230

the former are a number who have sufficient command of English to benefit from conversation with a British visitor who can speak with authority on conditions at home and on the international situation.[589]

Northern Department minuted that these comments would interest the Labour Party more than the Foreign Office. Hankey therefore wrote to Healey enclosing two copies of Collier's despatch and noting the beneficial results of Earnshaw's attendance on the question of the Atlantic pact. He also drew Healey's attention to Collier's comments on the desirability of maintaining and strengthening the personal contacts between the Labour Party and DNA. Hankey added that the Foreign Office agreed with his view that such contacts had an excellent effect and that, as Norwegian Labour Party leaders were particularly anxious to develop their connections with the British Labour Party, it would be a pity to disappoint them. He supported Collier's recommendation that a representative of the British Labour Party should if possible attend future conferences of this kind.[590] Healey replied that the Labour Party would lose no opportunity to maintain personal contact with DNA. Unfortunately, they did not invite foreign delegates to their own annual conference, but they hoped to invite Martin Tranmæl - who was due to retire as editor of *Arbeiderbladet* at the beginning of 1950 - to attend the fiftieth anniversary celebrations of the British Labour Party the following winter. He concluded by emphasising that he and fellow members of the Labour Party would of course be in continuous contact with individual members of DNA at International Socialist conferences.[591] In an intriguing postscript, he added that he had heard that the Norwegian government had been considering sending Arne Ording to their embassy in London as Commercial Counsellor. He very much hoped that this would happen, since he had quite an influence within DNA, as well as being a most likeable man. It is not clear where this report came from, and no further information is available in the archives:

---

[589] Collier to Bevin, 2 March 1949, N2243/1016/30, FO 371/77436.
[590] Hankey to Healey, 1 April 1949, N2243/1016/30, FO 371/77436.
[591] Healey to Hankey, 4 April 1949, N3254/1016/30, FO 371/77436.

8 THE RELATIONSHIP AT WORK AND ITS SUDDEN END: 1949 TO OCTOBER 1951

nor do Ording's diaries, which conclude on 4 April 1949, the day of Healey's letter and of the signature of the Atlantic Treaty, make any mention of it.

Earnshaw's report on the DNA conference noted that the British Labour Party was the only non-Nordic party to participate in the conference. He commented that all the parties represented were responsible for the government of their respective countries. Although he gave no details of his speech or the nature of his own participation, he wrote in some detail about the foreign policy debate. He observed that hitherto it had been estimated that between a quarter and a third of the membership of DNA had been opposed to Norwegian participation in the Atlantic pact. However, this had been based largely on the idea that some sort of joint Scandinavian defence would be possible. As a result of the unanimous resolution of the conference, this view had now ceased to be expressed.[592]

It is likely that Collier realised that the small size of the international department of the Labour Party, and its increasing number of foreign commitments, would make it difficult to sustain the level of contacts which had been achieved during the early post-war period. This probably encouraged him to write again as he did on a subject on which his opinions would already have been well known in London. Moreover, he soon found another opportunity to comment on both the quantity and quality of exchanges between the two labour movements. In early March he wrote to Hankey that Earnshaw's presence at the DNA conference had had a good effect. He added a further comment which echoed the views of Inman about Luke Fawcett in 1946:

> What I did not say there, was that the delegate in question, though he did his best and was far better than nobody at all, was not a very impressive personality and that it would be worthwhile in these cases to send out someone who is a good speaker and a good mixer and who can

---

[592] Report by Harry Earnshaw on the DNA Conference 17-18 February, written for the international sub-committee of the National Executive Committee, March 1949, Healey papers, Labour Party archive, Manchester.

talk to the leading Norwegian DNA personalities (who are usually very well educated and intelligent people) on their own level.[593]

Collier's initiatives to arrange British participation at LO's national conference

Collier did not allow his reservations about the quality of visiting representatives from the British labour movement to deflect him from trying to arrange further opportunities for their participation in significant events in Norway. He noted that a further chance for a visit would be provided by the national conference of LO in late May, especially since the Storting had invited a British delegation from the Inter Parliamentary Union (IPU) to visit for a week from 15 May. If that delegation could include an MP who was also a trade unionist, he could also attend the LO conference, thus saving money. Highlighting the possible advantages, he commented that if he were a prominent MP he would presumably be a better speaker. Collier was aware that the Foreign Office could not directly influence the choice of members for an IPU delegation, but he presumed that their political chiefs could find a means of doing this.[594] The Foreign Office did its best to implement Collier's suggestion. Etherington-Smith suggested to Hankey that Mayhew might mention these views confidentially to the TUC. He understood that the IPU chairman, Milner, would be consulting Mayhew about the composition of the delegation, and thought that it would be wise to discuss the subject informally with the TUC and IPU before

---

[593] There is no evidence to show that Collier's remarks were passed on to Healey or anyone outside the Foreign Office. As a member of the international sub-committee of the National Executive, Earnshaw frequently travelled abroad to party conferences. For example, he went to Stockholm in May 1948 to attend the conference of the Swedish Social Democratic party. Report for the international sub-committee, Healey papers, Labour Party archive, Manchester.
[594] Collier to Hankey, 3 March 1949, N2436/1016/30, FO 371/77436.

this approach.⁵⁹⁵ Mayhew agreed to speak to Tewson, the general secretary of the TUC.

The subsequent process was not entirely straightforward, partly because the Chief Whip was displeased to find that Milner had selected a delegation for this visit without consulting him first. However, a trade unionist MP, McLeavy, was considered suitable and was eventually chosen. It turned out that he was unable to play a large part in the conference: LO had decided not to invite foreign trade unions because of the prevailing tension in the international trade union movement, and because the question of Norwegian resignation from the WFTU was on the agenda for discussion. Only the ILO office and Scandinavian trades union organisations were invited. However, McLeavy was able to be present at the opening ceremony on the first day, though he did not make a speech or take any official part in the proceedings.⁵⁹⁶ After a long debate, the conference decided that LO should withdraw from the WFTU, and should start the process of contributing towards the establishment of a successor organisation.

It is interesting to note that there was some support for the idea that Haakon Lie should become the general secretary of the organisation which was subsequently created, the International Confederation of Free Trade Unions (ICFTU). Arnfinn Guldvog, the labour attaché in Washington, wrote to Nordahl that he had heard that both American labour organisations were ready to support Lie as a candidate for the post. However, they had heard that neither Sweden nor Denmark (particularly Sweden, which held strong views on the subject of Lie's suitability) would be willing to support this idea. They were opposed to Lie's candidature. The Americans did not wish to press their view against such opposition, even though they were not enthusiastic about either Schevenels or Oldenbroek, other possible candidates.⁵⁹⁷ It was Oldenbroek who was subsequently elected general secretary. There is, not surprisingly, archival evidence which shows that the

---

[595] Minuting in March 1949 between Etherington-Smith, Mayhew and Gee (Labour adviser), N2436/1016/30, FO 371/77436.

[596] Despatch by Crowe, chargé d'affaires, and minute by Inman, 9 June 1949, N5260/1016/30, FO 371/77436.

[597] Guldvog to Nordahl, 20 September 1949, Nordahl korrespondanse, D 0001, Arbeiderbevegelsens arkiv.

TUC and LO had for some time been closely involved in a discussion of policy and tactics relating to withdrawal from the WFTU and that the embassy had also facilitated some of the exchanges. Nordahl and Bell (the international secretary of the TUC) had discussed the issue when they met in Geneva in late 1948. Soon afterwards, Inman wrote to Bell in November 1948, asking for a meeting when he visited London the following month. He wanted information, on behalf of Nordahl, 'on the policy of the TUC towards the WFTU, about which the LO was much concerned'.[598] Inman subsequently wrote to Nordahl, outlining the views of Bell on the TUC's approach to several important tactical aspects.[599]

Visit of Vic Feather, assistant general secretary of the TUC

It is difficult to gauge the precise impact which Collier's renewed recommendations may have had on the Foreign Office, the Labour Party and the TUC. They would surely have helped to explain why Vic Feather, then assistant general secretary of the TUC, visited Oslo in October 1949. The embassy was much involved in arranging his programme. Mason wrote to Alfred Skar at LO in September, outlining the nature of the commitments which Feather might undertake. He would be willing to make one or two speeches on trade unions and nationalisation and full employment, and wished to study The LOorganisation. This was arranged, and Feather's visit took place from 19-22 October.[600] There was some follow-up from this, because during his visit, Feather met Asbjørn Larsen, the labour correspondent of *Arbeiderbladet*. Mason wrote to Feather about Larsen in the following month: Feather replied on 21 November that he would shortly be seeing him to discuss the International

---

[598] Inman to Bell, 26 November 1948, 292/948/2, TUC archive, Warwick University.
[599] Inman to Nordahl, 23 December 1948, Nordahl korrespondanse, D 0001, Arbeiderbevegelsens arkiv.
[600] Mason to Skar, 24 September 1949, and Skar to Mason, 29 September 1949, LO File, D Dd 0047, Arbeiderbevegelens arkiv.

which would be replacing the WFTU.[601] However, sometimes planned arrangements fell through. Healey wrote to Lie in December to say that despite an earlier commitment to do so, the national executive had decided not to invite Scandinavian prime ministers to the fiftieth anniversary jubilee of the Labour Party in February 1950. Apart from the difficulties of excluding representatives of socialist parties from outside Scandinavia, they had realised that there would be a problem over the timing of the general election. It could not be held later than June, and so the February jubilee would have something of the character of a pre-election meeting, in which it would be undesirable to have the heads of foreign governments involved. He nevertheless hoped that the opportunity for an invitation might arise later.[602]

The parties continued to keep in touch both with each other and with political developments through less formal means. For example, Bratteli, the labour attaché in London, continued to write to Lie quite regularly providing information and commentary on events in Britain. He wrote a congratulatory letter after the DNA conference in February 1949, noting that news of the outcome of the foreign policy debate had been received with the greatest interest in London, and it was remarkable to see how 'The Norwegian Labour Party' had taken the headlines in the newspapers. He also commented on favourable by-election results for the Labour Party, most recently in South Hammersmith. In reply, Lie observed that DNA was optimistic after the election in Hammersmith and were hoping for an election in Britain before the Norwegian election in the autumn.[603] This did not happen, but at the election on 10 October, DNA won a resounding victory, winning eighty-five seats (against seventy-six in 1945) providing an overall majority of twenty while the communist party (NKP) despite polling over

---

[601] Exchange of letters between Mason and Feather, November 1949, 292/948/2, TUC Archives.
[602] Healey to Lie, 14 December 1949, Lie arkiv, Internasjonale forbindelser, Dc 0003, Arbeiderbevegelsens arkiv.
[603] Bratteli to Lie, 25 February 1949, and Lie to Bratteli, 28 February 1949, Sosialattacheen i London, Bratteli privat post, UD utenriksstasjoner, ambassaden i London, Boks 684.99/9, Riksarkiv.

100,000 votes (about forty per cent down on their turnout in 1945), won none, losing all eleven of their seats.

Development of regular reporting on communist activities

In the immediate postwar period, the embassy had been reporting regularly on communist and NKP activities as a part of its general political work. Many of the early despatches were based on reporting from Inman. For example, he commented in May 1946 on relations between DNA and NKP, noting that DNA had embarked on an energetic campaign to discredit the leadership of NKP and to detach waverers from the rank and file.[604] A year later, Collier reported that the communists had been similarly trying to weaken DNA by infiltrating the trade unions and by propaganda, although they had been matched by a DNA counter-campaign. DNA had had no opportunity to make an all-out attack with good prospects of success until publicity over the Svalbard question enabled them to represent the communists as habitually subordinating the interests of their fellow countrymen of the working class to those of a foreign dictatorship. In this despatch, Collier noted the Machiavellian tactics of DNA, and praised them.[605] At the end of January 1948, Inman reported on the action which had been taken by the leadership of the Norwegian Seamens' Union against communist activities among Norwegian seamen, highlighting the suspension of Leif Vetlesen, a communist official of the union.[606] Shortly afterwards, the embassy reported that the NKP had taken delivery of ten new typesetting machines which had been manufactured in East Germany, five of which were given to *Friheten*, and three to *Arbeidet* in Bergen.[607]

---

[604] Despatch signed by Wardrop as chargé d'affaires (though drafted by Collier), covering report by Inman, 24 May 1946, N7061/16/30, FO 371/56277.
[605] Collier to Bevin, 6 June 1947, N6812/4496/30, FO 371/66059.
[606] Collier to Attlee, 30 January 1948, covering a report by Inman, N1525/1525/30, FO 371/71498.
[607] Chancery to Northern Department, 19 February 1948, N2056/1525/30, FO 371/71498.

8 THE RELATIONSHIP AT WORK AND ITS SUDDEN END: 1949 TO OCTOBER 1951

By the spring of 1948, as concerns continued to grow about the nature of the threat from Russia, the Foreign Office had decided that it needed to have regular reporting on communist activities in key countries. In March, Warner sent a telegram to the majority of posts which had not yet replied to the earlier circular announcing the establishment of IRD. In addition to reminding them of the need for comments on methods of implementing the new policy, he requested that they provide regular and detailed information about communist organisations and activities in their areas of responsibility.[608] Stockholm started to send in reports every week, and Northern Department – noting that they were giving particularly close attention to communist activities in Scandinavia and western countries at that time – asked other posts to copy the practice and ensure that their reports were also copied to IRD.[609] Collier felt this was too frequent. He wrote to Hankey to say that Oslo intended to provide monthly reports. He thought it would be a waste of effort to collect material for reports when there was likely to be nothing available. Moreover, if the reports were too frequent, then the information would come in such small driblets that the authorities at home would not pay proper attention to it. He preferred to wait until he had something important to say.[610] The first report (for June) in this series has been retained, as have several others later in the year.[611] The second report, at the end of June, referred to the earlier one, noting that it had described a quiet and in some respects uncertain month for the NKP. The highlights had been that DNA had successfully continued its campaign to isolate communist elements and that, in Sandefjord, the communist chairman and vice-chairman of the Iron and Metal Workers'

---

[608] Circular telegram from Warner, 4 March 1948, PR40/1/913G, FO 1110/2.
[609] Northern Department circular letter to Scandinavian posts, 1 April 1948, N3361/842/42, FO 371/71731.
[610] Collier to Hankey, 28 April 1948, N5148/1525/30, FO 371/71498.
[611] The June report was contained in N5148/1525/30, FO 371/71498. There is other material in linked jackets in N6513/1525/30, N6300/1525/30 and N6513/1525/30 which is probably on the same subject. All have been retained under Section 3 (4), and presumably therefore deal with intelligence-related aspects of this report.

Union had been voted out of office. It observed that communist activity of a more directly subversive nature was no doubt still continuing, but the only recent evidence of this was a report at the end of May (no source was cited) from the Swedish frontier near Stromstad, alleging that arms were being smuggled into Norway.[612]

Subsequent reports often tended to emphasise international exchanges rather than domestic activities, because they appeared to be of more significance, for example the visit by a Norwegian delegation to a peace congress in Wroclaw in August. The report for July commented that there was nothing new of any importance, though it added that the NKP was pursuing its routine tasks with an industriousness which some other Norwegian parties might well emulate. It also contained some interesting results from a Gallup poll conducted to obtain a general view of the loyalty of the NKP to Norway in the event of a war. Sixty per cent of respondents considered that Norwegian communists would work for the Russians, while only fifteen per cent thought that they would work for Norwegian interests.[613] Many of the subsequent reports for this year contained reporting by Inman on the strike at the Herøya chemical works, owned by Norsk Hydro. Inman observed that the strike had been denounced as a communist manoeuvre, and was thought to be part of Cominform policy designed to cause the maximum amount of trouble in countries receiving Marshall aid.[614]

Northern Department attached importance to these reports, but wrote to Oslo asking for them to be submitted in a different form. Collier baulked at this request. In a spirited and successful attempt to avoid additional and burdensome bureaucracy, he wrote to Hankey to express the opinion, based on a good deal of past experience, that such questionnaires and similar cast-iron regulations for reports caused on balance more trouble than they saved. Hankey

---

[612] Chancery to Northern Department, 30 June 1948, containing the monthly report on communist activities in Norway, N7595/1525/30, FO 371/71498.
[613] Monthly report on communist activities for July 1948, N9313/1525/30, FO 371/71498.
[614] Crowe to Bevin, 13 October 1948, covering a report by Inman, N10994/1525/30, FO 371/71498.

8 THE RELATIONSHIP AT WORK AND ITS SUDDEN END: 1949 TO OCTOBER 1951

minuted 'quite right' in the margin of this letter, and left Collier to make his own decisions concerning their format.[615] All reports on communist activities in Norway continued to be routinely copied to IRD. Watson asked for Oslo to report by telegram any appeal in a communist paper for a strike in the merchant navy, commenting that it was the sort of subject which IRD could make good use of.[616]

The embassy continued to report regularly on communist activities throughout 1949, although towards the end of the year they reduced the frequency of the reports to one every two months. One of the most significant was a despatch by Collier in March. In it, he reported that at an NKP meeting in Oslo, Emil Løvlien had made a declaration of solidarity with the view recently expressed by Thorez, Togliatti and Pollitt on behalf of the French, Italian and British communist parties. This view was that in the event of a war with the Soviet Union, the communists would fight on the Soviet side against the forces of their own countries. This was gleefully and widely reported by the non-communist press in Norway. IRD were predictably interested, describing it as most gratifying. They noted that the position of the Norwegian communists showed most clearly the extent of the tremendous handicap imposed on communist parties by compelling them slavishly to conform to Moscow. This robbed them of room to manoeuvre.[617] A further report later in the year noted that the left-wing MP Konni Zilliacus had visited Norway for a week in September and had made a series of attacks on the foreign policy of the British government. He had been invited by the 'nominally pacifist but really communist Temporary Peace Committee' under Mimi Sverdrup Lunden, whom he had met at the Paris Peace Conference in 1949. The same report observed that on foreign policy, the attack on the Atlantic pact had been subsumed into the general peace offensive, which was being pursued in Norway

---

[615] Northern Department to Collier, 5 August 1948, N5290/302/G, FO 371/71498. The subsequent exchange between Collier and Hankey is on N9313/1525/30 FO 371/71498

[616] Watson's minute to Northern Department, 24 December 1948, N12277/1525/30, FO 371/71498.

[617] Collier to Bevin, 5 March 1949, and subsequent minuting within IRD, N2437/1015/30, FO 371/77435.

as elsewhere by means of special peace committees such as the one which invited Zilliacus to Norway.[618]

Norwegian reporting on communist activities in Britain

Bratteli, the Norwegian labour attaché in London, like Inman, served several different masters and provided occasional detailed reporting on communist activities to DNA, to LO and to the Foreign Ministry as well as to the Ministry of Social Affairs which employed him. For example, Lie wrote to him in December 1947, asking for a copy of Harry Pollitt's 'Statement of Policy to the Executive Committee of the British Communist Party' and some of his other speeches which announced that the communists were going to start a production offensive. Lie assumed that the communists would be changing the signals which they were putting out in Norway as well, so he considered that it would be useful to be ready for them before they had started. He wrote that on a forthcoming visit to London, he would be meeting people who dealt with propaganda, with a view to starting a similar campaign in Norway early in 1948.[619] Some of Bratteli's reports, for example on the communist offensive against the government, were copied by the Ministry of Social Affairs to LO, as well as to the prime minister's office and the Norwegian employers' association.[620]

---

[618] Embassy report on communist activities for July, August and September, 5 October 1949, N8763/1015/30, FO 371/77435. Although they do not appear to have met during any of his visits to Norway, Zilliacus knew Collier quite well because they had been contemporaries at Bedales school. Furthermore, Collier was in no doubt that Zilliacus was a communist. (Conversation with his son, William Collier, 7 September 2006.) Others, such as Christopher Mayhew and Ian Mikardo, did not share this view: see for example Christopher Mayhew, *A War of Words* (IB Tauris, 1998), p107, which also quotes the opinion of Mikardo, who did not consider Zilliacus a communist.
[619] Lie to Bratteli, 19 December 1947, Bratteli to Lie, 29 December 1947, Kommunistene i England, Boks 556.25/4/12a, Riksarkiv. No archival record of this visit has been found.
[620] Bratteli to the Ministry of Social Affairs, 9 January 1948, Kommunistene i England, Boks 556.25/4/12a, Riksarkiv.

8 THE RELATIONSHIP AT WORK AND ITS SUDDEN END: 1949 TO OCTOBER 1951

In the course of the next year, Bratteli wrote a series of reports on communist activities in Britain. The subjects which he covered included the mineworkers and the communists, the position of the TUC towards the communists and the WFTU, British trade unionists and the communists, and British communists and the TUC. Keen to ensure that the Norwegian trade unionists acted in step with them, Tewson sometimes sent Bratteli confidential statements about TUC policy, which he forwarded to Nordahl.[621]

The split in NKP: how IRD exploited the propaganda opportunity

Not surprisingly, the embassy reported in some detail on the split in the NKP. The split occurred after the inquest which had examined why NKP had done so badly in the general election in October 1949, when it lost all its seats. The most detailed reporting is contained in IRD files, rather than in those of Northern Department. In October, Mason reported on the meeting of officials who gathered in Oslo to discuss the circumstances of the NKP's defeat, when Strand Johansen (a former NKP Storting member for Oslo) had violently attacked Peder Furubotn and his group and maintained that they were responsible for the electoral defeat. Following this, the Løvlien group, led by Johansen, had broken into NKP offices, as well as those of *Friheten* and the communist youth movement, and ejected the so-called 'Titoists'. The following day, *Friheten* published a story which criticised Furubotn as a hostile element in the party, 'who was of a Trotskyist and Titoist nature'. It concluded that only by getting rid of such subversive elements could the NKP solve its problems.[622] Mason reported shortly afterwards that the situation at that time

---

[621] Reports from Bratteli to the Ministry of Social Affairs on these subjects were sent between 14 October 1948 and 13 January 1949. The personal and confidential letter from Tewson to Bratteli contained a copy of a statement which had been sent to all TUC-affiliated organisations in Britain in connection with TUC policy towards the WFTU. It commented on disruptive activities being carried out by communists 'in servile obedience to the decisions made by the body calling itself the Cominform.' Kommunistene i England, Boks 556.25/4/12a, Riksarkiv.
[622] Mason to IRD, 27 October 1949, PR3268/62/G, FO 1110/262.

was still fluid and the results were unpredictable. However, Johansen had had a complete nervous breakdown and was in hospital. He appeared to be worried about the Furubotn group having a secret military organisation in Norway and he alleged that he had been exposed to threats of murder by the Furubotn group. The police were investigating the possible existence of a secret military organisation in the country: the press released a dated report, which had originally been suppressed at the time at police request, of some military exercises and training which Furubotn and his group were alleged to have been organising in the Valdres region in the autumn of 1948.[623] Mason also noted how *Arbeiderbladet* had used the opportunity to attack the NKP, its treachery and its willingness to accept direction from abroad. He quoted an editorial which commented that 'fear and terror are the Cominform's first weapon, but they can act as a boomerang against those who use them. Strand Johansen has been sacrificed to his own party's policy, tactics and strategy'.[624]

In internal minuting on this correspondence, IRD considered whether this material would be sufficient for an article, and concluded that it would fit with other material which was being prepared for a proposed article on the internal dilemma of the world's communist parties. The article concerned cannot be located, since it has not been released to the archives. It was very probably linked to an article entitled 'The case of Hr Johansen', which was quite widely circulated in late 1949. It was possible to establish the existence of this article by scrutinising the Index of Foreign Office documents at the National Archive. However, a search of the catalogue showed that this document, and other related material, had not subsequently been transferred into the archives. Thus, PR 3629/11/913, shown in the 1949 index under 'Communism in Norway', refers to an IRD paper entitled 'The Case of Hr Johansen'. An annex to Ralph Murray's report for the second half of 1949[625] shows that this was an article written by Paul Anderson (an author frequently used by IRD) which

---

[623] Mason to IRD, 2 November 1949, PR 3369/62/G, FO 1110/262.
[624] Ibid.
[625] Murray's report covering 1 August to 31 December 1949, 15 February 1950, PR110/5/G, FO 1110/359.

described the purges in the NKP in October 1949 following the poor performance of the party in the national elections earlier that month. Furthermore, an analysis of IRD reporting carried out by Harris, who assessed 110 reports during this period, showed that this article was replayed in Turkey, Holland, Greece, Trieste, Belgium, Burma and Colombia.[626] PR 3629/11/913 would no doubt have provided some useful insights into the genesis of the article, the process by which it was commissioned and circulated and how IRD had worked in Norway.

Continuing decline of the NKP

In his annual review for 1949, Collier commented that the NKP had been greatly weakened by the split and would feel its effects for a long time to come. Furthermore, he noted that the national opposition to communism, which had developed rapidly during the previous two years, had now become unshakeable and absolute. DNA was continuing to campaign to destroy NKP's influence in the trade unions, in which they had lost many posts.[627] A report in the following October noted that communist influence in the executives of trade unions had practically disappeared, and that only a handful of communist delegates had attended the annual LO conference.[628] The extraordinary congress of the NKP, which took place in February 1950, effectively put the seal on the attempts by Løvlien to extend his control over the whole of the party, though Furubotn remained active and continued to attract some support, as the membership of the NKP gradually declined further. It was shortly after this that the Foreign Office decided to request only quarterly reports on

---

[626] Analysis of IRD reporting in late 1949 by Harris, 10 May 1950, PR110/2/G, FO 1110/359.
[627] Oslo annual review for 1949, 23 February 1950, NN1011/1, FO 371/86534.
[628] Oslo quarterly report on communist activities, 14 October 1950, NN1016/9, FO 371/86536.

communist activities in future.[629] The format which was now required still covered a significant range of detail:
1. Organisation and strength of the party.
2. Penetration: effected or attempted. (This usually referred to penetrations of moderate trade union organisations.)
3. Cover organisations and fellow travellers.
4. Propaganda.
5. Trade Unions.
6. Domestic and foreign policy.
7. Foreign contacts.
8. Sabotage.

The Korean war also had an adverse influence on support for the NKP, which continued to dwindle. By the middle of 1951, the embassy was sending only a six-monthly report on communism, noting that the situation had been very quiet, especially during the first quarter, and they had not thought it worth sending a report in April. The embassy estimated that the NKP had an actual membership of about 8,600 and that this figure was very close to the hard core which was not likely to be much further reduced.[630] The NKP lost some further ground during the municipal elections which were held in the autumn of 1951, though not as much as the embassy had first been inclined to think.[631]

DNA's contribution to British and American reporting on communist activities

Bergh and Eriksen provide some details of methods used by both British and American intelligence services, as well as diplomats, to obtain information on communists and communist activities in Norway during this period. They note that Asbjørn Bryhn, the head of the Norwegian security service POT, later concluded a formal agreement on cooperation with the CIA during a visit to the United States

---
[629] Reference to Northern Department letter to Oslo, 14 March 1950, N2191/16, contained in Oslo letter to Northern Department, 12 April 1950, N1016/7, FO 371/86536.
[630] Six-monthly report on communist activities, July 1951, NN1016/2/G, FO 371/94665.
[631] Oslo to Foreign Office, 15 October 1951, NN1015/5, FO 371/94664.

8 THE RELATIONSHIP AT WORK AND ITS SUDDEN END: 1949 TO OCTOBER 1951

in 1953, and provide details of the wide range of information which was exchanged on this subject.[632] However, they found no record of any corresponding agreement between Norway and Britain.[633] Bergh and Eriksen also describe the extent to which the two embassies obtained information on communist activities in Norway through frequent contacts with DNA, and in particular with Haakon Lie. They note that the senior leadership of DNA would have been aware, and approved of, his activities. They also provide an example of material (party reports on communist activities in Finnmark) which he later passed to the British embassy in 1953.[634] These reports are interesting because they analyse the factors which enabled NKP to obtain an increase in votes at the 1953 municipal elections, at a time when DNA lost over 5,000 votes in the same area.[635] They are also significant because they are the only example in the archives of such explicit material being passed to the British embassy in written form by Lie or by DNA, although the manner of drafting of many of the embassy's regular reports on communist activities strongly suggests that they frequently drew on privileged, though perhaps oral, briefings from DNA.

IRD activities in Norway after 1948

There is less material in the archives on IRD activities and usage in Norway in the period after 1948. This is probably partly due to there generally being more work involved in establishing a new organisation such as IRD, in obtaining agreement on new policies and in determining how to implement them. The documents which have been released to the archives reflect the greater importance of most aspects of this work during the first few months of IRD's existence, compared with the relatively more routine work which was carried out in subsequent years. Nonetheless, sufficient information has survived to provide a clear picture of significant aspects of

---

[632] Bergh and Eriksen, *Den hemmelige krigen - overvåking i Norge 1914 -1997*, p499.
[633] Ibid, p504.
[634] Ibid, pp504-5.
[635] Cullis to Hohler, 20 November 1953, NN1016/3, FO 371/106363.

IRD work, the usage of its material in Norway, and the contacts through which it achieved its most significant objectives.

Among the first exchanges, there was a misunderstanding in London. Early in 1949, Collier reported a request from Lange for assistance in presenting the case for the Atlantic pact to the Norwegian public. The Foreign Office misinterpreted the nature of this report, and thought that the kind of assistance which Lange sought referred to propaganda work to be done in Norway which could best be provided though advice from IRD. They suggested that they should send Murray out to Oslo the following week. They added that any arrangement would have to be confidential, and wanted to be sure that their approach would not result in leakages concerning the existence of IRD. Murray minuted enthusiastically that this appeared to be a golden opportunity 'to have the Norwegian government working with us. I think that we can go further with them than with the Brussels powers, on the basis of the contacts made by Mr Kenney, and provide them with polemical stuff as well as with pure research material.'[636] However, Collier pointed out that the context of Lange's remarks made it clear that his appeal for help with the Norwegian public referred to something else: the need for the British and American governments to present the policy on the Atlantic pact so as to command maximum approval in Oslo, both by the answers to the questions to be put to them and by their public statements on that policy. He did not imply that he needed help in organising the means of putting the Alliance case before the Norwegian public if the case itself was unsatisfactory. It was unlikely that a visit by Murray would serve any useful purpose.[637] He therefore did not go.

Continuing widespread use of IRD material in Norway

In its early years, IRD considered that one of its most striking successes had been the campaign on the Forced Labour Codex. IRD asked posts abroad to report on the extent to which the information provided on the Codex had been

---

[636] Exchange of telegrams between Oslo and the Foreign Office, February 1949, and minute by Murray, 4 February 1949, PR 249/62/G, FO 1110/252.
[637] Oslo to Foreign Office, 5 February 1949, PR251/62/G, FO 1110/252.

used in their local media.⁶³⁸ Mason reported that Oslo had achieved maximum publicity for the material on this subject. *Arbeiderbladet* had carried a news item and two long leading articles. There had also been coverage in *Aftenposten, Morgenbladet* and *Morgenposten* and the right-wing press agency and DNA press agencies had both sent out specially written articles to the thirty to forty newspapers on their lists throughout the country.⁶³⁹ Runacres in IRD commented that Oslo had done well with the material.

In January 1950, Mason reported on usage for the previous month, listing twelve articles which had been placed in the local press. Miss C. S. Harris (IRD) commented that Oslo placed very little IRD material directly. The bulk of it was incorporated into two embassy bulletins which went to forty-six left-wing and forty conservative and liberal papers. This was considered a more effective procedure than using party news agencies. The conservative press agency had refused recently to handle any more IRD material following a disparaging reference to the League of Nations in an article by Wickham Steed. Harris noted that Mason estimated that seventy-five per cent of the material in Oslo bulletins was published. She was somewhat sceptical of this figure, but noted that in the last quarterly report, the ambassador had written that results of the new procedure were 'phenomenal' and that some provincial papers were practically filled with IRD material. She was, however, slightly critical of the statistics for December which had fallen a little by comparison with previous results – though an IRD colleague, Maclaren, minuted that there was little to complain about in the figures.⁶⁴⁰ In a separate assessment, Harris analysed the usage of 110 IRD articles, on the basis of feedback from local information officers, in an attempt to evaluate the marketability of IRD articles as a whole. She noted that regular monthly reports were received from Oslo, among other countries, although the report quoted here is the only one which has survived. Norway was among those most often mentioned as achieving

---

⁶³⁸ FO Circular, 4 July 1949, PR1757/5/913, FO1110/174.
⁶³⁹ Mason to IRD, 26 July 1949, PR 2101/5/913, FO 1110/174.
⁶⁴⁰ Mason to IRD, 2 January 1950, minute by Harris, 16 January 1950, PR 41/1, FO 1110/314.

publication of these listed 110 articles. A total of twenty-nine articles from the list were published. Many of those which were unused concerned Islamic or colonial subjects which would have been of no interest in Norway. Oslo was particularly pleased with the extent of the usage of material on the Nazi-Soviet pact, and Soviet genocide.[641]

Ineffective Russian reactions to anti-communist propaganda in Norway

The Russian foreign ministry contains records of several Russian complaints about anti-Soviet and anti-communist propaganda during this period. Ambassador Afanasiev wrote to Deputy Foreign Minister Zorin in August 1949, noting that the Norwegian press was publishing more and more such material, activity which he considered to be linked to the beginning of the general election campaign. He thought that it had been produced by enemies of the Soviet Union, including American and other experts. He quoted the titles of a series of articles which had been recently published in *Arbeiderbladet* which, he considered, had been 'cooked up' by the so-called American experts on the Soviet Union.[642] There is insufficient information to permit an assessment of whether IRD or some other agency might have provided the material on which these articles were based. However, it was noted in Chapter Five that in late 1948, Murray had offered Kenney 'a terrific document on trade unions in the Soviet Union' which he thought could be of use to DNA in developing their election propaganda, as well as a study of human rights in the Soviet Union, which Watson subsequently instructed Mason to pass to DNA.[643] DNA would therefore have had plenty of material to draw on during this period, as well as reasonable time to prepare it. To counter this propaganda, the Soviet embassy recommended making an attempt to increase the level of information provided in Norway about

---

[641] Report by Harris, 10 May 1950, PR110/2/G, FO 1110/359.
[642] Afanasev to Zorin, 9 August 1949, AVPRF f. 0116, op. 38 p. 150 d. 2, ll 53-54.
[643] Murray to Kenney, 17 November 1948, PR1069/60/913G, FO1110/112, Watson to Mason, 21 December 1948, PR1229/760/913G, FO1110/112.

the Soviet Union. This should include more use of material from TASS and an increase in radio broadcasts to Norway: Afanasiev provided advice on the subjects which should be covered in these areas, which should include the negative consequences for Norwegian workers of participation in the Marshall Plan, as well as the effects of joining the Atlantic pact.[644] It is not clear to what extent this recommendation was acted on, but the election results could scarcely have been more disappointing to the communists.

Afanasiev complained again the following year about the increasingly sharp tone of hostility towards the Soviet Union in the Norwegian press, in particular in *Arbeiderbladet*. He recommended that a strong protest should be made to the Norwegian government.[645] Orlov recommended to Zorin that a protest should be made, but not as strongly as on a previous occasion in January 1948, because this time the anti-Soviet statements had been made in the press and did not come from official sources. The protest note which he submitted specified a number of hostile editorials which had been published between March and June of that year. It maintained that the purpose of *Arbeiderbladet,* in publishing these articles, was to create a misleading picture in Norway about Soviet foreign policy and to create an atmosphere of open hostility towards the Soviet Union.[646]

In view of the extensive activity of DNA, supported by IRD and its American equivalent, it is perhaps surprising that there is little evidence to show why the Soviet embassy did not respond more strongly to the campaign which was being waged against the communists. Part of this work would have been carried out by the Soviet intelligence services, whose archives remain closed, and it is not therefore possible to make a judgment about its effectiveness. However, part of the explanation is also likely to be found in the indifferent quality of some of the work of the Soviet embassy in Oslo at that time, which provoked a complaint to Molotov by Maevsky, the deputy head of the fifth European

---

[644] Afanasev to Zorin, Ibid.
[645] Afanasev to Andrei Ia. Vishinsky, 8 June 1950, AVPRF f.07 op.23 p. 50 d. 325 ii. 1-4.
[646] Orlov to Zorin, 22 June 1950, AVPRF f. 0116 op. 39 p.156 d.16 i. 67.

department of the foreign ministry. In a long minute to Zorin, he noted that reports from the embassy were late and that they contained some significant errors. He also noted that the embassy had limited contacts in government and political circles, failed to update the assessments which they provided and did not always respond to requests from the foreign ministry for reports to be sent to them. These omissions included requests for reports on some of the subjects which would have been of greatest concern to the foreign ministry, and which included the peace movement, the trade unions and – most remarkably – DNA.[647]

It is difficult to think of subjects which could have been of greater concern to the foreign ministry than these. This probably contributed to the unusual situation in 1951 which was reported by the visiting Makins: the Russian Foreign Ministry used Konstantin K. Rodionov, the Soviet ambassador in Sweden, as the preferred channel for passing important messages to Lange via his Norwegian colleague in Stockholm. For example, Rodionov informed the Norwegian ambassador that Lange should not cooperate too enthusiastically with the Atlantic Pact and that in general Norway was too subservient to American policy. On a separate occasion, he said that the landing of American troops in Iceland was not regarded too seriously by the Soviet Union, but warned that the landing of American troops in western Norway would be a different matter and might have serious consequences.[648] Pharo and Eriksen take a similar view, based on material obtained by Holtsmark,[649] and a study of material in Norwegian Foreign Ministry archives, and conclude that the Soviet ambassador had a low status at that time. They note that his contacts were limited to formal ones, and to a small circle of communists and left-wing members of DNA. They consider that this probably contributed to the

---

[647] Note from Maevsky, acting deputy of the fifth European department, to Zorin, 27 April 1950, quoted in Holtsmark (ed.), *Norge og Sovietunionen 1917-1955, en utenrikspolitisk dokumentasjon*, pp443-444.
[648] Note by Makins, visiting deputy under secretary, enclosed with a despatch from Wright, 25 June 1951, N1052/1, FO 371/94444.
[649] Holtsmark (ed.), *Norge og Sovietunionen 1917-1955, En utenrikspolitisk dokumentasjon*.

fact that the embassy also gave a distorted picture of the political and economic situation in Norway.[650]

Budgetary cuts in information work in Western Europe: the Oslo information officer becomes the IRD regional representative

Information work in Western Europe was significantly cut back in 1951. The Foreign Office informed the embassy in Oslo that this would be necessary to meet the costs of maintaining the British defence effort, that the BBC service in Norwegian would cease, and that fifty per cent of the remaining information services in Norway would have to stop by the end of the financial year.[651] This had some significant effects, though in his half yearly report on information work, the new ambassador, Sir Michael Wright, commented favourably on what it was still possible to achieve through Cullis, who had replaced Mason as information officer. He noted that he was still hoping to obtain a replacement for the Labour attaché, Inman, who had left without being replaced. Northern Department minuted that the Labour Party and the TUC had a benevolent regard for Scandinavia and for that reason they hoped that a labour attaché could be posted to Oslo - though nothing came of this attempt.[652] It is worth noting that the Norwegian foreign service had also already suffered some cutbacks in 1950, when its budget had been cut by well over ten per cent and fifty-nine posts had been suppressed. Three press attaché posts were cut.[653] Norwegian labour attachés were not affected by economies during this period, although

---

[650] Pharo and Eriksen, *Kald Krig og internasjonalisering 1949-1962* (Universitetsforlaget, 1997).
[651] Foreign Office to Oslo, 13 January 1951, P1012/5/G, FO 953/1052.
[652] Information report for the first six months of 1951, Wright to Nicholls, 10 August 1951, PG 1304/1, FO 953/1144. In this report, Wright noted that budgetary cuts meant that Cullis had lost two of his staff of six in the information section, including his assistant whose post had been suppressed. At the same time, the American embassy had an information establishment of more than twenty, half-a-dozen of whom were officers of diplomatic rank. He slightly undermined his mild complaints about this situation by noting the compliments regularly paid by the press to his information staff, at the expense of the Americans.
[653] Minute by Mason, 3 March 1950, N1903/1, FO 371/86579.

there were occasional scares. For example, Salvesen wrote privately to Bratteli in 1949 to inform him that the Foreign Ministry was planning to cut the number of labour attachés from eight to one on budgetary grounds, without having asked the Ministry of Social Affairs for its view on this proposal – which in the event was not implemented.[654]

However, further economies in Britain soon became necessary, and in December the Foreign Office informed all posts in Scandinavia as well as Switzerland and Portugal that for pressing reasons of national economy, their information offices must be closed by the end of the financial year. In a personal letter, Nicholls in Northern Department explained the background to Wright, describing the problems which the Foreign Office had in finding any alternative areas to make the cuts. They could not touch the Middle East or South East Asia in the prevailing circumstances, and had cut posts in Latin America already.[655] However, it proved possible for Oslo to avoid closing their information office. Although the papers describing this have not survived, subsequent minuting on other issues makes clear that Cullis was retained in Oslo as the IRD representative, so that he could undertake work throughout Scandinavia on behalf of IRD. Apart from the posting of Adam Watson to Washington, this may have been the first time that IRD had its own representative abroad.[656] Separate minuting by Ching in IRD in the spring of 1953 also referred to the decision to offer Cullis employment as a member of IRD, and commented very favourably on the extent of his activities.[657] In a subsequent comment John Peck, who had succeeded Murray as head of IRD, noted that a member of the Norwegian Foreign Ministry had commented to a third party (not knowing that it would be reported back to the embassy) that Cullis was doing more to

---

[654] Salvesen, Ministry of Social Affairs, to Bratteli, November 1949, Sosialattacheen i London, Tjenestesaker, Boks 503.2/8, Riksarkiv.
[655] Foreign Office to Oslo, 27 December 1951, Nicholls to Wright 28, December 1951, P1032/1, FO 953/1175.
[656] There is minuting on PR44/11 (FO1110/496) in May and June 1952, on correspondence concerning a trip by Cullis to other posts in Scandinavia, which provides some background to this decision.
[657] Minute by Ching, 13 May 1953, PR 30/26/G, FO 1110/576.

damage communist interests in Norway than the whole of the American embassy put together.[658]

Cullis had earlier written to Peck to report on work he was doing with Haakon Lie to produce anti-communist propaganda. He noted that DNA and the Conservative Party had been busy attacking each other over the Price Control Bill, rather than their common enemy, the communists. Cullis discovered from Lie that his financial resources were limited, so he suggested that in their counter-propaganda over the Price Laws, DNA might emphasise that the opposition were not the only villains of the piece, but that the situation underlying the dispute was primarily the result of Soviet policy. Lie said that he was personally receptive, but that he would have to obtain the approval of DNA's central committee before taking such a line. He was successful. Cullis sent Peck a DNA leaflet which used just this argument, containing accusations against the communists for their responsibility in contributing to price increases, noting that they were responsible for starting the war in Korea and that in the two and a half years since the war had started there, prices in Norway had increased by over thirty per cent.

When was the Norwegian government briefed about the work of IRD?

In the early period after its establishment, IRD was determined to keep its existence secret. Sir Oliver Harvey wrote to Warner in April 1948, raising the question of whether the embassy should be doing anything covert in France. He did not believe that there was justification for starting a full-scale campaign on the territory of a close ally 'without at least informing the Minister of Foreign Affairs of our desire to do so and asking for his blessing'. After consulting Sir Orme Sargent, the PUS, Warner replied that there was no intention to go in for covert work in France – and that he was sure from recent indications that they would not obtain the approval of the Secretary of State for doing so. In such circumstances, he did not see a need to inform the French authorities that they were taking an anti-communist line

---

[658] Minute by Peck, 16 May 1953, PR30/26/G, FO 1110/576.

in their overt publicity.⁶⁵⁹ When the embassy in The Hague asked the same question shortly afterwards, they were told by Warner that they and the Belgians would be affected by the same decision as had been taken concerning the French – in other words, this ruling would apply to all the signatories of the Brussels pact.⁶⁶⁰ Warner acknowledged that the Foreign Office should aim at eventual co-operation with the governments of the Brussels pact and at the creation in due course of some inter-allied machinery for conducting anti-communist propaganda on behalf of the western democracies as a whole. However, this would take time.⁶⁶¹

IRD gradually became slightly less sensitive about providing at least a limited briefing to some of its closest allies. Murray's comments in February 1949, when it seemed as though he might need to visit Oslo to assist the Norwegian government ('I think that we can go further with them than with the Brussels powers, on the basis of the contacts made by Mr Kenney, and provide them with polemical stuff as well as with pure research material'), indicate that by then the Brussels powers had been given some sort of briefing – and that the Foreign Office would have been prepared to go even further with the Norwegian government.⁶⁶² Shortly afterwards, there was correspondence with Stockholm, when the embassy there reported that the Swedish Foreign Ministry was contemplating setting up the equivalent of an IRD, and Joedahl, the head of the press bureau in the ministry, sought some assistance. Murray was willing to encourage the initiative and, while asking how reliable the department could be considered to be, authorised a cautious initial briefing. However, there is no indication that this was taken further: a planned visit to London was not pursued.⁶⁶³

---

⁶⁵⁹ Harvey to Warner, 7 April 1948, Warner to Harvey, 10 May 1948, PR312/1/913G, FO 1110/9.
⁶⁶⁰ Chancery, The Hague to Warner, 20 May 1948, Warner to The Hague, 15 June 1948, PR346/1/913G, FO 1110/9.
⁶⁶¹ Circular telegram of 12 May 1948 to embassies in the countries of Brussels pact signatories, PR229/1/913G, FO1110/6.
⁶⁶² Minute by Murray, 4 February 1949, PR 249/62/G, FO 1110/252.
⁶⁶³ Exchange of correspondence between Bennett and Murray, March 1949, PR3/1/G, FO 1110/166.

8 THE RELATIONSHIP AT WORK AND ITS SUDDEN END: 1949 TO OCTOBER 1951

It is not clear when IRD may have authorised individual posts to take their host government into their confidence. However, several of the NATO powers were briefed in the course of 1949. Murray wrote to Sir Oliver Harvey in Paris in July to inform him about a visit by van Leetham, who had been directed by the French Foreign Ministry to establish a department in some respects similar to IRD, and who had been given a fairly full briefing, which lasted for four days.[664] The Dutch had also been given a briefing by the late summer. Replying to a letter from the ambassador who was pressing to take the Dutch fully into his confidence, Murray wrote, 'with regard to the subject of liaison with the Dutch over our anti-communist activities, I had hoped that our letter PR2263/39/G of 24 August 1949 gave you full discretion to keep the Dutch as fully informed as you felt desirable of the broad lines of our anti-communist activities, provided that this did not commit us to consulting the Netherlands government about everything we put out'.[665] When Peck addressed a conference of Western European information officers in September 1951, he said that members of NATO were obliged to do anti-communist work under the treaty and that IRD aimed to help smaller countries who had no Information Research Department of their own. They tried to make IRD work a combined operation with friendly states – but the fact that the British government was taking the lead in active anti-communism should still be kept as confidential as possible.[666]

No documents have been found – either in the National Archive or in any archive elsewhere – to show when a decision might have been taken to inform the Norwegian government of the nature of the work which IRD was performing. In view of the briefings carried out in 1949 in France, the Netherlands, other members of the Brussels Pact and fellow NATO members, it is likely that this happened around the same time. The material from this period gives plenty of evidence of the extent of activities by Cullis – for example,

---

[664] Murray to Harvey, 28 July 1949, PR2079/109/G, FO 1110/276.
[665] Murray to Nichols, The Hague, 6 February 1950, PR33/5/G, FO 1110/308.
[666] Minutes of a conference of Western European information officers, 12-14 September 1951, PR121/7, FO 1110/458.

the production and circulation of anti-communist pamphlets, printed locally by Schyberg. The first pamphlet, entitled 'Peace, as a Communist Weapon', ran to forty-eight pages. 5,000 copies were produced and it was to be sold at a price of one krone. IRD contributed to the costs of this venture.[667] They also provided some further assistance to DNA during its election campaign in 1953. For example, it was reported that an article based on 'Facts about the Soviet taxpayer' had been published by DNA as their main pamphleteering effort directed against the communists in the recent elections.[668]

The importance of the role played by labour attachés

Labour attachés were seen as very much the brainchild of Bevin, who had developed the system when he was minister of labour during the war. His first appointment was the posting of McDonald Gordon to Washington in September 1942: appointments to Paris, Rome and Stockholm followed in 1944 and to Cairo, Athens, Brussels and Helsinki in 1945.[669] However, the idea of appointing labour attachés had first been put forward before the first war, although it was not implemented then.[670] After the war, Bevin wanted to increase their number because he wanted the foreign policy of the Labour government to promote democratic socialism. Roger Murphy comments that Bevin believed the Foreign Office to be so elitist that diplomats could not understand working class conditions and movements abroad.[671] He would have been satisfied by the results. Labour attachés

---

[667] Cullis to Peck, 30 June 1953, PR30/31, FO 1110/576.
[668] Minutes of Western European regional meeting, 10 December 1953, PR103/14/G, FO 1110/615.
[669] Note prepared by the Foreign Office in reply to a request from the editor of the Industrial Welfare Journal, May 1946, FO366/1784.
[670] Maurice de Bunsen, ambassador in Vienna, recommended in May 1914 the appointment to embassies of attachés or secretaries whose 'special duty it would be to watch labour questions or social questions.' Fifth report of the Royal Commission appointed to inquire into the Civil Service, 1914-1916 (Cd7748) XI, P57. (Information provided by FCO Historians to Professor Patrick Salmon.)
[671] Roger Murphy, *Challenges from Within* (Ashgate Publishing, 2001), p74.

increased in number to twenty-three in 1952,[672] though they declined slightly thereafter as a result of cuts made by the Conservative government.

Although the Ministry of Labour considered that the job of an attaché was to report on labour conditions, industrial negotiating machinery and trade union organisations, most labour attachés quickly found themselves involved in political work and were able to develop wide-ranging sources of information and influence and to enjoy considerable freedom of action, as Inman did. Collier sent a considerable number of his reports on political, industrial and economic issues to the Foreign Office, which by mid-1947 had acquired Gee as its labour adviser. An example of Inman's involvement in sensitive political work was given in Chapter Three when it was described how he was used by Healey to brief Haakon Lie on the background to Bevin's Western Union speech, bypassing the Foreign Office and the embassy. It has already been noted that both Inman and Kenney were involved in passing messages between Healey and Lie. The frequency with which they did this does not appear to have been replicated elsewhere, a reflection of the closer relations which the Norwegian party enjoyed both with the British party and also with British officials. A contrasting picture can for example be seen in the Netherlands: the embassy in The Hague was concerned that when accepting a message from the Dutch Labour Party to pass to the British Labour Party, the labour attaché should be careful to avoid giving the impression that labour attachés were the representatives of political parties.[673] No such consideration was ever entertained in Oslo, where it has been demonstrated that links between DNA and many members of the embassy (not just the labour attaché) remained extremely close throughout this period. It is possible that Inman was able to act with greater flexibility

---

[672] Ibid, p74.
[673] The relevant document has not been deposited in the National Archive. The index description is 'Question of the labour attaché at The Hague accepting a message from the Dutch Labour Party for the British Labour Party; the importance of being careful to avoid giving the impression that that attachés are representatives of political parties.' The document reference is Z10674/1704/29 but it is not contained on FO371/67853C, where other documents on file 1704 have been placed.

because he was not appointed by the Ministry of Labour, but he would nevertheless have needed the support of Collier for most of his actions.

The decision to appoint an officer in the Foreign Office to specialise in labour relations was taken at the same meeting in November 1946 which discussed relations between the Foreign Office, the Labour Party and the TUC and which recommended that Healey be given confidential briefings via Mayhew. However, it took considerably longer to implement.[674] There were a number of reasons for this, not least because the Foreign Office wished to reach agreement with the Ministry of Labour on the responsibilities and terms of reference for the new post, the seniority of the job-holder, the number of staff who would support him and the department which he would work in.

During this period, there were also discussions about a proposal that labour attachés should collect information which would meet Joint Intelligence Bureau objectives. However, these papers have not been included in the file which has been sent to the archive. Since there are no references to this idea anywhere else in the indices in the National Archive, it is likely that it was mooted but then discarded as impractical.[675]

It was not only British labour attachés were able to fulfil this range of functions. Writing about Sam Berger, a close friend who was the labour attaché in the American embassy in London after the war, Healey commented that

---

[674] Minutes of the meeting chaired by McNeil to consider the question of relations between the Foreign Office, the Labour Party and the TUC, 5 November 1946, UNE/33/33/96, FO 371/67613. These papers show that Bevin developed the idea of closer contacts between these organisations after he had read the report written by Alice Bacon, Harold Laski, Morgan Phillips and Harold Clay on their goodwill visit to the Soviet Union in the summer of 1946. The visit included a meeting with Stalin which lasted well over two hours. This appears to have made Bevin realise the potential value of exchanges of information between the Foreign Office and the Labour Party. It was never possible to achieve similar results from the attempts to develop close links with the TUC.

[675] The relevant documents are UNE1919/33/96 and UNE 2374/33/96, described in the index as 'Collaboration between the Ministry of Labour and the JIB: proposals; discussions of;' and 'Proposals that HM Labour attachés should collect information on Joint Intelligence Bureau objectives: discussions on.'

8 THE RELATIONSHIP AT WORK AND ITS SUDDEN END: 1949 TO OCTOBER 1951

by developing good personal relations with many key figures in the British labour movement at the end of the war, including Sam Watson and Hugh Gaitskell, Berger exerted an enduring influence on British foreign policy.[676] There is evidence that Walter Galenson, the American labour attaché in Oslo immediately after the war, also played a similarly significant role in Norway. (Indeed, it would have been surprising if the American labour movement had not been attempting to develop contacts by using similar methods to those employed by the British labour movement. Some Norwegians, including Haakon Lie, had also spent time in the United States during the war and made use of the opportunity to develop their own links.) Lie wrote to Gerhardsen in early 1947 to pass on Galenson's comments about the views of State Department officials who were critical of the attitudes of the Norwegian UN delegation on Russia, but more particularly on Spain.[677] Norwegian labour attachés had similarly wide-ranging responsibilities, and also occasionally became involved in work of a sensitive political nature. For example Øksnes, the attaché in Paris, who frequently exchanged correspondence privately with Bratteli in London, wrote to him in April 1947 about a visit the previous month by Konrad Nordahl, the chairman of LO and Ingvald Haugen, the leader of the Norwegian Seamens' Union. They were concerned about a report that the Franco government was considering a ban on Norwegian ships entering Spanish ports. Øksnes told Bratteli that at Haugen's request, he had just had a further meeting with Trifon Gomez, the representative of the Spanish UGT in the Paris-based Giral government in exile. Øksnes sent him a copy of his letter to Haugen, asking Bratteli to treat it as confidential, because he had not sent any official report to the department on the subject.[678]

Although the dissemination of IRD material was the responsibility of information officers in posts abroad, labour

---

[676] Healey, *The Time of my Life*, p113.
[677] Lie to Gerhardsen, 27 February 1947, Lie arkiv, Internasjonale forbindelser, Dc0004, Arbeiderbevegelsens arkiv.
[678] Øksnes to Bratteli, 24 April 1947, Sosialattacheen i London, Tjenestesaker, UD utenriksstasjoner, ambassaden i London, Boks 503 2/8, Riksarkiv.

attachés had a valuable role to play in this work, not least through their ability to identify and often to approach key members of the labour movement who would be willing to receive and act upon material provided by IRD. For example, as was demonstrated in Chapter Five, Inman played an important role in drawing up the list of names of those who were considered suitable recipients of *Freedom First*. There are many similar examples to be found elsewhere: in 1950, the information officer in Athens wrote to Murray about his increased use of IRD material and his use of the labour attaché to send copies of the weekly digest to the main trade union leaders. He sought additional copies of the digest in French. In reply, Watson noted the increased importance of the labour field in Greece now that the civil war had ended.[679] The Foreign Office was always keen to arrange meetings with labour attachés when they came back to London on leave. A representative from IRD was invited to make a presentation to the labour attachés' conference in 1949, which was attended by nineteen of the twenty-one attachés who had by then been appointed. The agenda note stated that during the previous year a good deal of material, such as the digest and special pamphlets, had been published in various forms. It would be valuable to have the frank views of attachés on this material and the impact that it made.[680] Warner had earlier made clear his views on the value of labour attachés. He did so in a comment on the original response from the ambassador in Ankara to Bevin's circular No 6 announcing the establishment of IRD. As he rather ingeniously observed to Kelly (who had made no such specific proposal)

> It is not my province, in this connexion, to enquire whether a genuine labour attaché is in your mind, but in case you are thinking of putting the idea forward I may say that I should support it since such attachés are very valuable for

---

[679] Hebblethwaite to Murray, 7 February 1950, PR 60/6, FO 1110/329.
[680] Report on the conference of labour attachés in London, 1949, LAB 13/595. The minutes of this meeting, written several months after the event, give very few details of the discussion of IRD work, beyond noting – not surprisingly - that there were considerable variations in practice and requirements because of political and economic differences, language problems and the degree of literacy of the local population.

providing channels for the dissemination of information to the labour world.[681]

When John Inman left Oslo towards the end of 1949, he was not replaced, despite the best efforts of the ambassador and Northern Department to obtain Foreign Office agreement to provide a successor. The information officer, Mason, took over some of his functions. Both the other main Scandinavian posts, as well as Helsinki, had a labour attaché appointed by the Ministry of Labour during this period. The position in Oslo may have been weaker because it had been filled by a local appointment at quite an early stage, rather than by someone from the Ministry of Labour. Thus it was never considered to be a substantive post: this meant that Inman was not invited to the first labour attachés' conference in London in 1947, although he did receive an invitation to the following one in 1949.[682] There is some evidence to suggest that the Ministry of Labour wanted to preserve departmental control of labour attachés and prevent any increase in the small number of 'amateur' labour attachés.[683] It is also possible that the changing budgetary climate may have made the selection of a substantive successor more difficult. There are no other surviving documents which give further insights into this matter.

At a meeting of Scandinavian ambassadors in 1951, Wright said that he badly needed a replacement labour attaché, and that he did not think that it would be workable to share one with a neighbouring post.[684] The Foreign Office looked carefully at his suggestion for a replacement for Inman. Mason, who had replaced Gee as labour adviser when he was posted home from Norway, minuted that he thought that a labour attaché would be most valuable in Oslo and that he had suggested that a service attaché or two could be sacrificed to make way for such an appointment. He believed that when the labour attaché service had started, it

---

[681] Warner to Kelly, 22 June 1948, PR29/1/913G, FO1110/2.
[682] Minutes of these meetings are on LAB 13/594 and LAB 13/595.
[683] Loose note on 'The Labour Attaché', Healey papers, Labour Party archive, Manchester.
[684] Minutes of meeting of Scandinavian ambassadors in Stockholm in 1951, NN1891/14, FO371/94462.

had been the intention to staff it with foreign service officers as far as possible. He thought that Oslo would be an excellent place for a foreign service officer who wished to specialise for a while in labour affairs. He noted that Norway was 'largely run by trade unions, and much of Norwegian pacifism and fellow travelling is to be found in the trade union ranks.' A labour attaché could do a job in Norway which would be out of proportion to the normal character of the job, and he hoped that it would be possible to obtain sanction for such a post there.[685] He noted subsequently that the proposal was not to be pressed for the time being for tactical reasons – and nothing came of the idea. Further, Wright's preference to avoid having a labour attaché who was shared with other posts was also later ignored. The labour attaché based in Helsinki became responsible for covering the Nordic region: the post was filled from 1961 to 1965 by Kit Kenney, who had by then transferred to the Ministry of Labour and who would have been well qualified to do the job.

Momentum maintained: exchanges and visits between the labour movements after 1950

In view of the close connections which were built up through regular meetings and the transaction of party business, it is perhaps not surprising that personal favours were also occasionally sought. Healey wrote to Haakon Lie in March 1950 on behalf of the prime minister, Clement Attlee. He said that Attlee's daughter Felicity, who was a trained nursery teacher currently working in a nursery school under the London County Council, would like to find a similar job abroad, preferably in Scandinavia. Healey asked whether Lie had any suggestions about how this might be arranged.

---

[685] Minute by Mason, 11 September 1951, PG1304/1, FO 953/1144. In view of Mason's close co-operation with Inman in Oslo, and the fact that he subsequently performed some of his functions, it is not surprising that he was sympathetic to the arguments for replacing him. It is not clear how much support the Foreign Office had actually given to the idea that their officers might be trained to do labour attaché work – probably not very much in view of the evident opposition in the Ministry of Labour as reflected in the note described in footnote 683 above. But it is interesting that on his return from Oslo, Mason was posted to succeed Gee as labour adviser.

8 THE RELATIONSHIP AT WORK AND ITS SUDDEN END: 1949 TO OCTOBER 1951

She would like to live with a decent socialist family, paying for her keep. He emphasised that Attlee was a most modest man, and would not wish to use his position as prime minister in any way to further his daughter's personal position. Indeed, he was very diffident about raising the matter at all. Lie replied that Felicity should not come to Oslo. Norway simply could not give her training opportunities similar to those which Sweden could offer. Norway itself had to send teachers to Sweden to give them proper training.[686]

There were few visits in 1950, although bilateral party contacts continued at much the same level during frequent meetings on agenda items for COMISCO and through discussions in the margins of committee meetings, as well as through written exchanges on a variety of topics, including the coordination of policy issues. Thus Healey wrote to Lie in July 1950 to inform him that he was preparing a memorandum on the official attitude of the various European socialist parties towards European unity. He asked Lie to send him details of any resolutions passed on this subject either by DNA's national executive committee, or its annual conference.[687] However, in 1951 the number of visits and exchanges increased considerably and marked a high point in the level and number of contacts in the post-war period. The first took place in April, when the former Colonies Minister Creech Jones, a prominent Fabian, visited Oslo to undertake a series of meetings with both DNA and LO.[688] At the same time, Phillips wrote to Lie to invite him to visit Britain as the guest of the Labour Party to address one of a series of weekend meetings arranged by the NEC, to which they were inviting foreign speakers. Lie was invited to choose whatever dates suited him: he preferred to avoid the autumn because of the impending municipal elections, and so came at the beginning of June. He spoke to a meeting of the London Labour Party, and again the following evening to a new group, the Socialist Union, on 'International

---

[686] Healey to Lie, 22 March 1950, Lie to Healey 27 March 1950, Internasjonalt utvalg 1950, D Da 36, Arbeiderbevegelsens arkiv.
[687] Healey to Lie, 21 July 1950, Lie arkiv, Internasjonale forbindelser, Dc0003, Arbeiderbevegelsens arkiv.
[688] Cullis to Lie, 3 April 1951, Internasjonalt utvalg 1951, D Da 43, Arbeiderbevegelsens arkiv

Socialism Today', sharing the platform with Alice Bacon, who was chairman of the Labour Party in 1951.[689]

The high point: four British ministerial visits in August 1951

In 1951, it was still unusual for Britons to holiday abroad. However, four British ministers, including Attlee and Morrison (who had succeeded Bevin as foreign secretary in March) visited Norway at almost the same time during the summer. This was unprecedented and prompted one of Morrison's secretaries to observe that it would be easier to transport Sir Norman Brook (the cabinet secretary) to Norway if a Cabinet meeting were required.[690] Not surprisingly, the visits provoked a rather more serious Russian response: *Pravda* imputed sinister motives to all this tourism, noting that Morrison had decided to tour in Northern Norway right up to the Soviet border.[691] The other two ministers were Philip Noel Baker, the minister of fuel and power, who spent a month in Norway from 10 August, staying with the widow of Fridtjof Nansen in Asker, and Tomlinson, the minister of education who visited Oslo for a week from 19 August, as a guest of the Foreign Ministry and the Ministry of Education.[692]

In his autobiography, Morrison wrote that he had visited Sweden in 1950 through the Workers' Travel Association and had met Erlander, the prime minister, who had viewed his trip as a significant step in the official rapprochement between Britain and Sweden since their breach over Sweden's wartime neutrality.[693] He wished to visit Norway and Sweden again. Randall, British ambassador

---

[689] Phillips to Lie, 6 April 1951, subsequent correspondence in May between Lie and Frank Mennell, assistant secretary of the International Department of the Labour Party, Lie arkiv, Internasjonale forbindelser, Dc0003, Arbeiderbevegelsens arkiv.
[690] Marginal comment by K.M. Wilford, assistant private secretary to Morrison, 2 August 1951, NN1361/12, FO371/94696.
[691] *Pravda*, 20 August 1951, NN1361/13, FO 371/94696.
[692] Baker, private secretary to Tomlinson, Ministry of Education, to Barclay, FO, 28 July 1951, NN1631/10 FO371/94696
[693] Herbert Morrison, *An autobiography* (Odhams, 1960), p494.

8 THE RELATIONSHIP AT WORK AND ITS SUDDEN END: 1949 TO OCTOBER 1951

in Denmark, heard of the planned trip, and asked Morrison to visit Copenhagen as well, noting that the Danes had not been entirely satisfactory members of NATO and there were some economic problems which could be smoothed over by a visit. This was supported by the Foreign Office, but Morrison chose to ignore their advice and kept to his original plan.[694] When he visited Oslo at the end of his trip to Norway, he had a meeting with Lange and also went to DNA headquarters for meetings with senior DNA officials. There is no record of the talks which he had on either occasion. However, in a general comment the ambassador, noted that Norway was settling down to acceptance of her responsibilities as a NATO power and was in sympathy with British policy towards the development of the organisation. Since Norway had some reservations about American policy, the Norwegian government was keen to remain in close and constant contact with the British government and to feel that they were both trusted and consulted by them. Lange and his colleagues were consequently much pleased that he had had the opportunity to meet the foreign secretary, both in Strasbourg and also in Oslo.[695]

Attlee went abroad on holiday very rarely. Kenneth Harris observed that with the exception of two other trips, one to Ireland and one to France, Attlee and his wife had

---

[694] Randall to Makins, 5 July 1951, N1052/3. FO 371/94444. Morrison minuted by hand on the recommendation from Makins and Mason: 'I follow, but if I may say so, you are all wrong. Apparently it is not realised that this is a holiday – I'm paying! It isn't a series of state visits. True, I want to see Oslo and once I am there I can't very well help seeing ministers. As to Sweden I am staying with friends and the Swedish PM is a friend of theirs and mine so it is quite likely that I shall meet him.... Have a heart!' In his book about Bevin, Sir Roderick Barclay, who had worked as his private secretary, observed that while Morrison was in Norway, the situation in the Middle East became so acute that the Foreign Office sent him a telegram advising him to return. He refused to do so, maintaining that he needed more of a break. This also meant a late departure for San Francisco for the signing of the Japanese Peace Treaty, so Younger, the minister of state, had to be sent to speak at the opening ceremony. Sir R. Barclay, *Ernest Bevin and the Foreign Office* (London, 1975), pp99-101.

[695] Wright to Morrison, 4 September 1951, reporting Morrison's visit to Oslo, 28-29 August 1951, NN1631/15, FO371/94696.

spent all their holidays at Chequers.[696] On this occasion, he sailed to Bergen in a naval frigate and drove through the mountains before arriving in Oslo on 10 August. There he had lunch as a guest of DNA and met the king, prime minister, foreign minister and several other ministers in the course of his visit. At a dinner that evening, Gerhardsen referred to the community of ideas between Britain and Norway which had its realisation in the Atlantic pact, which was the only hope for the free world. In his reply, Attlee said that he was grateful for the hospitality of the Norwegian government, which had given him his first real holiday for many years.[697]

Again, there is no detailed report available of the discussions which Attlee had with Gerhardsen and Lange. However, a subsequent minute in December 1951 from the PUS, Sir William Strang, to Eden gives an indication of some of the substance of one of Attlee's meetings:

> Early in 1951, the Norwegian Minister of Justice, O.C. Gunderson intimated that he would welcome closer co-operation on security. In August, when Mr Attlee was on holiday in Norway, Mr Gunderson suggested that he might come to London to discuss this, and Mr Attlee said that he would be pleased to receive him and other officials who might come. By agreement with the Norwegians, the visit was postponed because of the British general election. It has now been brought up again by Mr Gunderson, who wishes to bring the head of the security police with him. In addition to liaison on security matters, he wishes to put forward a proposal for closer Anglo-Norwegian co-operation in co-ordinating information on subversive activities in the merchant navies of NATO countries. SIS and the Security Service would not have regarded a visit as essential, but it would be impossible to choke Mr Gunderson off without giving offence. The British ambassador supports the visit and suggests that the Lord Chancellor should host the visit as Mr Gunderson hosted the Lord Chancellor in Norway in 1949 and the

---

[696] Kenneth Harris, *Attlee* (Weidenfeld and Nicholson, 1982), p413.
[697] Wright to Morrison, 3 September 1951, reporting Attlee's visit to Oslo 10-12 August 1951, NN1631/16, FO 371/94696.

Lord Chancellor is the nearest equivalent to a Minister of Justice.[698]

Eden noted that there seemed to be little to be gained by this, but that he was committed by the invitation of the previous prime minister, and there was no choice but to proceed as Strang had suggested. It is not clear what lay behind the reluctance of SIS and the Security Service to be involved in such a visit – whether they were not interested in coordinating information on subversive activities in the merchant navies of merchant countries (a subject about which Norway, with its large merchant fleet, was bound to be closely concerned) or whether they had other reservations. At any rate, Eden wrote to Wright to instruct him to convey the invitation. There are no documents available to show when the visit subsequently took place.[699] However, in an interview with *Aftenposten* in 1987, Gundersen recalled that he had had a meeting with Eden in either 1951 or 1952 to discuss the relationship with the British security and intelligence services, and that he had been accompanied by Bryhn, who was the head of the Norwegian security service at that time.[700]

Labour's election defeat: the aftermath

The Norwegians were quick to attempt to maintain their links after the Labour Party lost the election in October 1951. In November, Anders Buraas, the foreign editor of *Arbeiderbladet*, wrote to James Griffiths MP to invite him to visit Oslo. Griffiths was a senior MP who had been chairman of the Labour Party in 1948-49 and minister of national insurance from 1945 until he succeeded Creech Jones as minister for the colonies in 1950, after Creech Jones had lost his seat at the general election in that year. Buraas told him that in the Norwegian labour movement there was immense interest in questions arising from the change of government

---

[698] Minute from Strang to Eden, 20 December 1951, NN1632/2/G, FO 371/94697. These documents were released under the Freedom of Information Act.
[699] Eden to Wright, I January 1952, NN1632/2/G, FO 371/94697.
[700] Interview in *Aftenposten*, 28 November 1987, quoted by Bergh and Eriksen, *Den hemmelige krigen – overvåking i Norge 1914-1997*, p504.

in Britain. There was also anxiety about the possible effects on European, colonial and international politics. He invited him to speak at a meeting of the Arbeidersamfunnet (the Labour Society) and to address a meeting of the DNA party executive. Griffiths visited Oslo at the end of November. In a subsequent letter to Griffiths, Buraas wrote that both Gerhardsen (who resigned shortly after this visit, after over six years as prime minister) and Lange had asked him to inform Griffiths how valuable his visit had been. They both felt that the British and Norwegian labour movements were as like as their different national backgrounds allowed them to be.[701] However, once the Labour Party had lost power in Britain, it was inevitable that the relationship could no longer be so effective.

It is clear that the Norwegians became concerned that the change of government would affect the nature of their relationship with Britain. This was certainly borne out by subsequent events, as the level of contacts and exchanges declined. Eden wrote to Churchill in February 1953 that there was a feeling in Norway that the Conservative government was being less friendly to the Norwegian Labour government than its socialist predecessor, and that the ambassador in Oslo had recommended a visit to Oslo either by Eden or another Foreign Office minister. He noted that when they had met at the UN General Assembly the previous autumn, Lange had specifically invited either him or Selwyn Lloyd to visit Norway. Eden recommended that Selwyn Lloyd go to Oslo during the Easter recess in April.[702] In his subsequent report, Selwyn Lloyd wrote that the visit had been interesting and useful: the Norwegians had been very friendly and had emphasised that they wanted to strengthen their friendship with Britain.[703]

The embassy took care to try to maintain its contacts with members of the Norwegian labour movement, although

---

[701] Letters from Buraas to Griffiths, 9 November and 13 December 1951, Internasjonalt utvalg D Da 43, Arbeiderbevegelsens arkiv. Griffiths visited Oslo from 30 November – 2 December 1951.
[702] Minute from Eden to Churchill, 26 February 1953, SC/53/6, Avon papers.
[703] Report by Selwyn Lloyd on his visit to Oslo, April 1953, SC/53/7, Avon papers.

8 THE RELATIONSHIP AT WORK AND ITS SUDDEN END: 1949 TO OCTOBER 1951

they do not appear to have remained as close once Cullis subsequently moved the regional office of IRD to Copenhagen. However, the embassy still met Arne Ording frequently. They noted that

> he is the member of the Foreign Ministry whom we see most frequently. He has no executive responsibilities but is a valuable channel for securing direct contact with Lange. He therefore comes into the embassy every week, and we have a general chat with him about current questions. The channel is two way and is often most useful to us in providing information about Norwegian political developments in the internal field.[704]

During this period, the embassy produced a number of imaginative suggestions for developing relations, building for example on an idea raised by Erik Brofoss, the trade minister, that Norway might join the Sterling Area, so as to develop a closer relationship with Britain, as well as enabling Norway to negotiate with Germany with more authority and to feel politically safer.[705] However, this did not happen: minuting by Eden showed that he was not in favour of these ideas. Wright also tried on several occasions, both here and in his valedictory despatch, to promote the idea that Norway might join the Commonwealth, though the suggestion foundered on a series of well-based objections raised by both the Foreign Office and the Commonwealth Office.[706]

Although there might not be quite so much documentary evidence available describing party exchanges during this period, there is sufficient to show that they continued frequently and at a high level. Moreover, as Healey noted to Hankey, he and fellow members of the Labour Party were in continuous contact with members of DNA at International

---

[704] Crawford to Hohler, 6 April 1955, NN1051/2, FO371/116470.
[705] Wright to Foreign Office, 19 December 1953, minute by Eden, 31 December 1953, NN1061/1, FO 371/106370.
[706] Wright to Foreign Office, 24 December 1954, NN1051/20 and subsequent minuting in various jackets in FO371/116470. These aspects are covered in much greater detail by Arve Rollag in his unpublished thesis, 'A special relationship? Norge og Storbritannia 1949-1960' (Universitetet i Oslo, 2000).

Socialist conferences. Unfortunately for the researcher, they did not always record in writing the outcome of their discussions. Thus, for example, shortly before a COMISCO meeting in London in January 1950, Haakon Lie wrote to both Healey and Phillips saying that he wanted to discuss with them a project on which he had been working for some time. There is nothing further to show what this was, or what the outcome of their discussion may have been.[707]

A notable aspect of this period was the extent of the information which was collected – mainly in Norway, but also to a lesser extent in Britain – about the activities of communist organisations in the two countries. It is to be expected that the security services would have been much involved in such work, and there is limited confirmatory evidence available to that effect. What is striking, though, is the extent to which the two labour parties contributed both officially and unofficially to this process, providing information in a variety of ways. The role of labour attachés during this period was also clearly important even if, as in Inman's case, they were locally recruited and not members of the mainstream labour attaché cadre. Indeed, it is possible that it was precisely because Inman had been locally recruited that he was able to enjoy a greater degree of flexibility in how he did his job than his colleagues from the Ministry of Labour . Although IRD was an avid customer for the reports which were provided, it is not often possible to determine the precise uses to which this information was put. IRD material also continued to be disseminated in significant quantities during this period.

Throughout his time in Oslo, Collier regularly emphasised to the Foreign Office the need to continue to encourage the development of links between the labour movements so as to foster further improvement in the bilateral relationship. While his successor, Sir Michael Wright, did not maintain this policy with the same enthusiasm, it is likely that he did not think it necessary, because the relationship was already about as close as it could possibly be in the prevailing circumstances. For example, in mid 1951 after a meeting with

---

[707] Lie to Healey and Phillips, 28 January 1950, Internasjonalt utvalg, D Da36, Arbeiderbevegelsens arkiv.

8 THE RELATIONSHIP AT WORK AND ITS SUDDEN END: 1949 TO OCTOBER 1951

Lange which discussed European and Atlantic integration, he concluded

> Lange's remarks again illustrate the remarkable similarity between the Norwegian and the British approach... On this, as on many other matters, the views of Norway are closer to Britain than those of any other country in Western Europe.[708]

The visits of Attlee, Morrison and two other British ministers in August 1951 provide the most telling evidence of this. So do the comments of Gerhardsen and Lange, relayed by Buraas to Griffiths, that the British and Norwegian labour movements were as like as their different national backgrounds allowed them to be. It was of course inevitable that the Labour defeat in the 1951 general election would have an impact on the overall relationship between Britain and Norway, as Eden noted. This did not prevent the relationship between the parties from remaining close and productive, but it significantly limited the impact which it could have in such changed circumstances.

---

[708] Wright to Eden, 25 June 1951, N1052/1, FO 371/94444.

9 Conclusion

In May 1945, Norway regained its independence after five years of German occupation. The north of the country was still occupied by one of the liberating powers, the Soviet Union. Its economy had been badly damaged by the war, and most of the energy of the government was directed towards reconstruction. During the period of the coalition government before the election in the autumn of 1945, all the political parties agreed on a joint programme for the reconstruction period. In its reference to defence and foreign policy, this programme emphasised the Norwegian intention to make a contribution to the construction of an international security system based on international law, and to safeguard the rights of small nations. These ideas provided the basis of Norwegian support for the United Nations.[709] They helped to ensure that Norway did not revert to isolation. Instead, Norway chose carefully to avoid linking itself to any of the Great Powers and developed its policy of bridgebuilding, distancing itself from too close a strategic involvement with any of them. Pharo quotes public opinion surveys from 1946-47 which show how deeply DNA was split over East-West questions. A large segment of labour voters was very critical of the United States.[710]

It was nonetheless scarcely surprising that Norway should have maintained and developed such close military, economic and diplomatic relations with Britain in the aftermath of the war. Norway, after all, would have been considered to be just

---

[709] Olav Riste, 'Was 1949 a Turning Point? Norway and the Western Powers 1947-1950', in Riste (ed.), *Western Security: the Formative Years* (Universitetsforlaget, 1985), pp130-131.

[710] Helge Pharo, 'Bridgebuilding and Reconstruction: Norway faces the Marshall Plan', *Scandinavian Journal of History* (1976), p129.

about Britain's most loyal wartime Western European ally. It was very much in Britain's interest that this remained the case. Archer quotes Turner's observation that

> During 1945-1947, the main objective of British policy towards Scandinavia was to tie Denmark and Norway as closely as possible to the British sphere of interest, and also to steer the direction of Swedish foreign policy in a more westerly direction'.[711]

He notes that decision-makers in the Foreign Office were concerned that Norway might become too influenced by Sweden and its policy of neutrality. He also quotes a recommendation from Collier, who stressed the importance of keeping Norway under British influence and who in late 1946 advised the Foreign Office to do everything to get the Norwegians 'into our pockets both militarily, and to a large extent, politically as well'.[712] This policy was pursued. Military links, in particular, continued to be developed and remained strong. Hauge and Alexander, the respective defence ministers, enjoyed a relationship of considerable confidence in each other. Britain supplied a large quantity of military equipment to Norway at greatly reduced prices. Norway sent a unit to take part in the occupation of Germany and in return benefited from extensive training both there and in Britain.

During the immediate post-war period, Norway also retained close economic links to Britain, which benefited from Germany's temporary disappearance as a trading partner. Udgaard quotes calculations to demonstrate that, based on the assumption that Germany would normally have retained the position she had held in 1937-39, estimates for 1947 showed that forty-four per cent of the imports replacing

---

[711] Howard Turner, 'Britain, the United States and Scandinavian Security Problems, 1945-1949', unpublished PhD Thesis, Aberdeen University (1982), p89, quoted by Archer, 'Uncertain Trust. The British-Norwegian Defence Relationship', *Forsvarsstudier*, (2/1989), p11.
[712] Collier to Foreign Office, 28 December 1946, FO 371/66018, quoted by Archer, 'Uncertain Trust', p12.

German goods came from Britain.[713] Udgaard also shows that although the total value of British trade to and from Norway declined slightly from a pre-war average of 20.1% of Norway's total imports and exports, to an average of 17.1% between 1946 and 1948, this was still only slightly less than the average of American trade (18.1%) during the same period[714] – quite an achievement given the damage done by the war to the British economy. On diplomatic issues Norway took a more independent line, consistent with its bridgebuilding philosophy, and often abstained in votes at the United Nations. Spain was, of course, a prominent exception. However, when the Great Powers dissented, Norway would more often vote with Britain and the United States – a point brought critically to Molotov's attention by the Russian Foreign Ministry, which noted that at the Paris peace conference, Norway had voted with Britain and the United States on all the most important questions.[715] There is, moreover, plenty of archival material which demonstrates the intimacy of the relations which existed between the respective ambassadors and foreign ministries, the frequency of their contacts and the frankness of their exchanges, particularly over the most important issues concerning the Marshall plan and Norwegian accession to the Atlantic pact.

In these circumstances, where relationships were already close, how were the two parties able to contribute further to that which already existed, and what did they achieve?

The answer lies in the unusual combination of circumstances which enabled the relationship between the parties to function as effectively as it did. The respective positions of Healey and Lie, and the closeness of their relationship, were of particular significance. Most important was the position of confidence which Healey enjoyed within the Foreign Office. This not only gave him access to a range of detailed

---

[713] Helge Seip, 'Tyskland og de norske valutaproblemene', Økonomisk Revy (1948), p4, quoted by Udgaard, *Great Power Politics and Norwegian Foreign Policy,* p169.
[714] Appendix I: the geographical pattern of Norway's foreign trade, Udgaard, *Great Power Politics,* p302.
[715] Memorandum from K. V. Novikov, member of the collegium of the Foreign Ministry, to Molotov, 5 January 1947, Holtsmark (ed.), *Norge og Sovietunionen 1917-1955 En utenrikspolitisk dokumentasjon,* p392.

and relevant briefing material, it also allowed him to become involved in meetings with ministers and the development of foreign policy in areas where the Labour Party had something to contribute. In return, he was able to provide briefings obtained from Labour Party contacts, used to best advantage in countries where the Foreign Office did not at that time have access to such information. He was also able to carry out commissions on behalf of the Foreign Office, meeting or entertaining visiting socialists on their behalf on occasions when they could not do so for themselves. The visit of U Ba Swe provides a good example of this. Healey's circumstances were unique. There is no other occasion when a senior Labour Party official has enjoyed such a position in the Foreign Office, and he used the authority which it gave him to good advantage.

The situation was somewhat different in Norway, where DNA enjoyed a closer relationship with the government. The international committee of DNA, which was appointed in the autumn of 1945 and chaired by Haakon Lie, included both the current foreign minister and his successor, as well as the chairman of LO and the editor of *Arbeiderbladet*. It was more authoritative than its British counterpart. Senior DNA members were occasionally despatched by senior ministers on government missions.[716] In such cases they reported back to the foreign minister as much as to their own party, and often shared their reporting with ministers anyway.[717] Similarly, diplomatic reporting was sometimes shared with DNA.

As Pharo points out, the foreign policy of the government and the labour party was the source of great dispute in the period before Norway joined NATO.[718] In these circumstances the Norwegians, who were described by Collier in

---

[716] Although LO sent John Sanness to London and Paris to investigate the possibilities of an international blockade of Franco -Spain, it was the Foreign Ministry which agreed to meet his costs. Sanness sent his detailed report and recommendations to Lange.

[717] Copies of Haakon Lie's report on his visit to London in March 1946, and of Arne Ording's report on the international conference in Paris in August 1946 to discuss Spain, are in the Foreign Ministry archives in the Riksarkiv.

[718] Helge Pharo, 'The Cold War in Norway and International Historical Research', *Scandinavian Journal of History* (1985), p169.

March 1946 as 'wishing to see the development of relations with Britain in all possible ways',[719] were well placed to exercise a positive influence on those policies which Britain considered important. It was in this connection that the relationship between Healey and Lie was of most significance in dealing with a range of issues: they were regularly in contact with each other. It has been shown that Healey passed Lie some classified material on the background to Bevin's Western Union speech, as well as arranging for him to be informally briefed.[720] He also used Foreign Office channels to arrange for the embassy to give Lie support before the meeting of the executive committee of DNA which was going to discuss Western Union, in advance of a meeting of Scandinavian socialist parties in Stockholm shortly afterwards.[721] No material has been discovered describing any exchanges between Lie and Healey in the weeks before the crucial DNA conference in February 1949, which resolved to support Norwegian accession to the Atlantic pact. But in view of the evidence of the closeness of their co-operation hitherto, it is reasonable to conclude that if advice or assistance had been sought by either side, then it would have been provided by the other.

The role played by Sir Laurence Collier and members of his embassy was also of crucial importance. It has been shown how, from an early stage, Collier identified the importance of encouraging closer links between the labour movements as a means of strengthening the relationship between Britain and Norway. It was a theme to which he frequently returned and echoes of it are to be found in many of his despatches containing policy recommendations throughout the five years he served as ambassador in Norway. He was also quick to see the significance of labour movement links as a key method of facilitating the work of IRD when it was established at the beginning of 1948. While he was not always approving of the quality or political views of some of the Labour Party or trade union representatives who came to Norway, he well understood that their overall impact was

---

[719] Collier to Bevin, 20 March 1946, N4417/219/30, FO 371/56284.
[720] Lie, *Skjebneår*, p241.
[721] Foreign Office to Oslo, 29 January 1948, N1336/34/30, FO 371/71485.

positive. In addition, he was closely involved in a variety of ways in promoting the exchanges of ideas as well as visitors in support of this overall objective. His recommendations were generally accepted and implemented by the Foreign Office; on many occasions during this period it is possible to observe how either the embassy or the Foreign Office acted as an intermediary in facilitating the relationship.

In this respect, Collier was well supported by members of his staff, several of whom were by reason of background or inclination, particularly sympathetic to Norway and its labour movement. Collier was fortunate to have the first editor of the *Daily Herald*, Rowland Kenney, as a member of his staff for a year after he returned to Oslo in 1945. Kenney's son Kit, half Norwegian and with experience of working with Norwegians both before and during the war, was also able to play a prominent role. So was John Inman, who may have been an amateur (i.e. not cadre) labour attaché, but who was considered by Haakon Lie to have been 'one of the family', so close did he become to DNA. It is occasionally difficult to distinguish whose interests they were representing when they undertook some of their initiatives, so closely were foreign policy and party political interests intertwined. A compelling example is provided by Kit Kenney's involvement in identifying the need for a senior Labour Party visitor to counteract the impression which had been made by Konni Zilliacus during his visit to Oslo in the autumn of 1947. It was he who took the initiative to propose Healey's visit, as well as subsequently undertaking many of the arrangements in co-operation with Haakon Lie. It has also been shown how both Kenney and Inman frequently corresponded directly with Healey, while Kenney also occasionally wrote to Healey through the Foreign Office when he wished to keep them directly informed as well.

The embassy had close contacts with a wide variety of Norwegians in the labour movement who had played a part in the war effort in Britain, many of whom were as a result both Anglophone and Anglophile. This would have facilitated both communication and cooperation. Some of these Norwegians later went back to work in Britain. Although, in general, the Norwegian Foreign Ministry and embassy in London did not play a prominent role in facilitating contacts between the labour movements, there were occasional exceptions. The role played by Olav Bratteli, who had worked for the Norwegian Seamens' Union in London during the war, and returned there as the first labour attaché, is one such exception. He was in frequent contact with Healey and represented DNA at London meetings when it could not send over someone from Oslo. Furthermore, while Anders Buraas may not always have been *persona grata* with the Foreign Office or the embassy in Oslo, he was the only foreign correspondent to enjoy the privilege of a weekly briefing from Healey.

It has been noted on a number of occasions that cooperation between the TUC and LO fell short of what Collier and the Foreign Office were hoping to achieve, often because the TUC was either insufficiently internationally minded, or because its interests lay elsewhere and it was not willing to subordinate its activities to Foreign Office direction. It is worth recalling the comment made by Nordahl when he attended the TUC conference in Southport in 1955. He observed that British trade unionists had changed a great deal since before the war, when they would have been unwilling to buy so much as a cup of tea for their Norwegian visitors – a reflection of the attitude of many to the Norwegian labour movement at that time. However, Nordahl went on to contrast this with the situation which he now found, commenting that there was no limit to what the British were prepared to do. They were beginning to understand that it was Europe which they should stick together with.[722] This provides an interesting context for the more critical Foreign Office comments: while the TUC at that time may not have been able to deliver what was required by the Foreign Office and the embassy, it appears that it was at least able to meet the more modest needs of the Norwegians.

The closeness, indeed intimacy, of the relationship between the two parties during this period has been noted and commented on. The views of Adam Watson support that assessment. However, this research is able to demonstrate that the relationship was much deeper and more extensive

---

[722] Nordahl, *Dagbøker Bind I. 1950-1955,* p386.

than has hitherto been believed to be the case – to such an extent that it has sometimes been impossible to distinguish foreign policy objectives from party political objectives. Compared with the practice in countries such as Holland where the niceties were more regularly observed, staff in the Oslo embassy did not always pay attention to the boundaries.

Healey commented in his autobiography that during this period the Scandinavian governments with socialist majorities collaborated closely with Attlee and Bevin, but that, like the Labour Party, they were pragmatic rather than ideological in their attitudes.[723] While he was referring particularly to their rejection of the federal approach to European unity, it is a judgement which may also be valid here. It is likely to have influenced the way in which members of DNA agreed to cooperate with requests for assistance in the dissemination of anti-communist propaganda. It is worth noting incidentally that whereas in other areas it has been possible to piece together aspects of a story (for example that concerning British attempts to remove Franco) from fragments discovered in different archives, this was not the case with IRD material. IRD work remained so sensitive that no significant references to it have been found outside the FO 1110 series. The only material which describes this extensive and wide-ranging co-operation is to be found in the National Archives. It has not therefore been possible to find any evidence describing the Norwegian side of this important issue.

In his valedictory, Collier observed that when he arrived in Norway in 1945, Anglo-Norwegian relations seemed to be at the crest of a wave. He expected that there would be some diminution in cordiality, not least as a natural reaction from the emotional high tension of the war years. There were some grounds for friction with former allies, and if the Soviet government had played their cards well, they might have taken advantage of these factors to drive a wedge between the allies. However, starting from the Spitzbergen demands of 1946, they did not play their hand well.[724]

---

[723] Healey, *The Time of My Life*, p95.
[724] Collier valedictory despatch, 22 November 1950, NN1015/18, FO 371/86535.

Separately, Korobochkin has commented on the extent of uncertainty and passivity, in spite of intensive planning, in Russian policy towards Norway.[725] Makins also reported on the most unusual situation where the Russians used their ambassador in Stockholm, rather than their ambassador in Oslo, to pass important messages to Lange.[726] But however awkwardly the Soviet government may have developed and implemented its policies in Norway, it was doing so from an initial position of strength. There continued to be concerns in Norway about the direction of Russian foreign policy, and the threat of communist influence, throughout this period. The collaboration undertaken between the two parties in facilitating the work of IRD can therefore be considered to have been of great importance.

It is not surprising that the intimacy and effectiveness of the co-operation between the two parties could not be matched by their collaboration in other areas. While the parties may have held similar views on Spain, they were never able to exert a telling influence over their governments. Nonetheless, the two parties used their links to the greatest extent possible to explore the limits of what might be achieved together. McNeil's actions showed how far the British government would have been prepared to go to help Norway resolve a serious complication in its relations with Spain in 1947. But this was to deal with a problem, rather than to explore the possibilities for changing the overall policy. DNA gradually realised that there was no identity of national interest with Britain, nor a reason for the two countries to work more closely together, as there was in their co-operation against communist influence. This remained the case even after Norway discovered in late 1946 that Britain did indeed have an undisclosed policy of working to remove Franco.

On international socialist co-operation, while the views of both parties were practically identical, particularly on the question of delaying the re-establishment of the International, this work was not of particular significance

---

[725] Maxim Korobochkin, 'Soviet policy towards Finland and Norway 1947-1949', p206.
[726] Note by Makins, enclosed with a despatch from Wright, 25 June 1951, N1052/1, FO 371/94444.

9 CONCLUSION

in terms of the overall relationship between the parties. Its value probably lay in ensuring that the movement remained as free as possible of communist influence, and in providing support for some of the weaker parties. Further, it provided a forum which enabled frequent exchanges. It was probably this - the opportunities which it offered for regular contacts between socialists to exchange ideas and experiences as they struggled to rebuild their societies and economies – which can be considered its most significant benefit.

In his autobiography, Denis Healey wrote that

> the Labour Party made good use of the exceptional influence it enjoyed after the war as the only socialist party to hold power on its own in a major country. The period of the Attlee government marked the high point of the Labour Party's role in Europe...[727]

In his valedictory, written at a time when it was becoming apparent that Norway was turning increasingly towards the United States for some of its security guarantees, Collier wrote that

> The Norwegian is essentially a European with no great liking for the American way of life, and indeed with a certain prejudice against it, particularly if he is a member of the Labour Party. His political and social ideals are those of Britain (or at least those of left wing Britain) rather than those of America. The members of the present Norwegian government have discovered, during and since the war, the affinity of their political and social ideas with those of the British labour movement.[728]

Assisted by Collier's facilitation, Healey, Lie and their colleagues made what was surely a unique contribution to the development of the links between these two Labour parties, to an extent which was greatly to the advantage of both countries.

---

[727] Healey, *The Time of My Life*, p95.
[728] Collier valedictory despatch, 22 November 1950, NN1015/18, FO 371/86535.

Bibliography

Unpublished sources

National Archives, Kew

British Council

BW 1	British Council: General
BW 83	British Council: Visits and Tours by Specialists

Cabinet Office

CAB 121	Cabinet Office Special Secret Information Centre 1939-1955
CAB 146	Cabinet Office Historical Section

Director of Public Prosecutions

DPP 1	Case papers: old series

Ministry of Education

ED 50	Board of Education: Special Services

Foreign Office

FO 188	Correspondence: British embassy Stockholm
FO 211	Correspondence: British embassy Copenhagen
FO 337	Correspondence: British embassy Oslo
FO 366	Chief Clerk's Department: Administration

FO 369   Consular Department: General correspondence
FO 370   Library and Research Department
FO 371   General correspondence: Political
FO 425   Confidential Print: Western Europe
FO 490   Confidential Print: Northern Affairs
FO 491   Confidential Print: Norway
FO 800   Private Collections: Ministers and Officials
FO 898   Political Warfare Executive and Foreign Office: Political Intelligence Department papers
FO 930   Ministry of Information and Foreign Office: General Publicity
FO 953   Foreign Publicity
FO 954   Avon Papers
FO 962   Correspondence: British embassy Reykjavik
FO 1110   Information Research Department
HD3/133   Permanent Under Secretary's Department: Correspondence and papers (Secret Service up to 1909)

Ministry of Labour

LAB 13   International Labour Division and Overseas Department

Prime Minister's Office

PREM 8   Prime Minister's Office Correspondence and Papers 1945-1951
PREM 15   Prime Minister's Office Correspondence and Papers 1951-1964

Security Service

KV 2   Security Service: Personal Files
KV 4   Security Service: Policy Files

Riksarkiv, Oslo

Files covering the following subjects:

Embassy in London: political reporting
Great Britain
Spain
Communist, Labour and other political parties
International Socialist Conferences
Trades Union Congress
Labour attachés
Judicial
Press

Labour Party Archive, Manchester.

CP/CENT/INT Communist Party International Department
LP/WG/SCAN Gillies papers on Scandinavia
LP/ID (International Department) Healey papers
LP/NEC International sub-committee 1945-1952
LP/JSM/INT/ 12 Middleton papers
LP/GS Phillips papers
LSI/Norway papers
LP/ID/SPA Spain
LP/SCW Spain

Arbeiderbevegelsens arkiv og bibliotek, Oslo

ARK - 1001 DNA papers, including international committee, international relations, pre-war files and conference reports
ARK – 2483 Haakon Lie papers
ARK – 1398 Konrad Nordahl papers
ARK – 1554 Trygve Bratteli papers
ARK – 1764 Erik Brofoss papers
ARK – 1507 Aksel Zachariassen papers
ARK – 2367 Anders Buraas papers
ARK – 1579 LO papers, including secretariat and international relations

BIBLIOGRAPHY

TUC Archive, Warwick University

Relations with the Norwegian Labour movement

Socialist International Archive, Amsterdam

Files covering the following subjects:
COMISCO meetings
General correspondence 1947-1950
General correspondence 1951-53
International Socialist Conferences
Expert conferences
SILO Newsletters
Britain
Norway

London School of Economics

Fabian Society archive

Russian Foreign Ministry

Correspondence on Norway and NATO

Collections of Private Papers

Avon papers, Birmingham University Archives
Butler Papers, Trinity College Archives, Cambridge
Christopher Mayhew papers, Liddell Hart Military Archive, King's College London

Books

Adelman, Paul, *The Rise of the Labour Party 1880-1945 (Third edition)* (Pearson Education, 1996)
Aldrich, Richard, *The Hidden Hand. Britain, America and Cold War Secret Intelligence* (John Murray, 2001)
Attlee, Clement, *As it happened* (Heinemann, 1960)
Archer, Clive, and Sogner, Ingrid, *Norway, European Integration and Atlantic Security* (Sage, 1998)

Aunesluoma, Juhana, *Britain, Sweden and the Cold War, 1945-54. Understanding neutrality* (Palgrave Macmillan, 2003)
Barclay, Sir Roderick, *Ernest Bevin and the Foreign Office: 1932 – 1969* (Latimer, 1975)
Barnett, Correlli, *The Lost Victory. British Dreams, British realities 1945-1950* (Pan, 1995)
Bennett, Gill, *Churchill's Man of Mystery. Desmond Morton and the World of Intelligence* (Routledge, 2006)
Berdal, Mats, *The United States, Norway and the Cold War, 1954-60* (Macmillan, 1997)
Berg, Roald, *Norge på egen hånd* (Universitetsforlaget, 1995)
Berg, Trond, and Pharo, Helge, (ed), *Vekst og Velstand. Norsk politisk historie* (Universitetsforlaget, 1981)
Bergh, Trond, and Eriksen, Knut Einar, *Den hemmelige krigen. Overvåking i Norge 1914-1997. Overvåkingssytemet bygges opp 1914-1955* (Cappelen Akademisk Forlag, 1998)
Bergh, Trond, and Eriksen, Knut Einar, *Den hemmelige krigen. Overvåking i Norge 1914-1997. Storhetstid og stormkast 1955-1997* (Cappelen Akademisk Forlag, 1998)
Brown, Gordon, *Maxton* (Mainstream, 1986)
Bullock, Alan, *Ernest Bevin. A biography* (Politico's Publishing, 2002)
Burridge, Trevor, *Clement Attlee. A Political Biography* (Jonathan Cape, 1985)
Butler, R. A. *The Art of the Possible: The Memoirs of Lord Butler* (Hamish Hamilton, 1971)
Citrine, Sir Walter, *My Finnish Diary* (Penguin, 1940)
Clarke, Peter, *The Cripps Version. The Life of Sir Stafford Cripps 1889-1952* (Penguin, 2002)
Cole, Margaret, and Smith, Charles, (eds), *Democratic Sweden: A Volume of Studies Prepared by Members of the New Fabian Research Bureau* (London, 1938)
Coleman, Peter. G, *The Liberal Conspiracy: the Congress for Cultural Freedom and the struggle for the mind of post-war Europe* (Free Press/Macmillan, 1989)
Collier, Sir Laurence, *Flight from Conflict* (Watts & Co, 1944)

Collier, Sir Laurence, *North House* (Unpublished manuscript)
Crossman, Richard, *The diaries of a Cabinet Minister Volume One* (Hamilton, 1975)
Curry, John, *The Security Service 1908-1945: The Official History* (PRO, 1999)
Defty, Andrew, *Britain, America and Anti-Communist Propaganda 1945-1953* (Routledge, 2004)
Derry, Kingston, *A History of Modern Norway 1814-1972* (OUP Clarendon Press, 1973)
Eriksen, Knut Einar and others (ed), *Arbeiderhistorie. 2005 Årbok for Arbeiderbevegelsens arkiv og bibliotek* (Valdres, 2005)
Eriksen, Knut Einar, *DNA og NATO* (Gyldendal Norsk Forlag, 1972)
Eriksen, Knut Einar, and Pharo, Helge, *Kald Krig og Internasjonalisering 1949-1962* (Universitetsforlaget, 1997)
Eriksen, Knut Einar, and Lundestad, Geir, *Kilder til moderne historie: Norsk Utenriks Politikk* (Universitetsforlaget, 1972)
Fostervoll, Kaare, *Norges Sosialdemokratisk Arbeiderparti 1921-27* (Det Norske Samlaget, 1969)
Fure, Odd-Bjørn, *Mellomkrigstid* (Universitetsforlaget, 1996)
Ganser, Daniel, *NATO's Secret Armies* (Frank Cass, 2005)
Garnett, David, *The Secret History of PWE* (St Ermin's Press, 2002)
Geyer, Robert, *The Uncertain Union – British and Norwegian Social Democrats in an Integrating Europe* (Avebury, 1997)
Grove, Eric, *From Vanguard to Trident. British Naval Policy since World War Two* (Annapolis, Maryland: Naval Institute Press, 1987.)
Hauge, Jens Chr, *The liberation of Norway* (Gyldendal Norsk Forlag, 1950 Reprinted in English, 1995)
Hauge, Jens Chr, *Manuskripter* (Tiden Norsk Forlag, 1988)
Healey, Denis, *Healey's Eye (*Jonathan Cape, 1980)
Healey, Denis, *The Time of my Life* (Michael Joseph, 1989)
Healey, Denis, *When Shrimps Learn to Whistle* (Michael Joseph, 1990)

Hennessy, Peter, *The Secret State. Whitehall and the Cold War* (Penguin, 2002)
Holtsmark, Sven, (ed), *Norge og Sovietunionen 1917-1955. En utenrikspolitisk dokumentasjon* (Cappelens Forlag, 1995)
Holtsmark, Sven, Pharo, Helge and Tamnes, Rolf, (eds), *Motstrøms. Olav Riste og norsk internasjonal historieskrivning* (Cappelen, 2003)
Howard, Anthony, *Rab: the life of R A Butler* (Cape, 1987)
Jones, Bill, *The Russia Complex. The British Labour Party and the Soviet Union* (Manchester University Press, 1977)
Kenney, Rowland, *Northern Tangle* (J M Dent, 1946)
Kenney, Rowland, *Westering* (J M Dent, 1939)
Kersaudy, Francois, *Norway 1940* (Collins, 1990)
Lange, Halvard, *Norges Vei til NATO* (Pax Forlag A/S Oslo, 1966)
Lashmar, Paul, and Oliver, James, *Britain's Secret Propaganda War 1948-1977* (Sutton Publishing, 1998)
Lie, Haakon, *Aust-Vest* (Noregs boklag, 1964)
Lie, Haakon, *Krigstid* (Tiden Norsk Forlag, 1982.)
Lie, Haakon, *Loftsrydding* (Tiden Norsk Forlag, 1980)
Lie, Haakon, *Martin Tranmæl. Et bål av vilje* (Tiden Norsk Forlag, 1988)
Lie, Haakon, *Martin Tranmæl. Veiviseren* (Tiden Norsk Forlag, 1991)
Lie, Haakon, *Skjebneår 1945-50* (Tiden Norsk Forlag, 1985)
Lie, Haakon, *...slik jeg ser det* (Tiden Norsk Forlag, 1975)
Lie, Haakon, *Søkelys på Sovjet* (Fram Forlag, 1953)
Lindsey, Donald, *Forgotten General. A life of Andrew Thorne* (Michael Russell, 1987)
Lundestad, Geir, *America, Scandinavia and the Cold War, 1945-1949* (Columbia University Press, 1980)
Lundestad, Geir, *East, West, North, South Major Developments in International Politics since 1945.* (Oxford, 1999)
Maisky, Ivan, *Memoirs of a Soviet Ambassador. The War 1939-1943* (Hutchinson, 1967)

Misgeld, Klaus, (ed), *Creating Social Democracy: a Century of the Social Democratic Party in Sweden* (Pennsylvania State University Press, 1992)
Morgan, Kenneth O, *Labour People* (OUP, 1987)
Murphy, Roger, *Challenges from Within* (Ashgate Publishing, 2001)
Morrison, Herbert, *Herbert Morrison: an autobiography* (Odhams, 1960)
Nordahl, Konrad, *Minner og meninger* (Tiden Norsk Forlag, 1967)
Nordahl, Konrad, *Med LO for friheten* (Tiden Norsk Forlag, 1969)
Nordahl, Konrad, *Gode arbeidsår* (Tiden Norsk Forlag, 1973)
Nordahl, Konrad, *Dagbøker Bind 1* (Tiden Norsk Forlag, 1991)
Nordahl, Konrad, *Dagbøker Bind 2* (Tiden Norsk Forlag, 1992)
Njølstad, Olav, *Jens Chr. Hauge – fullt og helt* (Aschehoug, 2008)
Olstad, Finn, *Einar Gerhardsen: en politisk biografi* (Universitetsforlaget, 1999)
Arne Ordings dagbøker: 19 juni 1942 – 23 juli 1945 (Tano Aschehoug, 2000) Opsahl, Erik, (ed)
Arne Ordings dagbøker: 24 juli 1945 - 4 april 1949 (Universitetsforlaget, 2003) Mordt, Gerdt, (ed)
Pearce, Robert, *Attlee's Labour Governments 1945-1951* (Routledge, 1994)
Pimlott, Ben, *Hugh Dalton* (Harper Collins, 1995)
Pimlott, Ben, *The political diary of Hugh Dalton 1918-1940 and 1945-1960* (Jonathan Cape, 1986)
Popperwell, Ronald G, *Norway* (Benn, 1972)
Potts, Archie, *Zilliacus. A Life for Peace and Socialism* (Merlin Press, 2002)
Preston, Paul, *A concise history of the Spanish Civil War* (Fontana, 1996)
Preston, Paul, *Franco* (Fontana, 1995)
Preston, Paul, *The triumph of Democracy in Spain* (Routledge, 1986)
Price, John, *The International Labour Movement* (OUP, 1945)

Price, John, *Organised Labour in the War* (Penguin, 1940)
Radice, Giles, *Friends and Rivals: Crossland, Jenkins and Healey* (Abacus, 2002)
Reed, B, and Williams, G., *Denis Healey* (Sidgwick and Jackson, 1971)
Reid, Alastair J, and Pelling, Henry, *A Short History of the Labour Party (Twelfth Edition)* (Palgrave, 2005)
Riste, Olav, *London Regjeringa 1940-1942* (Det Norske Samlaget, 1973)
Riste, Olav, *London Regjeringa 1942-1945* (Det Norske Samlaget, 1979)
Riste, Olav, *Norway's Foreign Relations – A History* (Universitetsforlaget, 2001)
Riste, Olav, *The Norwegian Intelligence Service 1945-1970* (Cass, 1999)
Riste, Olav, (ed), *Western Security: The Formative Years. European and Atlantic Defence 1947-1953* (Universitetsforlaget, 1985)
Salmon, Patrick, *Scandinavia and the Great Powers 1890-1940* (Cambridge, 1997)
Salmon, Patrick, (ed), *Britain, Norway and the Second World War* (HMSO, 1995)
Saunders, Frances Stonor, *Who Paid the Piper? The CIA and the Cultural Cold War* (Granta, 1999)
Skodvin, Magne, *Norden eller NATO?* (Universitetsforlaget, 1971)
Sverdrup, Jakob, *Inn i storpolitikken 1940-1949* (Universitetsforlaget, 1996)
Tamnes, Rolf, *The United States and the Cold War in the High North* (Dartmouth, 1991)
Thorpe, Andrew, *A History of the British Labour Party* (Palgrave, 2001)
Thorpe, D. R., *Eden* (Pimlico, 2004)
Udgaard, Nils Morten, *Great Power Politics and Norwegian Foreign Policy.* (Universitetsforlaget, 1973)
Warbey, William, *Look to Norway* (Secker / Warburg, 1945)
Warbey, William, and others, *Modern Norway. A Study in Social Democracy* (Fabian Publications Ltd, 1948)
Weiler, Peter, *Ernest Bevin* (Manchester University Press, 1993)

Wilford, Hugh, *The CIA, the British Left and the Cold War: calling the tune?* (Cass, 2003)
Worley, Matthew, *Labour inside the Gate. A History of the British Labour Party between the Wars* (I. B. Tauris, 2005)

Theses

Heidar, Knut Martin, *The Deradicalisation of Working Class Parties: a study of three Labour party branches in Norway* (London School of Economics, 1980)
Rollag, Arve, A *Special Relationship? Norge og Storbritannia 1949-1960* (Universitetet i Oslo, 2000)
Turner, Howard, *Britain, the United States and Scandinavian Security Problems 1945-1949* (University of Aberdeen, 1982)

Articles

Archer, Clive, 'Uncertain Trust: The British Norwegian Defence Relationship', *Forsvarsstudier* (2/1989)
Aunesluoma, Juhana, "Our Staunchest Friends and Allies in Europe': Britain's Special Relationship with Scandinavia, 1945-1953', in M. Hopkins, M. Kandiah and G. Staerck (eds) *Cold War Britain, 1945-64 New Perspectives* (Palgrave Macmillan, 2003)
Blidberg, Kersti, 'Just good friends. Nordic Social Democracy and Security Policy 1945-1950', *Forsvarsstudier* (5/1987)
Christopherson, Jens A., "Mot Dag' and the Norwegian Left', *Journal of Contemporary History* Vol 1 No 2 (1966) pp136-150
Cole, Robert, 'The other 'Phoney War': British Propaganda in Neutral Europe, September – December 1939', *Journal of Contemporary History* Vol 22 No 3 (July 1987) pp455-479
Collier, Sir Laurence, Obituary *The Geographical Journal* Vol 143 No 1 (March 1977) pp162-163
Collier, Sir Laurence, 'The Old Foreign Office', *Blackwood's Magazine* (September 1972)

Clive, N., 'Labour and the Cold War', *Government and Opposition* Vol 28 No 4 (1993) pp553-8

Cullis, Michael, 'Review of '.....slik jeg ser det' by Haakon Lie', *International Affairs* Vol 53 No 1 (January 1977) pp132-133

Defty, Andrew, 'Co-ordinating Cold war Propaganda: British and American liaison in anti-communist propaganda, 1950-1951', *European Studies Research Institute, University of Salford* (November 2002)

Eriksen, Knut Einar, 'Great Britain and the Problem of Bases in the Nordic Area 1945-1947', *Scandinavian Journal of History* Vol 7 (1982) pp135-163

Foreign Office Historians, Library and Records Department, 'Origins and Establishment of the Foreign Office Information Research Department 1946-48', *FCO History Notes* (August 1995)

Halvorsen, Terje, 'Stalinist Purges in the Communist Party of Norway 1948-1949', *Scandinavian Journal of History* Vol 18 No 1 (1993) pp148-161

Healey, Denis, 'The International Socialist Conference 1946-1950', *International Affairs* 26 (July 1950) pp363-373

Hetland, Tom, 'The Soviet View of the Nordic Countries and NATO, 1948-1952', *Scandinavian Journal of History* Vol 11:1 (1986) pp149-181

Holtsmark, Sven, 'A Soviet Grab for the High North. USSR, Svalbard and Northern Norway 1920-1953', *Forsvarsstudier* (2/1993)

Holtsmark, Sven, 'Enemy springboard or benevolent buffer? Soviet attitudes to Nordic co-operation 1920-1955', *Forsvarsstudier* (6/1992)

Holtsmark, Sven, 'Between 'Russophobia' and 'bridge-building'. The Norwegian Government and the Soviet Union 1940-1945', *Forsvarsstudier* (5/1988)

Korobochkin, Maxim, 'Soviet Policy towards Finland and Norway 1947-1949', *Scandinavian Journal of History* Vol 20 No 1 (1995) pp185-207

Majander, Mikko, 'Britain's Dual Approach: Labour and Finnish Social Democracy 1944-1951', in Juhana Aunesluoma (ed) *From War to Cold War. Anglo-*

Finnish Relations in the 20th Century (SKS/Finnish Literature Society, 2005)

Merrick, Ray, 'The Russia Committee of the British Foreign Office and the Cold War, 1946-1947', *Journal of Contemporary History* Vol 20 No 3 (July 1985) pp453-468

Misgeld, Klaus, 'As the Iron Curtain Descended: the Co-ordinating Committee of the Nordic Labour Movement and the Socialist International between Potsdam and Geneva (1945-1955)', *Scandinavian Journal of History* Vol 13 No 1 (1988) pp49-63

Pharo, Helge, 'Bridgebuilding and Reconstruction. Norway faces the Marshall Plan', *Scandinavian Journal of History* Vol 1:1 (1976) pp125-153

Pharo, Helge, 'The Cold War in Norway and International Historical Research', *Scandinavian Journal of History* Vol 10:2 (1985) pp163-189

Riste, Olav, 'The Foreign Policy-Making Process in Norway: An Historical Perspective', *Forsvarsstudier Årbok* (1982) pp232 – 244

Rothwell, Victor, 'Robin Hankey', in John Zametica (ed) *British Officials and British Foreign Policy* (Leicester University Press, 1990) pp156-189

Røksund, Arne, 'Vestmaktagent eller god nabo? Norge i sovjetisk utenrikspolitikk 1945-1949', *Forsvarsstudier* (6/1996)

Skodvin, Magne, 'Nordic or North Atlantic Alliance? The Postwar Scandinavian Security Debate', *Forsvarsstudier* (3/1990)

Smith, Lyn, 'Covert British Propaganda: The Information Research Department, 1947-1977', *Millennium: Journal of International Studies* Vol 9 No 1 (1980) pp67-83

Tamnes, Rolf, (ed), 'Soviet 'reasonable sufficiency' and Norwegian security', *Forsvarsstudier* (5/1990)

Tamnes, Rolf, 'Svalbard og stormaktene. Fra Ingenmannsland til Kald Krig 1870-1953', *Forsvarsstudier* (7/1991)

Taylor, P. M., 'The Foreign Office and British Propaganda during the First World War', *Historical Journal* 23 (1980) pp.876-98

Weiler, P., 'Labour and the Cold War: The Foreign Policy of the British Labour Governments 1945-51', *Journal of British Studies* 26 (1987) pp54-82

Wilford, Hugh, 'The Information Research Department: Britain's secret Cold War weapon revealed', *Review of International Studies* (1998), 24, pp353-369

Index

A

Acheson, Dean 90
Adler, Fritz 204
Afanasiev, Sergei 53, 157, 158, 249, 250
Aftenposten 27, 137, 148, 248, 268
Alexander, A. V. 139, 159, 274
Andersson, Sven 71, 72
Andvord, Rolf 44
Arbeiderbladet 23, 51, 54, 56, 65, 75–77, 81, 85, 88, 95, 96, 102, 120, 136, 146–148, 152, 156–158, 170, 192, 197, 214, 223, 231, 235, 243, 248–250, 268, 276
Arbeidet 237
Armata Italiana Liberta 113
Artajo, Alberto Martin 170
Aspaas, Leonard 25, 28
Attlee, Clement 13, 43, 55, 57, 77, 101, 165, 179, 180, 187, 237, 263–267, 272, 280, 282, 286, 287, 290

B

Basso, Lelio 112, 114, 214, 216
Bell, Ernest 43, 62, 70, 74, 174, 235
Berger, Sam 171, 259, 260
Berg, General Ole 159, 160, 184
Bevan, Aneurin 129, 176
Bevin, Ernest 14, 18, 29, 30, 39–43, 48–50, 52–54, 58, 61–63, 66, 67, 69–80, 82–85, 90–97, 101, 103–110, 113, 116, 130, 135–141, 144, 164, 166, 169–172, 175, 176, 181, 183–185, 187, 192, 195, 213, 231, 237, 239, 240, 257–259, 261, 265, 266, 277, 280, 287, 291
Bidault, Georges 168, 213
Bjørk, Kaj 147
Blum, Léon 121, 122, 180, 181
Bojer, Halvard 26
Bowker, Sir Reginald 124, 126, 127
Braathen, Gunnar 152
Braatoy, Bjarne 34

297

INDEX

Bratteli, Olav 42, 53, 54, 60, 65, 88, 152, 193, 208, 209, 211, 213, 236, 241, 242, 253, 260, 279
Bratteli, Trygve 152
Braunthal, Julius 171, 197, 198, 217, 221–223
Brimelow, Thomas 71, 72
Brockway, Fenner 31
Brofoss, Erik 270
Brutelle, Georges 121, 147
Bryhn, Asbjørn 245, 268
Bull, Edvard 32
Bunkholdt, Bjørn 148
Buraas, Anders 9, 54, 56, 81, 82, 85–88, 141, 192, 268, 269, 272, 279, 285
Burgess, Guy 130, 131
Burmese Socialist Party 125, 127–130

C

Caballero, Largo 39
Cadogan, Sir Alexander 40, 42
Cards on the Table 83, 84, 104
CGIL 115
Cherkasov, Mikhail 53, 157
Citrine, Sir Walter 40, 41, 43, 62, 69–71, 287
Codex 122, 123, 154, 247
Colban, Eric 34, 54, 167, 171, 175, 176, 182–184, 188, 194
Collier, Sir Laurence 14, 19, 31–33, 37–40, 42, 48–53, 57, 58, 60–70, 73–76, 81–84, 86, 89, 94–97, 101, 102, 107, 119, 135–145, 158–161, 170, 171, 179, 184, 185, 192, 195, 229–233, 235, 237–241, 244, 247, 258, 259, 271, 274, 276–280, 282, 287, 288, 292
Comintern 21, 23, 24, 28, 30, 106, 136
COMISCO, Committee of the International Socialist Conference 11, 90, 91, 115, 197, 209, 214–216, 218, 220, 221, 223, 224, 264, 271, 286
Creech Jones, Arthur 55, 171, 264, 268
Cripps, Sir Stafford 129
Crossman, Richard 59, 84, 132, 133
Cullis, Michael 150, 151, 246, 252–254, 256, 257, 264, 270

D

Daily Herald 20, 37, 79, 278
Dallas, George 35
Dalton, Sir Hugh 32, 33, 35, 41, 78, 95, 104, 106, 116, 176, 204, 205
De Gasperi, Alcide 115
de Gaulle, Charles 168
DNA, Det norske arbeiderpartiet 11, 20, 21, 23, 24, 27–35, 41, 44, 45, 47, 48,

50–54, 60, 64–67, 69, 73–76, 78, 81, 83–86, 88, 93, 94, 97, 102, 115, 119, 135, 136, 138, 142, 148–153, 155, 161, 166, 171, 173–176, 180, 192, 205–209, 211, 213, 227, 229–233, 236–238, 241, 244–246, 248–251, 254, 257, 258, 264, 266, 267, 269, 270, 273, 276–281, 285, 288
Dormer, Sir Cecil 33, 37
Drogseth, Arne 217

E

Earnshaw, Harry 227, 229–232
Ebbell, Sven 166, 188–191, 193–195, 198
Eden, Sir Anthony 16, 42–44, 267–270, 272
Egeland, Erik 87
Elster, Torolf 51, 75, 76
ERD, European Recovery Programme 78, 79, 211
Etherington-Smith, Raymond 233, 234
Evang, Vilhelm 94, 160
Evensen, Lars 41, 191

F

Fabian Society 22, 36, 59, 74, 89, 177
Falk, Erling 24
Fawcett, Luke 62–65, 232
Feather, Vic 235, 236

Fierlinger, Zdenek 213
Flanders, Allan 88
Franco, General 15, 18, 39, 63, 163–173, 177–188, 191–193, 195, 197, 199, 200, 260, 276, 280, 281
Franc Tireur 123
Freedom First 108, 145, 151–153, 261
Friheten 75, 156, 237, 242
Furubotn, Peder 242–244

G

Gaitskell, Hugh 36, 66, 260
Galenson, Walter 157, 260
Gee, H. G. 115, 125, 129, 234, 258, 262, 263
Gerhardsen, Einar 34, 47, 57, 60, 63, 96, 136–138, 141, 158, 173, 190, 191, 196, 197, 229, 260, 267, 269, 272
Gerhardsen, Rolf 165
Gillies, William 34, 35, 42, 55
Giral y Pereira, José 178–180, 182, 183, 260
Gomez, Trifon 18, 183, 184, 200, 260
Gordon Walker, Patrick 60, 66
Gore-Booth, David 81
Greenwood, Arthur 35
Griffiths, James 268, 269, 272
Gromyko, Andrei 13, 167
Guldvog, Arnfinn 234
Gunderson, O. C. 267

H

Halifax, Lord 40, 41
Hankey, Robin 18, 64–66, 68, 71, 72, 79, 81, 83, 89, 93–95, 102, 105, 115, 137, 158–160, 209, 231–233, 238–240, 270
Hansteen, Viggo 136
Haraldson, Harald 152
Hardie, Keir 36
Harvey, Sir Oliver 118–122, 186, 254–256
Hauge, Jens Chr 44, 139, 155, 158–160, 274
Haugen, Ingvald 192, 193, 196, 197, 260
Healey, Denis 1, 13–18, 20, 42, 52, 54–57, 59, 65, 68, 71, 74–81, 83–85, 90–95, 97, 104, 108, 109, 111, 114–117, 121, 125–129, 133, 146, 147, 161, 164, 169, 171, 174, 176, 180–183, 185, 187, 192, 199, 200, 203–213, 215–217, 219–221, 230–232, 236, 258–260, 262–264, 270, 271, 275–280, 282, 285, 288, 291, 293
Heller, Phil 205
Henderson, Arthur 33, 43, 144
Hodann, Max 28, 29
Howie, Chris 56
Hoyer Millar, Robert 178, 179

Huysmans, Camille 43

I

IFTU, International Federation of Trade Unions 21, 24, 30, 38, 39, 45, 62
ILP (Independent Labour Party) 22, 24, 31, 36, 44, 45
Il Tempo 113
Inman, John 14, 18, 20, 49, 58, 59, 62, 64–66, 70, 74–76, 81–84, 89, 90, 92, 93, 136, 152, 229, 230, 232, 234, 235, 237, 239, 241, 252, 258, 261–263, 271, 278
IPU, Inter Parliamentary Union 125, 233
IRD, Information Research Department 11, 15, 17–19, 37, 56, 59, 79, 86, 96, 98–100, 103, 105, 106, 108–111, 113–115, 117–120, 122–127, 129–133, 140, 141, 143–154, 158, 161, 169, 203, 218–221, 228, 238, 240, 242–244, 246–250, 252–257, 260, 261, 270, 271, 277, 280, 281
ITWF, International Transport Workers Federation 29, 191–193, 197

J

Jebb, Gladwyn 32
Jenkins, Roy 111, 133
Jerram, Sir Cecil 72, 93, 95
JIC, Joint Intelligence Committee 158
Johansen, Strand 242, 243
Johnson, Carol 47, 66

K

Keep Left 84, 104, 132
Kennan, George 80
Kenney, Asta 37
Kenney, Kit 18, 37, 57–59, 66, 69, 75, 76, 82, 84–86, 94, 97, 101, 102, 138, 142, 146–150, 152, 153, 247, 255, 258, 263, 278, 289
Kenney, Rowland 20, 36–38, 42, 48, 57, 60, 64, 278
Kildal, Birger 87
Kirkpatrick, Sir Ivone 103, 119, 120
Koht, Halvdan 33, 34, 165, 229
Kun, Bela 26
Kuznetsov, N. D. 155

L

Labour Party 22–24, 30, 31, 33, 34, 36, 40, 44, 45, 47–49, 53, 55, 56, 60, 68, 71, 73, 76–79, 81, 83, 84, 88, 91, 93, 94, 98, 99, 102, 104, 108, 110–112, 115, 120, 121, 124, 125, 127–130, 132, 133, 144, 147, 153, 155, 164, 165, 169, 171–173, 175, 176, 182, 187, 193, 200, 203, 204, 206–211, 215, 217–220, 222, 227, 228, 230–232, 235, 236, 252, 258, 259, 264, 265, 268, 270, 276–278, 280, 282
Lamming, G. N. 71, 72
Lange, Halvard 18, 25, 28, 31, 57, 67, 77, 86, 93–96, 171, 174–180, 183–185, 188, 190–192, 194–198, 200, 229, 247, 251, 266, 267, 269, 270, 272, 276, 281, 289
Lang, Rev Gordon 111
Larock, Victor 223
Larsen, Asbjørn 235
Laski, Harold 48, 57, 77, 78, 121, 155, 176, 207, 208, 214, 259
Lie, Haakon 1, 9, 13–15, 17, 18, 20, 23, 34, 41, 43, 44, 49, 52–60, 65–67, 73–78, 83–85, 88, 90–95, 119, 136, 146–148, 150, 152, 157, 158, 161, 165, 169–173, 175, 176, 192, 197, 198, 201, 205–209, 211–218, 227–229, 234, 236, 241, 246, 254, 258, 260, 263–265, 271, 275–278, 282, 285, 289, 293

INDEX

Lie, Trygve 41, 43, 44, 77, 171–173, 188, 190, 196
Lionæs, Aase 75, 77, 148, 149
Llopiz, Rodolfo 180–182
Lloyd George, David 27
LO, Landsorganisasjonen 21, 24, 30, 38–41, 43, 45, 47, 52, 60–63, 70, 73, 74, 77, 96, 147, 152, 173, 175, 192, 233–235, 241, 244, 260, 264, 276, 279
Lozovski, Solomon 53
LRC, Labour Representation Committee 22
LSI, Labour and Socialist International 24, 35, 42, 43, 45, 204
Lunden, Mimi Sverdrup 240
Løvlien, Emil 240, 242, 244

M

MacDonald, Ramsay 22
Maevsky, I. V. 250
Maisky, Ivan 167
Makins, Sir Roger 251, 266, 281
Mallet, Sir Victor 40, 111–113, 115–117, 170, 186, 188
Mann, Jean 66
Mann, Tom 23
Marshall, George 79, 89–92, 96, 113, 114, 138, 211, 213–215, 239, 250, 273, 275

Marshall plan 79, 90, 113, 114, 213–215
Marthinsen, Rosa 52
Martin, Mary 29
Masaryk, Jan 135
Mason, Frederick 147–150, 154, 235, 236, 242, 243, 248, 249, 252, 262, 263, 266
Maxton, James 24, 32, 44
Mayhew, Sir Christopher 10, 13, 36, 56, 65–68, 71, 79–81, 91, 92, 103–109, 114, 116, 121, 125, 130–132, 148, 149, 151–153, 171, 209, 210, 212, 228, 233, 234, 241, 259, 286
McKinlay, Adam 65
McNeil, Hector 54, 64, 65, 72, 73, 79, 80, 83, 95, 103–105, 108, 130, 133, 169, 174, 175, 182, 185, 191, 192, 259, 281
Mennell, Frank 125, 227, 228, 265
Miall, Leonard 90
Middleton, James 34, 42
Midelfart, Willi 165
Moe, Finn 77, 136, 190, 197
Mollet, Guy 122
Molotov, Vyacheslav 43, 44, 119, 155–157, 213, 251, 275
Morgenbladet 87, 93, 148, 248
Morgenposten 248
Morgenstierne, Wilhelm 138

Morgontidningen 81
Morrison, Herbert 13, 265–267, 272
Mot Dag 23, 24
Murray, Ralph 99, 107, 108, 110, 111, 113, 117–124, 126, 127, 129, 130, 133, 134, 145, 148, 149, 151, 153, 154, 169, 220, 243, 247, 249, 253, 255, 256, 261
Møller, Gustaf 35
Mørk, Anders 152

N

Nasjonen 93
NATO 13, 229, 256, 266, 267, 276
Neal, Harold 66
Negrin, Juan 180–182
Nenni, Pietro 112–114, 216
NKP, Norges Kommunistisk Parti 11, 24, 48, 51, 59, 61, 101, 102, 136–138, 171, 208, 236–240, 242–246
Noel Baker, Francis 74
Noel Baker, Philip 43, 67, 74, 175–177, 265
Nordahl, Konrad 16, 17, 30, 38–43, 52, 61, 63, 69, 77, 97, 152, 191–193, 196, 197, 208, 234, 235, 242, 260, 279, 285, 290
Norwegian Employers Union 29
Norwegian Seamens' Union 27
Norwegian Shipowners Association 29
Novikov, K. V. 156, 157, 275
Nutting, Sir Anthony 130
Ny Tid 23

O

Oldenbroek, J. H. 174, 193, 222, 234
Ollenhauer, Erich 218, 219
Ording, Arne 16–18, 24, 25, 28, 34, 45, 65, 75–77, 86, 93, 180–185, 200, 229, 231, 232, 270, 276
Ording, Molla 28
Ording, Åke 65, 75, 135, 136, 176–178, 206–208
Orwell, George 126

P

Pankhurst, Sylvia 25, 27
PCI, Italian Communist Party 111, 112
Peck, John 124, 220, 253, 254, 256, 257
Peterson, Sir Maurice 100
Pettersen, Anker 27
Phillips, Morgan 17, 18, 42, 48, 68, 74, 76, 78, 80, 109, 110, 121, 125, 171, 176, 185–187, 203, 204, 206, 207, 210, 212, 215, 219, 222–224, 228, 259, 264, 265, 271, 285
Plotnikov, Viktor 53
Pollitt, Harry 240, 241

POT, Politiets
    Overvåkingstjeneste
    138, 245
Prebensen, Per 54, 55, 188,
    191, 192, 194, 197,
    198
Price, John 22, 24, 41, 43,
    254
Prieto y Tuero, Indalecio
    183
PSI, Italian Socialist Party
    112, 114, 216

Q

Quisling, Vidkun 137, 166

R

Randall, Eric 219, 227, 228
Randall, Sir Alec 265, 266
Reddaway, Norman 109,
    131, 132
Rio Tinto Zinc 177
Roberts, Sir Frank 100, 167
Rodionov, Konstantin 251
Roosevelt, Theodore 55
Russell, Bertrand 221
Ruud, Arthur A. 70

S

Salvesen, Kaare 253
Sanness, John 77, 148, 175,
    180, 276
Saragat, Guiseppe 112,
    115, 116
Sargent, Sir Orme 79, 81,
    95, 100, 101, 103–105,
    140, 143, 183, 184,
    186, 254
Schapiro, Leonard 221
Schevenels, W. 234

Schumacher, Kurt 85, 212
Security Service 28, 29,
    221, 267, 268
Selwyn Lloyd, John 269
SFIO, French Socialist
    Party 121, 122, 147
Shaw, George Bernard 56
Shinwell, Manny 78
SILO, Socialist Information
    and Labour Office
    145, 207, 217
SIS, Secret Intelligence
    Service 28, 106, 267,
    268
Skar, Alfred 152, 235
Social Demokraten 23, 27,
    35
Socialist International 15,
    21, 35, 42, 53, 56, 96,
    176, 203, 204, 218,
    222–224
Special Branch 17, 26
Stalin, Joseph 55, 164, 172,
    259
Stewart, Robert 30
Strachey, Lytton 129
Strang, Sir William 267,
    268
Ström, Fred 26
Sunday Times 96
Sutherland, Mary 49
Sverdrup, Jacob 24, 56,
    196, 199, 200, 240,
    291
Svolos, Aleksandros 80
Swingler, Stephen 66, 67

T

Tennant, Peter 118–120,
    122

Tewson, Vincent 63, 72, 73, 97, 117, 208, 234, 242
Thakin Nu 127, 129
Thompson, Edward 218, 220
Thomson, Basil 17
Thomson, Sir Basil 26
Tillett, Ben 23
Tomlinson, George 265
Tracey, Herbert 58, 108, 151
Tranmæl, Martin 22, 23, 30, 42, 43, 64, 77, 136, 152, 180, 231, 289
TUC, Trades Union Congress 17, 21, 34, 39–41, 43, 47, 58, 61–63, 65, 69, 70, 72–74, 81, 83, 88, 96, 104, 108, 115, 117, 125, 127, 129, 151, 153, 172, 174, 175, 183, 187, 233, 235, 242, 252, 259, 279

U

U Aung Than 127
U Ba Swe 125, 127–129, 133, 276
U Kyam Nyein 125
Undén, Osten 95

V

Vilfan, Dr Josa 111
Vogt, Benjamin 26
Voluntari Civili 113
Vorrink, Koos 147
Vougt, Allan A. 95

W

Warbey, William 59, 60, 63–66, 89, 169, 171, 174, 175, 291
Wardrop, James 18, 68, 85, 237
Warner, Christopher 57, 61, 64, 86, 94, 95, 100–102, 105, 108, 109, 113, 114, 117–122, 130, 143, 145, 148, 149, 151, 167, 209, 228, 238, 254, 255, 261, 262
Watson, Adam 37, 99, 117, 126, 146, 147, 150, 151, 161, 219, 220, 240, 249, 253, 260, 261, 279
Watts, Stephen 221
Western Union 14, 18, 53, 75, 92–95, 137, 258, 277
WFDY, World Federation of Democratic Youth 81
WFTU, World Federation of Trade Unions 70, 79, 81, 97, 109, 127, 129, 234–236, 242
Whyte, Anne 89
Wickham Steed, Henry 248
WIDF, World International Democratic Federation 81
Width, Trygve 148
Wilson, Walter 148
Wingfield, Charles 32, 33
Wold, Terje 180
Woolwych, S. H. C. 86, 119

Wright, Sir Michael 252, 253, 262, 263, 266–268, 270, 271, 281
Wyatt, Woodrow 129

Z

Zachariassen, Aksel 17, 25–27, 45, 285
Zilliacus, Konni 84, 85, 97, 240, 241, 278
Zorin, Valerian 53, 157, 158, 249–251

Ø

Øksnes, K. E. 260
Øverland, Arnulf 148